# THE BLACK PANTHERS SPEAK

By Philip S. Foner

Frederick Douglass on Women's Rights

The Voice of Black America, 1797–1971

The Black Panthers Speak

The Life and Writings of Frederick Douglass (4 vols.)

History of the Labor Movement in the United States (10 vols.)

A History of Cuba and Its Relations with the United States (2 vols.)

The Complete Writings of Thomas Paine (2 vols.)

W. E. B. Du Bois Speaks (2 vols.)

Business and Slavery: The New York Merchants and the
Irrepressible Conflict

The Fur and Leather Workers Union

Jack London: American Rebel

Mark Twain: Social Critic

The Jews in American History: 1654–1865

The Case of Joe Hill

The Letters of Joe Hill

The Bolshevik Revolution: Its Impact on American Radicals,
Liberals, and Labor

The Autobiographies of the Haymarket Martyrs

Helen Keller: Her Socialist Years

The Basic Writings of Thomas Jefferson

The Selected Writings of George Washington

The Selected Writings of Abraham Lincoln

The Selected Writings of Franklin D. Roosevelt

# THE BLACK PANTHERS SPEAK

Edited by Philip S. Foner

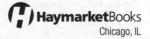

Chicago, IL

First published by J.B. Lippincott Company, Philadelphia/New York.
This edition published in 2014 by Haymarket Books
PO Box 180165
Chicago, IL 60618
773-583-7884
info@haymarketbooks.org
www.haymarketbooks.org

Trade distribution:
In the US, Consortium Book Sales and Distribution, www.cbsd.com
In Canada, Publishers Group Canada, www.pgcbooks.ca
In the UK, Turnaround Publisher Services, www.turnaround-uk.com
In Australia, Palgrave Macmillan, www.palgravemacmillan.com.au
All other countries, Publishers Group Worldwide, www.pgw.com

ISBN: 978-1-60846-328-2

Cover design by Ragina Johnson. Cover image of Black Panther Party members
demonstrating on the steps of the Alameda County Courthouse for the release
of Huey Newton (Copyright Bettmann/Corbis and AP Images).

Published with the generous support of Lannan Foundation
and the Wallace Global Fund.

Printed in Canada by union labor.

Library of Congress Cataloging-in-Publication data is available.

10 9 8 7 6 5 4

## Acknowledgments

Excerpts from *The Wretched of the Earth*, by Frantz Fanon, copyright © 1963 by *Presence Africaine*, are published with the permission of Grove Press, Inc. "Huey Newton Talks to the Movement about the Black Panther Party, Cultural Nationalism, SNCC, Liberals and White Revolutionaries"; "You Can Murder a Liberator, but You Can't Murder Liberation," by Fred Hampton; and "Black Caucus Program: An Interview" are published with the permission of the *Movement*. "Bobby Seale Explains Panther Politics" is published with the permission of the *Guardian*. "An Open Letter to Stokely Carmichael," by Eldridge Cleaver, is published with the permission of *Ramparts*. "We Will Win: Letter from Prison," by Afeni Shakur, and "To Judge Murtagh: From the Panther 21" are published with the permission of *Ray*. "People's Medical Care Center" is published with the permission of *Daily World*. "Ten-Point Health Program of the Young Lords" is published with the permission of the Y. L. O. Tom Foner generously furnished copies of *The Black Panther* from his personal files.

# Contents

# Foreword to the New Edition

The Black Panther Party for Self-Defense, later simply the Black Panther Party (BPP), was founded in Oakland, California, in 1966 by Huey Newton and Bobby Seale, two students at Merritt College who were influenced by the political upsurge in the country and angered by the continued police violence and harassment in African American communities, including Oakland. They were later joined by Eldridge Cleaver, David Hilliard, and others. Estimates are that at their peak, the Panthers claimed thousands of members and many more supporters, including a number of prominent celebrities, artists, and intellectuals. Romanticized by some and vilified by others, they became icons of the Black Power movement, but the organization was eclectic and complex and its story is a nuanced one. Its macho image disguises a reality where the struggle against sexism was intense and ongoing. The stoic, militant urban-warrior profile camouflaged a profound commitment to the organization's survival and service programs. And the "all-things-Black" exterior cloaked the internal politics of solidarity and internationalism.

I was nine years old when the Black Panther Party was founded, but its emergence would have a profound impact on my evolving consciousness as a young Black woman growing up in the late 1960s and early '70s. I remember the familiar image of large Afro-wearing men and women hawking Panther newspapers on Detroit street corners: "Black Panther paper, young sister?" And then I remember the funeral of a friend's brother who died way too young. He was a Panther. The funeral took place in a local Catholic church with a casket draped in a red, black, and green flag and pallbearers wearing black berets, leather jackets, and Black Panther buttons, fists raised as they honored a fallen comrade and brother. Their slogan, "All Power to the People," was ubiquitous. It was on posters, buttons, T-shirts, even bumper stickers. I did not really understand the politics of the Panthers at the time, or the seriousness of what those politics represented in the real world. All I knew was that their bold defiance to unjust authority was contagious and exhilarating.

The BPP was one of the most audacious and influential organizations of the 1960s and 1970s, but it was also an organization that has been vastly misread and misunderstood. When historian Philip Foner first edited and published *Black Panthers Speak* in 1970, he disrupted the mythmaking by creating a platform for Panther voices to be accessed directly by a larger audience than those who experienced the organization firsthand. In recent years, a new generation of scholars (and activists) are engaging the Panther legacy with rigor and a resolve to get the story right and to position the Panthers not at the margins, but at the center of the storm of political activity that, against all odds but with some margin of success, attempted to confront racism and injustice, militantly strike a blow against empire, build new communities and social practices, and change the world.

What these documents also demonstrate is something radical Trinidadian intellectual C.L.R. James recognized decades ago: that, above all, we must remember that history and revolutionary movements are made by human beings: flawed, inconsistent and sometime misguided, brilliant and confused, kind and vengeful, selfless and self-promoting—all in the same moments of intensity and passion.

The Panthers represented the militant spirit of urban Black youth who refused to be broken by the policeman's baton, refused to defer to the authority of a racist state apparatus, and refused the fundamentally skewed logic of American capitalism. They were bold and brazen, defiant, sometimes to the point of recklessness. And for this they paid a terrible price. When most of these documents were written, the leaders of the BPP were under serious surveillance and assault. Many chapters had been infiltrated by the FBI's famed COINTELPRO (counterintelligence) program. COINTELPRO sought to disrupt, divide, and destroy the organization. The

Panther leadership knew at the time that they were being targeted, but later, with the release of formerly classified documents through the Freedom of Information Act, the vastness and ruthlessness of the government campaign against the Panthers was revealed. FBI director J. Edgar Hoover insisted, "The Black Panther Party, without question, represents the greatest threat to [the] internal security of the country."[1] COINTELPRO was designed to eliminate that perceived threat.

From 1968 on, there was a series of killings and court cases that devastated the organization. In April 1968, seventeen-year-old Bobby Hutton was shot dead by police after his arrest in Oakland. In January 1969, John Huggins and Alprentice (Bunchy) Carter were killed during a confrontation with cultural nationalists in Maulana Karenga's US organization after a meeting on UCLA's campus. Huggins left behind his wife and comrade Erica Huggins and their infant daughter, Mai. The following December, young Panthers Fred Hampton and Mark Clark were killed in a bloody nighttime police raid on Chicago's West Side. And there were arrests and trials that further tapped the resources of the group and undermined its ability to carry out its work. The Panther 21 trial in New York and the New Haven Nine in Connecticut were two of the most high-profile cases, but the most dramatic was the surreal courtroom scene that surrounded Bobby Seale's indictment as a part of the 1969 Chicago Eight trial, an outgrowth of the 1968 protests at the Democratic National Convention. During the trial, the judge ordered Seale bound, gagged, and shackled in his chair in order to silence his outbursts, after which his trial was separated from his co-defenders, leaving them as the Chicago Seven.

By 1970 dozens of Panther leaders had been jailed, their offices had been raided in multiple cities, members had been wounded and killed, and two prominent leaders, Eldridge and Kathleen Neal Cleaver, were in exile in Algeria. It was a violent and tumultuous time in the United States and the world, and the Black Panther Party was in the thick of the fray.

In the words of the Panthers' eloquent young Chicago martyr Fred Hampton, "You can kill a revolutionary, but you can never kill the revolution." The revolutionary ideas and ideals that the Panthers embraced were indeed bigger than them. Their reach was long and it touched young radicals around the globe. More important even than what the Panthers did or said is what they represented. The organization's powerful symbolism extended well beyond its membership and has lived long after its demise. A narrow read of what the Panthers symbolized would focus on its youthful, militant defiance to the violent racism and police brutality suffered by urban Black populations. The actions that first earned them notoriety were their armed police-monitoring efforts and their insistence on the right to bear arms for community self-defense. But there was more. The Panthers also engaged in the gender-bending practice of promoting women warriors and male community servants. They, like the Student Nonviolent Coordinating Committee (SNCC), also recalibrated notions of intergenerational work. No longer was the accepted protocol simply to defer to wise elders and seasoned political experts. Equally significant was their broad and forward-looking Third World internationalism. Finally, their class politics were pivotal. Working-class Black youth were not viewed as angry rebels or as young protégés of successful movement veterans, but as strategists and revolutionary change agents in their own right—at least, that was the aspiration. This praxis was informed by the Panthers' appreciation of Marxist, and specifically Maoist, ideas about class struggle, nationalism, and revolution.

Over the years there has emerged a growing body of scholarship on the Panthers, including significant research on the role of gender in Party politics and the importance of the organization's "survival" or community service programs. These scholars are re-engaging the Black Panther Party with the benefit of hindsight as well as the challenges of distance and time. But this re-engagement is not simply an academic pursuit. The Panthers remain a source of political fascination and inspiration, even as their legacy is hotly contested, their mistakes fully acknowledged, and their losses deeply mourned. Panels, conferences, reunions, memorials, and memoirs have provided opportunities for new revelations, insights, and debates regarding the history of the Black Panther Party.

The issue of gender, the role of women in the Party, and the idealized notion of Black manhood continue to be significant points of interest and analysis when it comes to the Panthers. Initially, the gender discourse around the Panthers was male-centered, grounded in the assertion of Black manhood through self-defense. Even some women in the Party expressed their own humanity in masculine terms in those days. Elaine Brown's poem in this volume is a good example. She ends it with: "We'll just have to get guns and be men." At the same time, Panther ideas and symbolism may have both inhibited and ignited radical Black feminist (or womanist) consciousness and actions. Angela Davis, the late June Jordan, and other Black feminists trace their political lineage, in part, to a critical engagement with the politics and practices of the BPP.

*Black Panthers Speak* foregrounds, above all, the sense of urgency that characterized the historical moment in which the BPP existed. The Panthers believed, for good, reason that in the late 1960s Black urban communities were under siege and had to be defended. They refused to turn a blind eye to the threats, intimidation, police beatings, and killings that occurred. In cities like Detroit, for example, there was a police decoy unit called S.T.R.E.S.S. (Stop the Robberies Enjoy Safe Streets), which was notorious and feared for its extreme entrapment methods, which led to many arrests and shootings on city streets and alleyways.[2] Militant resistance seemed at the time to be a necessary tactic for survival.

Police brutality and harassment were not the only threats to Black survival, however. The problem, as the Panthers saw it, was systemic and required a dual set of responses that were both defensive and proactive. The survival programs of the BPP were intimately bound up with their notions of personal transformation, liberation, and community defense. The defenses they sought to provide were against poverty, despair, unemployment, physical illnesses, and miseducation as much as against police tyranny. They radically and idealistically organized thousands of young Black people and their white supporters to help create alternatives to existing institutions, a process through which they hoped both communities and individuals would be transformed. One example of this effort was the Oakland Community School, founded by the Panthers as an innovative model for community-based education, which lasted until 1983. The Free Breakfast for Children program, held in community centers, schools, and church basements around the country, was another such program. A site for political education as well as nourishment, this program showcased the Panthers' compassion for the suffering of poor Black folks and exposed the unwillingness of the government to adequately meet community needs. The Panthers' ethos was a spirit of self-help coupled with a practice of protest and confrontation.

Similarly, the People's Free Medical Clinics, which historian Alondra Nelson chronicles in her book *Body and Soul*, were set up in Portland, Washington, D.C., Oakland, and elsewhere. The clinics relied on donated labor and supplies and held up a different view of medicine and health that promoted prevention and health education and stressed the social and political context in which health and illness occur, pointing out racialized health disparities that negatively affected Black and Brown communities.[3]

All of this work was undergirded by an analysis of the racialized nature of Western capitalism and imperialism that is as relevant today as it was in 1966. The Panthers focused their organizing efforts on the so-called "lumpenproletariat," those at the very bottom of the social and economic hierarchy who make a living on the margins or in the illegal underground economy. In other words, those bearing the brunt of what Beth Richie calls the "prison nation" and Michelle Alexander calls "the new Jim Crow" today. Even as they recruited young people who had previously been in street gangs or in jail, the Panthers also reached out to college students. Martha Biondi's book *The Black Revolution on Campus* argues that the BPP had considerable sway among Black campus activists in the 1970s.[4]

The Panthers also stood in solidarity with the rising new nations of the former colonial world, with the expectation that many of those countries, from Cuba to Algeria to Vietnam, were headed toward a more humane alternative to capitalism. History did not unfold the way they hoped. Still, into the twenty-first century, the need for transnational solidarity campaigns remains a critical part of any serious transformative politics, from post-apartheid South Africa to Palestine.

Woman-of-color feminism and "queer of color" analyses of gender and sexuality emerged after the Panthers' demise as an organization, but to their credit, and despite some pretty inexcusable sexism by individual leaders, there was a persistent push within the organization for women's leadership, sexual freedom, and independence from the conservative confines of traditional heterosexual family structures. Collective childrearing practices, community nurseries, and schools were alternatives to privatized parenting and male-headed nuclear families where women were expected to do the domestic work. Scholars Tracye Matthews and Robyn Spencer have written on the complex gender dynamics in the Party; in former Party leader Elaine Brown's memoir, *A Taste of Power*, she offers her own take on the nexus between sex, power, and violence in the Panthers.[5]

In this volume, a 1969 message from a male party leader reads: "It is mandatory that all manifestations of male chauvinism be excluded from our ranks and that sisters have a duty and the right to do whatever they want to do to see that they are not relegated to an inferior position." Saying this did not make it so, but the formal position represented an advance over other Black organizations and most white organizations in 1969, which did not even see gender inequality as a problem.

In terms of the BPP's stance on gender and sexuality, Huey Newton's 1970 statement on homophobia was also hugely important. One year after the Stonewall rebellion in New York's Greenwich Village credited with igniting the modern gay rights movement, Huey wrote:

> Whatever your personal opinions and your insecurities about homosexuality and women (and I speak of homosexuals and women as oppressed groups), we should try to unite with them in a revolutionary fashion. . . . We must gain security in ourselves and therefore have respect and feelings for all oppressed people. . . . We have not said much about the homosexual at all,

but we must relate to the homosexual movement because it is a real thing. And I know through reading, and through my life experience and observations that homosexuals are not given freedom and liberty by anyone in society. They might be the most oppressed people in society. . . . There is nothing to say that a homosexual cannot also be a revolutionary. . . . Maybe a homosexual could be the most revolutionary. . . . We should be careful about using those terms that might turn our friends off. The terms "faggot" and "punk" should be deleted from our vocabulary. . . . We should try to form a working coalition with the gay liberation and women's liberation groups.[6]

Finally, something must be said of Philip Foner, the prolific white leftist historian who edited the first edition of this powerful collection of primary documents in 1970, when the history of the BPP was still unfolding. Shaped by the radical interracial organizing of the 1930s, Foner understood not only the importance of a group like the Panthers to Black communities and to the left in general, but to our collective understanding of late-twentieth-century United States history overall. His antiracist consciousness and selfless service to a people's history and a useable past were truly exemplary.

Forty-eight years after the Panthers' founding, it is important to revisit what the organization meant in its own time and what it means in ours. What is the lesson for this historical moment? It is a different time and we are in a different place. Yet many of the problems, challenges, and threats the Panthers faced remain with us. COINTELPRO surveillance is mirrored in the far-reaching high-tech surveillance of the US National Security Agency. With the wanton murder of Black Florida teenager Trayvon Martin by a white vigilante in 2012 and the court's subsequent refusal to hold his killer accountable, we are reminded of the continued devaluation of Black life, even as we witness a greater display of power wielded by privileged Black politicians and elites than ever before. In the language of the Panthers, poor black folk are still "catching hell." The epidemic of mass incarceration is but one symptom; continued disparities in health, education, and income are others.

Many of the brave, idealistic, and committed young people who gave themselves, as Nelson's book title reminds us, "body and soul" to the struggle for Black liberation, and by extension human liberation, in the late 1960s and '70s are elders now. Some did not survive. Some were set up by COINTELPRO and spent decades in prison. Panther political prisoners like Dhoruba bin-Wahad and the late Geronimo ji-Jaga finally had their convictions overturned and were released. Others like Ahmad Rahman, jailed at age nineteen in Detroit for Party activity, did their time, got out, rebuilt their lives, and continue to "serve the people." Still others remain in prison or exile. There is the well-known case of Mumia Abu-Jamal, but there are the lesser known cases of Black Liberation Army members Mutulu Shakur and Sundiata Acoli, who have spent most of their adult lives in prison for their political activities in the 1970s. A campaign continues to win their freedom and that of others, including their Puerto Rican nationalist comrade and fellow political prisoner Oscar López Rivera. Former BLA member Assata Shakur has lived in exile in Cuba since soon after her escape from a New Jersey prison in 1979, for a crime most who know her and the details of the case insist she did not commit. Others took different paths after the Panthers split in 1971 and the organization gradually unraveled. Some former Panthers wrote books, others became lawyers and college professors, and one, Bobby Rush, was elected to the US Congress from Illinois's First Congressional District. Many former Panthers remain committed, in various ways, to ongoing struggles for freedom and justice.

The legacy of the Panthers is not defined, however, by the life and career trajectories of individuals. It is defined by how the current generation of activists has learned from its strengths and its mistakes and how they read Panther history into current Black political realities. The coercive arm of the state still polices young Black bodies on the streets of major cities, demanding that they justify congregating together, walking in certain areas, and even wearing their clothes a certain way, but much more sinister is that more than a million Black and brown bodies are policed inside the walls of prisons and correctional facilities of various types. The United States cages and confines more of its citizens than any other society in history. Young people in groups like Students Against Mass Incarceration (at Howard and Columbia Universities), the Black Youth Project 100, the Florida-based Dream Defenders, and the intergenerational and interracial activists in prison-abolition groups like Critical Resistance are responding with steady challenges, mobilizations, popular education, courage, and creative determination to confront and change that reality, as are networks of activists like Ella's Daughters. The documents, speeches, essays, and poems in this volume represent the militant voices of resistance in the twentieth century. The voices of the twenty-first century may speak, chant, scream, and "flow" in a different rhythm and register, but they are no less outraged at the injustices of their time and no less hungry for something different and better.

—Barbara Ransby, 2014

Barbara Ransby is a writer, historian, and longtime political activist. She is the author of an award-winning biography of civil rights activist Ella Baker, *Ella Baker and the Black Freedom Movement: A Radical Democratic Vision.*

1.  Curtis J. Austin, *Up Against the Wall: Violence in the Making and Unmaking of the Black Panther Party* (Fayetteville: University of Arkansas Press, 2006), xxvii.
2.  Dan Georgakas and Marvin Surkin, *Detroit: I Do Mind Dying: A Study in Urban Revolution* (Chicago: Haymarket Books, 2012).
3.  Alondra Nelson, *Body and Soul: The Black Panther Party and the Fight Against Medical Discrimination* (Minneapolis: University of Minnesota Press, 2011).
4.  Beth Richie, *Arrested Justice: Black Women, Violence and the Build Up of the Prison Nation* (New York: NYU Press, 2012); Michelle Alexander, *The New Jim Crow: Mass Incarceration in the Age of Colorblindness* (New York: New Press, 2010); and Martha Biondi, *The Black Revolution on Campus* (Berkeley: University of California Press, 2012). See also Peniel E. Joseph, ed., *The Black Power Movement: Rethinking the Civil Rights—Black Power Era* (New York: Routledge, 2013), and Donna Murch, *Living for the City: Migration, Education and the Rise of the Black Panther Party in Oakland, California* (Chapel Hill: University of North Carolina Press, 2010).

5. Robyn Spencer, "Engendering the Black Freedom Struggle: The Black Panther Party and Revolutionary Black Womanhood," *Journal of Women's History* 20 (2008); Tracye Matthews, "'No One Ever Asks, What a Man's Role in the Revolution Is': Gender and the Politics of the Black Panther Party, 1966–1971," *Black Panther Party Reconsidered,* ed. Charles E. Jones, (Baltimore: Black Classic Press, 2005).

6. Huey P. Newton, "The Women's Liberation and Gay Liberation Movements" (August 15, 1970), in *The Huey Newton Reader,* ed. David Hilliard and Donald Weise (Boston: Seven Stories Press, 2002).

# Foreword to the 1995 Edition

How do oppressed people with few resources overcome their oppression? The Black Panther Party's grassroots insurgency and ideological innovation produced suggestive answers to this enduring question. More than any other group of the 1960s, the Black Panther Party (BPP) inspired discontented urban African Americans to liberate themselves from oppressive conditions. They provided distinctive guidance for the black struggles of the late 1960s and 1970s, borrowing eclectically from past liberation movements, testing ideas through intense struggle, and sometimes bravely questioning their own approaches and assumptions. As this definitive anthology demonstrates, the Panthers forged their radical ideas through sustained militancy. *The Black Panthers Speak* provides comprehensive documentation of their fascinating and instructive effort to build an insurgent African-American movement in the face of vicious repression.

The Black Panther Party grew out of the African-American political agitation and grassroots militancy of the 1960s. While attending Oakland's Merritt Junior College, Huey P. Newton and Bobby G. Seale had become familiar with the period's various currents of black political thought, identifying initially with Donald Warden's Afro-American Association, one of the pioneering black nationalist groups on the West Coast. The Association enlarged their understanding of African-American history, but Newton's and Seale's goal was to change history rather than simply to study it. After breaking with Warden, they briefly affiliated with the Revolutionary Action Movement (RAM), inspired by Cuban-based guerilla warfare advocate Robert F. Williams. In 1965, Newton and Seale assumed leading roles in the Soul Students Advisory Council, which campaigned for black history courses at Merritt. Working with these groups expanded the two men's political awareness and contacts in the San Francisco Bay Area, but they remained unsatisfied in their search for a way to transform discontent into militant collective action.

Like other grassroots black activists of the period, Newton and Seale saw the need for an organization that would appeal particularly to young urban blacks from working-class backgrounds. Greatly influenced by Marxist literature and Frantz Fanon's revolutionary handbook, *The Wretched of the Earth* (1963), they also identified with Malcolm X's rhetorical attacks against white authority and black middle-class leadership. The two saw Malcolm as a model leader who combined erudition with an ability to communicate with black people of all educational levels: "He knew what the street brothers were like, and he knew what had to be done to reach them," Newton wrote. For Newton and Seale, Malcolm's message went beyond nationalist rhetoric about racial pride. They were drawn to his harsh criticisms of established civil rights leaders who were deemed too cautious, dependent on white support, and unwilling to retaliate against white racist violence. Their responsiveness to Malcolm's call for freedom "by any means necessary" increased during 1964 after he broke away from Elijah Muhammad's apolitical Nation of Islam to form the Organization of Afro-American Unity (OAAU). Newton later described the Panthers as "a living testament" to Malcolm's life work.[1]

Following Malcolm X's assassination in February 1965, Newton and Seale became even more determined to find or create a black militant group that embodied Malcolm's political ideas. The massive rebellion in Los Angeles during August 1965 demonstrated that conditions were ripe for a new direction in African-American politics. "At this point, we knew it was time to stop talking and begin organizing," Newton later recalled.[2] In October 1966, Newton and Seale drafted the Platform and Program of the Black Panther Party at the offices of the North Oakland Service Center, a federal anti-poverty agency. Their list of ten demands combined basic needs—full employment and decent housing—with more radical objectives, such as exemption of black men from military service and freedom for all black men held in federal, state, county, and city prisons and jails. The last item on their list summarized their goals: "We want land, bread, housing, education, clothing, justice, and peace. And as our major political objective, a United Nations-supervised plebiscite to be held throughout the black colony in which only black colonial subjects will be allowed to participate for the purpose of determining the will of black people as to their national destiny."[3]

Assuming the posts of defense minister and chairman, respectively, of the Black Panther Party for Self-Defense, Newton and Seale directed the group's rapid growth during the winter and spring of 1967. Their first recruit was a sixteen-year-old Oakland resident, Bobby Hutton, who became the Party's treasurer. Another important early recruit was David Hilliard, a childhood friend of Newton's who became the Party's chief of staff, responsible for coordinating its daily activities. Initially concentrated in the San Francisco Bay Area, the Black Panther Party ("for Self Defense" was dropped from its name) would attract dozens of new members during 1967 and 1968.

The Party's considerable appeal among young African Americans was based less on its program or its leaders' Marxist rhetoric than on its willingness to confront police. The issue of police brutality was of great concern to black urban residents, and the Panthers articulated these widespread anti-police sentiments. The first issue of the Party's newspaper, *The Black Panther*, published in April 1967, called on the black community to protest the police killing of Denzil Dowell, who was shot while allegedly running from a stolen car. During this period the Party's principal activity was to "patrol the pigs"—that is, to monitor police activities to insure that civil rights of black people were respected. When Panther members saw police pull over a black driver, they stopped and observed the incident, usually with weapons in hand. Newton carried law books in his car, and, despite police objections, he would question police conduct, often drawing a crowd as he read aloud the relevant portions of the California legal code. As their numbers increased, the Panthers doubled and tripled their patrols, expanding their operations from Oakland to Richmond,

Berkeley, and San Francisco. They patrolled at irregular intervals and in various areas to thwart any attempts by the police to track them. In addition to discouraging police harassment, the Panther patrols educated black residents about their ability to contest violations of their rights.

The Black Panther's most publicized early action came after legislation was proposed in the California State Assembly that would make the Panther armed patrols illegal. Seale led a group of Panthers to Sacramento to protest the bill by parading across the State Capitol lawn with guns in plain view. Among the startled witnesses of the protest was Governor Ronald Reagan, who happened to be talking to a group of students on the Capitol lawn. After reporters gathered, the Panther contingent distributed copies of Executive Mandate #1 and Seale read the document to the media. The mandate called upon "the American people in general and the Black people in particular to take careful note of the racist California Legislature, which is now considering legislation aimed at keeping the Black people disarmed and powerless at the very same time that racist police agencies throughout the country are intensifying the terror, brutality, murder and repression of Black people." Charging that the government was preparing to place African Americans in concentration camps, Seale proclaimed:

> The Black Panther Party for Self-Defense believes that the time has come for Black people to arm themselves against this terror before it is too late. . . . We believe that the Black communities of America must rise up as one man to halt the progression of a trend that leads inevitably to their total destruction.[4]

Thirty BPP members, including Seale, were prosecuted as a result of the incident, but the Party nevertheless gained valuable publicity as the new symbol of black militancy in America. According to Newton, "even those who did not hear the complete message saw the arms, and this conveyed enough to black people."[5] The Panthers were soon overwhelmed with new members and calls from people across the country who wanted to establish new chapters. During the months afterward, the Panthers made the transition from a local group to a national organization.

One of those attracted to the Black Panther Party as it became increasingly visible outside the Bay Area was Eldridge Cleaver, a former convict and author whose autobiographical essays were later collected in the bestseller *Soul on Ice* (1968). The Party first attracted Cleaver's attention in February 1967 when he witnessed a tense standoff between police and an armed contingent of Panthers guarding Betty Shabazz, the widow of Malcolm X. Impressed by their brash militancy, he attended the Sacramento protest, and, despite his claim that he was merely an observer, was arrested with other Panthers. Threatened with return to prison for violating his parole, Cleaver began a highly publicized legal battle against California authorities. Determined to maintain his ties with the Panthers, Cleaver quickly became one of the Party's most effective and best-known spokespersons. His position as a writer for the New Left journal *Ramparts* brought the group additional publicity and created a link between the Panthers and white leftist sympathizers. After Cleaver became editor of the Party's Black Community News Service and a public speaker on behalf of the group, his uniquely caustic, bombastic verbal attacks on white authorities became part of the Black Panther Party's public image.[6]

Cleaver's prominence in the Black Panther Party increased after October 28, 1967, when Newton was arrested after an altercation ending in the death of an Oakland police officer. The Panthers immediately mobilized to free Newton, who faced a possible death sentence if convicted. As part of this support effort, Cleaver and Seale contacted Stokely Carmichael, former chairman of the Student Nonviolent Coordinating Committee (SNCC) and a nationally known Black Power proponent. The Panther leaders recognized that they could benefit from SNCC's extensive support network and learn from SNCC's years of community organizing experience (indeed, the Party's name was derived from the black panther symbol used by Lowndes County Freedom Organization, an Alabama political party organized by Carmichael and other SNCC workers). Cleaver and Seale "drafted" Carmichael to be the Panther's Prime Minister, and offered administrative positions

to other SNCC officers, including H. Rap Brown and James Forman. Newton later wrote that "we were in effect voting to give
leadership of the Party to SNCC. We even considered moving
our headquarters to Atlanta, where we would be under SNCC, in
their buildings, with access to their duplicating equipment and
other sorely needed materials."[7] Carmichael, Brown, and Forman
agreed to join leaders from other black militant groups in "Free
Huey" rallies to be held in Los Angeles and Oakland during February 1968. These well-attended events increased the national vis-
ibility of the Black Panther Party and broadened support for the
effort to free Newton.

Despite the success of the February rallies, Panther leaders experienced considerable difficulties in their efforts to build lasting
ties with other black militant groups. The internal and external
factors that were responsible for these difficulties were evident in
the ill-fated effort to build an alliance between the BPP and SNCC.
Although Cleaver presumptuously announced at a "Free Huey"
rally in Oakland that SNCC had merged with the Panthers, he
and Panther leaders wrongly assumed that former SNCC chairman Carmichael and other SNCC officers spoke for the SNCC
rank-and-file. At a deeper level, the Panther leaders failed to
recognize that the BPP's hierarchical leadership style contrasted
sharply with SNCC's decentralized structure. The self-conscious
effort of Carmichael and other black activists in SNCC to separate
themselves from former white allies also adversely affected their
relations with the Panthers, who welcomed white support. Moreover, the Panther's recognition that they were under deadly attack
made them distrustful of and impatient with black activists who
questioned their ideological orientation. By August 1968 relations
between the two groups had soured to the point of open conflict.
Afterwards, Carmichael decided to ally himself with the Panthers
rather than remain in SNCC. His BPP ties helped the group establish strong chapters in the eastern United States, but his advo-
cacy of racial unity rather than interracial coalitions continued to
put him at odds with other Panther leaders.[8] The ideological and
personal tensions between Carmichael and other Panther leaders

signaled the beginning of a period of pervasive, vicious infighting within the black militant community.

Constant confrontations with police and covert disruptive activities of the FBI's counterintelligence program (COINTELPRO) exacerbated these conflicts within the black community. As explained in a February 1968 memorandum, the FBI's COINTELPRO operations were intended to "neutralize militant black nationalists" and forestall "a coalition of militant Black nationalist groups" and prevent the emergence of a "Black messiah" "who might unify and electrify these violence-prone elements."[9] Numerous FBI "dirty tricks" directed against the Panthers seriously disrupted its organizing efforts and strengthened the tendency of Panthers to suspect the motives of black militants who questioned the group's strategy or tactics. FBI disinformation campaigns-anonymous phone calls or letters and planted newspaper stories—exploited the Black Panther Party's vulnerabilities, especially its tendency toward rhetorical excess and its heavy-handed efforts to intimidate critics.

Even as the Panthers deliberated their future course,[10] direct and covert external attacks threatened their existence. On April 6, 1968 police attacked a house containing several Panthers, killing Hutton, the seventeen-year-old treasurer of the Party, and wounding Cleaver, who was briefly returned to prison as a parole violator. In September 1968 Newton was convicted of voluntary manslaughter and sentenced to two-to-fifteen years in prison. Soon after finishing his 1968 presidential campaign as candidate of the Peace and Freedom Party, Cleaver left for exile in Cuba and then Algeria to avoid returning to prison for parole violation.

During 1969 continued FBI COINTELPRO plots directed against the Black Panther Party decimated its leadership and disrupted its relations with other militant organizations. In southern California, these covert activities exacerbated conflicts between the Party and followers of black cultural nationalist Maulana Karenga. The FBI's disinformation efforts and the Panther's escalating verbal attacks against Karenga (described in Panther literature as a "pork chop" nationalist) culminated in a gun battle in January 1969 on the UCLA campus that left two Panthers dead.

In March 1969 Seale was arrested for conspiracy to incite rioting at the 1968 Democratic convention in Chicago, and in May Connecticut officials charged Seale and seven other Panthers with murder in the slaying of Party member Alex Rackley, who was believed to be a police informant. In New York, 21 Panthers were charged with plotting to assassinate policemen and blow up buildings. Then in December 1969 police killed two Chicago Panther leaders, Fred Hampton and Mark Clark, while they were sleeping at Hampton's apartment. The police raid was planned with the help of a police informer and coordinated with the United States Department of Justice. Other covert operations by the FBI and local police forces further intensified the sometimes vicious factionalism within the Black Panther Party.

This was particularly the case after Cleaver, speaking from exile in Algeria, stepped up his calls for violent revolution while Newton and Seale were seeking to moderate the Party's image. FBI heightened mutual suspicions through anonymous letters and other actions that transformed leadership competition and ideological differences into deadly conflicts. Newton, for example, reacted to a planted story that Los Angeles Panther leader Elmer "Geronimo" Pratt was a police agent by expelling him. The FBI later conspired to have Pratt convicted of robbery and murder. In 1971 Newton expelled the New York 21 shortly before their trial on conspiracy charges after the FBI led him to believe that they were plotting with Cleaver to take over the Party.[11]

In 1970, when Newton was released on bail after his conviction on a manslaughter charge was reversed on appeal, he returned to find the Party in disarray. Seale still faced conspiracy charges in the murder of Rackley (they were dropped the following year). Chief of staff David Hilliard awaited trial on charges of verbally threatening the life of President Nixon. Some chapters, particularly those in the eastern United States, resisted direction from the Oakland headquarters. Many chapters were heavily infiltrated by police or FBI informants. One of these informants, Earl Anthony, had been active in disrupting the Party's operations in Los Angeles.[12]

Newton sought to revive the Party and reestablish his control

by de-emphasizing police confrontations in favor of survival programs that would meet the everyday needs of black communities
while also educating black people. During the late 1960s and early 1970s the Black Panther Party concentrated on developing four
main programs: the petition campaign for community control of
police, free breakfast for school children, free health clinics, and
liberation schools. Such programs attracted new members, allowed
Panthers to interact with diverse segments of black communities,
and helped to counter the Party's negative image in the media.[13]

Newton's decision to shift course prompted an open break with
Cleaver, who continued to argue from exile that the black "lumpen
proletariat" were ready for revolution. Newton charged that Cleaver
had been unduly influenced by the confrontation he had witnessed
between police and Panthers guarding Betty Shabazz and, as a result, placed too much emphasis on armed rebellion. Cleaver's attitude, according to Newton, "was that either the community picked
up the gun with the Party or else they were cowards and there was
no place for them." Newton asserted that Cleaver's leadership had
caused the Black Panther Party to become "a revolutionary cult
group" that had lost touch with the black community. The group's
emphasis on police confrontations had increased the Black Panther
Party's appeal among young blacks, but maintaining a "macho"
image lessened the Party's actual ability to effectively organize the
black community toward concrete political ends. Cleaver's profane,
bombastic rhetoric, according to Newton, made the Panthers vul-
nerable to external repression and increased the influence of those
more concerned with displays of bravado than with community
organizing. In addition, Cleaver encouraged the Party to develop
close ties with white radicals without influence in their own communities. "The Black Panther Party defected from the community
long before Eldridge defected from the Party," Newton concluded.[14]

Newton's efforts to shift the Black Panther Party's emphasis
from revolutionary rhetoric and armed confrontations to survival
programs did not prevent further external attacks and internal
conflicts from plaguing the group. Throughout the late 1960s
and early 1970s, efforts to purge members considered disloyal or

unreliable were at times counterproductive and disrupted Panther chapters. In addition, the Party's hierarchical, military-style structure exposed the limitations of Newton and other officers. As Elaine Brown later conceded, the Party was "not a democratic organization," and by the early 1970s its principle of "democratic centralism" generally was "reduced to one man, Huey Newton, though the Central Committee still influenced the governance of the Party, since its members held individual fields of sway."[15] After years of external attacks, internal conflicts, and legal prosecutions, Newton and other Panther leaders suffered from battle fatigue, and Newton was further debilitated by his increasing use of cocaine and other drugs. Moreover, the Party's authoritarian male leaders were increasingly out of step with the substantial and growing involvement of female rank-and-file members.

In ways that distinguished it from other black militant groups of the period, the Black Panther Party encouraged the participation of women by condemning "male chauvinism" and lessening its reliance on a paramilitary style of organization.[16]

By the mid-1970s, the Panthers had been weakened by years of external attacks, legal problems, and internal schisms. Nevertheless, some chapters maintained their activities during the period. In 1973 Bobby Seale ran an unsuccessful, though formidable, campaign for mayor of Oakland, and following Newton's departure for exile in Cuba, Elaine Brown experienced some success in continuing Newton's emphasis on community service programs. Nevertheless, in a hostile political climate, the group could not reverse its decline as a political force. Most Panther veterans, including Seale and Cleaver, left or were expelled from the group. Popular support for the Party declined further after newspaper reports appeared describing the group's involvement in illicit activities such as drug dealing and extortion schemes directed against Oakland merchants.[17] After Newton returned from exile in 1977, the Black Panther Party never regained its former prominence.

The rapid rise and decline of the Panthers reflected the general course of black political militancy during the late 1960s and 1970s. One of only a few militant political groups to gain widespread support in urban black communities, the Party's achievements and its failures provided instructive lessons for a generation of activists. The Party demonstrated the ability of urban, grassroots, political activists to offer intellectual and tactical guidance for the ongoing African-American freedom struggle. Although the group was unable to prevent the deterioration of urban black communities that resulted from poverty, powerlessness, and pessimism, the Black Panther Party at its best offers a historical example of brave activists willing to "die for the people" and thus continues to provide discontented African-American youth an alternative to self-destructive despair.

—CLAYBORNE CARSON Stanford University November 1994

Clayborne Carson is professor of history at Stanford University and director of the Martin Luther King, Jr., Research and Education Institute. He is the author of *In Struggle: SNCC and the Black Awakening of the 1960s* and *Malcolm X: The FBI File.* He is an editor of *The Eyes on the Prize Civil Rights Reader* and *The Papers of Martin Luther King, Jr.* (volumes I and II).

---

1.  Huey P. Newton with the assistance of J. Herman Blake, *Revolutionary Suicide* (New York: Harcourt Brace Jovanovich, 1973), p. 71, 113.
2.  Newton, *Revolutionary Suicide,* p. 113.
3.  "Black Panther Party Platform and Program—What We Want/What We Believe," reprinted in this volume, p. 2.
4.  Newton, "In Defense of Self-Defense: Executive Mandate Number One," *The Black Panther,* June 2, 1967, reprinted in this volume, p. 40.
5.  Newton, *Revolutionary Suicide,* p. 150.
6.  Cleaver's writings as a member of the Black Panther Party appear in this volume and in Robert Scheer, ed., *Eldridge Cleaver: Post-Prison Writings and Speeches* (New York: Random House, 1969).
7.  Newton, *Revolutionary Suicide,* p. 113, 154, 155.
8.  For a fuller discussion of the SNCC-Panther ties, see "Huey Newton Talks to the Movement About the Black Panther Party', Cultural Nationalism, SNCC, Liberals and White Revolutionaries" and Eldridge Cleaver, "An Open Letter to Stokely Carmichael," in this volume (p. 50 and p. 104 respectively); David Hilliard and Lewis Cole, *This Side of Glory: The Autobiography of David Hilliard and the Story of the Black*

*Panther Party* (Boston: Little, Brown and Company, 1993), pp. 161, 171-175, 202-204; Clayborne Carson, *In Struggle: SNCC and the Black Awakening of the 1960s* (Cambridge, Mass.: Harvard University Press, 1981), pp. 278-285.

9. Memorandum is reprinted in Ward Churchill and Jim Vander Wall, *The COINTELPRO PAPERS: Documents from the FBI's Secret Wars Against Domestic Dissent* (Boston: South End Press, 1990), p. 107.

10. See, for example, Huey Newton's statement, "The Correct Handling of a Revolution," in this volume, p. 41.

11. On the repression campaign against the Panthers, see "To Judge Murtagh: From the Panther 21," and Charles R. Garry, "The Old Rules Do Not Apply," in this volume (p. 196 and p. 257 respectively); Huey P. Newton, "The War Against the Panthers: A Study of Repression in America," Ph.D. dissertation, University of California at Santa Cruz, 1980; Kenneth O'Reilly, *"Racial Matters": The FBI's Secret File on Black America, 1960-1972* (New York: The Free Press, 1989), chapter 9; *Search and Destroy: A Report by the Commission of Inquiry into the Black Panthers and the Police* (New York: Metropolitan Applied Research Center, 1973); and Assata Shakur, *Assata: An Autobiography* (Chicago: Lawrence Hill Books, 1987).

12. See Earl Anthony, *Spitting in the Wind: The True Story Behind the Violent Legacy of the Black Panther Party* (Malibu, California: Roundtable, 1990).

13. See documents in section on Community Activities in this volume, pp. 167-181.

14. Newton, "On the Defection of Eldridge Cleaver from the Black Panther Party and the Defection of the Black Panther Party from the Black Community," *Black Panther Intercommunal News Service,* April 17, 1971, reprinted in this volume (p. 272). See also Lee Lockwood, *Conversation with Eldridge Cleaver, Algiers* (New York: McGraw-Hill, 1970).

15. Brown, *A Taste of Power: A Black Woman's Story* (New York: Pantheon Books, 1992), p. 320).

16. See section Black Panther Women Speak, and Eldridge Cleaver, "Message to Sister Erica Huggins of the Black Panther Party," in this volume (pp. 145-165 and p. 98 respectively); also Bobby Seale, *Seize the Time: The Story of the Black Panther Party and Huey P. Newton* (New York: Random House, 1970), pp. 393-403.

17. See, for example, Kate Coleman with Paul Avery, *New Times,* July 10, 1978. The unsavory aspects of the Party's activities are emphasized in Hugh Pearson's *The Shadow of the Panther: Huey Newton and the Price of Black Power in America* (Reading, Massachusetts: Addison-Wesley, 1994).

# Preface

In April, 1970, I was asked by Edward P. Morgan, Correspondent for the American Broadcasting Companies, how black people feel about the Black Panthers. I replied (and the reply was broadcast on the ABC-TV program "The Panthers"):

> what the Panthers do more than anything else is they set a standard, that young black people particularly want to measure up to.... It's a standard of aggressiveness, of militance, of just forcefulness, the sort of standard we haven't had in the past. Our idols have been Dr. King who, for all of his beauty as a man, was not an aggressive man, but the Panthers, and I think Malcolm X, have set this new kind of standard that a great many people want to adhere to.

Mr. Morgan then asked, "But figurative[ly] speaking, you're not about to become a Panther?" I replied, "No, not today or tomorrow at any rate. Maybe the day after."

*The Black Panthers Speak* should give the American people a clear idea of why I answered as I did. So much has been written and spoken about the Black Panthers in the press and over the radio and TV that one might suppose that most people know what the organization really stands for and seeks to achieve. But this is far from the case. Only rarely does the press report what the Panthers are actually saying and doing and how they view the problems of black people in our society. The result is that most Americans have obtained their impression of the Panthers from statements issued by those who wish to see them eliminated as a factor in American life.

The language of the Panthers is often shocking to those accustomed to the ordinary expressions of political figures, but we might as well get accustomed to it, for it expresses the sentiments of a vast section of oppressed Americans. The Panthers articulate what the people in the ghettoes feel and, in so doing, enable all of us to gain insight into deep-set anger of so many of our deprived citizens as well as their determination to change these conditions.

Mr. Morgan observed back in April that throughout his talks with black Americans, it became clear that "there is a great deal of truth in what the Panthers have been saying." Now all of us have the opportunity to learn what that is.

—JULIAN BOND

Julian Bond (1940–2015), was a civil rights activist and co-founder of the Student Nonviolent Coordinating Committee.

# Introduction

In 1919 Paul R. Brissenden, Professor of Economics at Columbia University, wrote in his pioneer study of the Industrial Workers of the World: "The public still knows but little about the organization and its members. . . . The public has not been told the truth about the things the I.W.W. has done or the doctrines in which it believes. The papers have printed so much fiction about this organization and maintained such a nationwide conspiracy of silence as to its real philosophy—especially to the constructive items of its philosophy—that the popular conception of this labor group is a weird unreality." If one were to substitute the words "white Americans" for "the public" and "Black Panther Party" for "I.W.W.," Professor Brissenden's statement could be reprinted today without any other alteration.

To the average white American the Black Panther Party conjures up the picture of an anarchistic band of gun-toting, white-hating thugs. This is hardly surprising, for the Black Panthers have been subjected to a campaign of vilification (to say nothing of terror) from the inception of their organization, and this was intensified as the movement grew. FBI Director J. Edgar Hoover (who spearheaded the drive against the I.W.W. and other radical groups in the post-World War I era) described the Panthers as a "black extremist organization" consisting mostly of "hoodlum-type revolutionaries" who stockpile weapons, espouse Marxist-Leninist doctrines, and terrorize black communities. Vice-President Spiro Agnew, exceeding his usual caustic language when dealing with dissenters, declared that the Panthers are a "completely irresponsible, anarchist group of criminals." Attorney-General John Mitchell has ruled that "the Panthers are a threat to national security and thus subject to FBI wiretapping."

Even liberals have gotten into the popular act of vilifying the Black Panthers. Daniel P. Moynihan obviously had the Panthers in mind when, in his notorious "benign neglect" memorandum to President Nixon, he referred to "black extremists" who used "lower-class" blacks "to threaten white society with the prospect of mass arson and pillage." Daniel J. Boorstein, an American historian, director of the Smithsonian Institution's National Museum of History and Technology, in a paper presented to the House Committee on Science and Astronautics, referred to the "aggressive ethnicity and racism of groups like the Black Panthers," and accused them of "destructive and illegal acts." [1] Writing in *Dissent* (March–April, 1970) under the provocative title, "Panthers: Black Men in Extremis," Jervis Anderson accused the Black Panthers of deliberately provoking the police to kill them because of a psychological desire for "martyrdom." He advises the Panthers to cease playing with "martyrdom," and devote themselves to the business of "getting your work done," adding the sneering comment—"assuming, in the case of the Panthers, that there is something worthwhile they would like to do, and that they have some idea of how to do it."

In general, the attacks on the Black Panthers, whether from diehard reactionaries or liberals, boil down to the theme that they deserve what they get. A letter to the editor of *Life* (February 20, 1970), put it this way: "If the Panthers didn't preach the overthrow of society and didn't make their homes arsenals, there would be no raids. One has but to reflect back a few years to the raid on conservative 'Minutemen'—all white—to see that social justice is against armed camps of revolutionaries and not against Black Panthers *per se*." This sweeping judgment has about as much substance to it as

1 In addition to being labeled "black racists," the Panthers have also been accused of being anti-Semitic. (See the document issued by the American Jewish Committee, February, 1970, entitled "The Black Panther Party—the Anti-Semitic and Anti-Israel Component," and the article by Gerald Emanuel Stern in the *New York Times Magazine*, March 8, 1970.) The Black Panthers, however, insist that they are not anti-Semitic and "do not lump all Jews with slumlords." But they do contend that they are anti-Zionist and view Israel as a "puppet imperialist state." While one can certainly argue that this is a simplistic view of a complex issue, it is difficult to see how being anti-Zionist and anti-Israel makes one *ipso facto* anti-Semitic. Certainly the American Jewish Committee is on weak ground when it asserts in its document: "While we do not necessarily equate anti-Israel or anti-Zionist sentiment with anti-Semitism, the Panthers' expression of support for Al Fatah has been so strident and distorted as to make it impossible to make the distinction." But thousands of Jewish Americans who have rallied to the support of the Black Panthers do make that distinction. Moreover, on January 13, 1970, at the winter leadership meeting of the Jewish Cultural Clubs and Societies, representing sixty-six New York organizations, the persecution of the Panthers was protested. "We will do everything in our power," the clubs' resolution stated, "to oppose those forces that are now trying to use repression, terror and police brutality against the black people and other minorities in our land, a repression that will soon be applied to Jews, labor, students and others fighting for full freedom and equality for all peoples if it is not halted by the united action of all Americans who cherish democracy." And Rabbi Arthur J. Lelyveld, head of the American Jewish Congress, declared on December 16, 1969, in calling for the defense of Panther civil liberties, "No consideration of which we can conceive would justify lawless activity on the part of the police." A criticism of a different nature, most sharply voiced by Harold Cruse, is that for all its revolutionary rhetoric, the Black Panther Party works for essentially reformist demands. Of course, those who voice such criticisms are clearly unaware of the essential unity between immediate demands and a long-term revolutionary goal.

the other comments on the Black Panthers cited above. The writer ignored the easily ascertainable facts that though the Minutemen were arrested with an arsenal that included $140,000 worth of arms, including an anti-tank weapon and a bazooka, two of the Minutemen were released on their own recognizance pending trial, and were ultimately given a suspended sentence of six months. Robert Boliver De Pugh, national coordinator of the Rightist paramilitary organization, was sentenced to four years in prison, to be followed by five years' probation, for conspiracy and violation of the Federal Firearms Act after a cache of machine guns was seized in rural Missouri. Minutemen have been treated gently and never harassed by arresting officials. Contrast this with the treatment meted out to the New York Panthers, who were arrested and charged with "conspiracy"—no actual act at all was charged—to bomb and destroy property and lives all over the city. All twenty-one had bail immediately set at one hundred thousand dollars for each alleged conspirator, and were not even given a hearing on reduction of bail—a request for it was denied—until three and a half months after their arrest.

In an address on March 4, 1911, delivered before the Republican Club of New York City, Dr. W. E. B. Du Bois, the distinguished black scholar, declared: "If the question before the court was simply one of justice between individuals the task would be an easy one, but a man enters court today to be tried and convicted according to the class he belongs to. . . . The Negro never enters a court in the South as a man, but always as a Negro. He knows that individual virtues will not weigh in the court's decision. The natural result of this is that the Negro has no faith in the courts." On April 24, 1970, Kingman Brewster, president of Yale University, brought Dr. Du Bois's observation up to date when he said that he was "skeptical of the ability of black revolutionaries to achieve a fair trial anywhere in the United States." And on July 6, 1970, *The New York Times* quoted the courageous black jurist, Judge George Crockett of Detroit's Recorders Court, as saying that while "the public likes to believe that the courts are crystallized in majestic neutrality, the truth is that they are not. The legal system does not work for blacks now. We have all the laws we need but we have too many police and government officials who do not live by the laws we have." Certainly the experience of the Black Panthers in court bears out the truth of these comments.

The fearsome picture painted of the Black Panthers by men who have little understanding of their program and little desire to understand it is not shared by the black community. Three black members of Local 1199 (Drug and Hospital Workers Union), interviewed by the union's magazine in January, 1970, as to their reaction to the Black Panthers, expressed admiration for them. The report noted:

When asked about the charges that the Panthers are a violent group, the feelings of all three men were summed up in the comment of one of them, Ed Mayo of Clara Maass Hospital in New Jersey: "They're fighting for the same cause as we are in the union—to be free and have human dignity. Some people don't see clearly what the fight is about because they see only violence. But these people don't see the disgusting things that are happening to us in this country. Every organization has its own way of fighting these things."

It may be argued that this finding is hardly convincing since it reflects the views of members of a militant and progressive trade union. But it is not so easy to dismiss reports in the established mass media. On January 13, 1970, *The Wall Street Journal* featured on its front page a lengthy article headed, "Panther Supporters" and sub-headed: "Many Black Americans Voice Strong Backing for Defiant Militants." Four reporters had investigated a sampling of opinion among black citizens of San Francisco, New York, Cleveland, and Chicago, and concluded that "a clear majority of blacks support both the goals and methods of the Black Panthers. An even larger percentage believes, moreover, that police officials are determined to crush the party by arresting or killing its key officials." Here is a response from one of the blacks who were interviewed:

> "I dig the Black Panthers. I think a lot of them," says Evord Connor who is head of an antipoverty center in Yonkers, N.Y., and who is black himself. "They appeal to young kids and create a lot of black awareness. They're not just advocating militancy; they're talking about economic and political power. Right now, they're backing up what they preach, and that's why the man is coming down on them."

Much of the support for the Black Panthers, *The Wall Street Journal* pointed out, came from young people who were attracted by the distinctive uniforms of black berets and black leather jackets, their display of guns, "their avowed determination to overturn the American 'system,' their refusal to back down under intense police pressure." It continued:

> But a sizeable number of blacks support the Panthers because they admire other, less-publicized activities of the Party such as its free-breakfast program for ghetto youngsters, its free medical care program and its war on narcotics use among black youth.
> "The news media never says how strong the Panthers are against narcotics," says Mr. Conner of the Yonkers antipoverty center. "You take the kids in Harlem, they sort of envy hustlers—guys who take numbers, push dope. But the Panthers are telling kids from grade school level, don't mess with dope. It works."

*The Wall Street Journal* concluded that "Mr. Conner's view may be surprising to those whites who regard the Panthers as a radical splinter group without wide support among black Americans. But his views may be more widely shared among blacks than many whites suppose."

In the next two months "those whites" were further surprised. A nationwide poll of black people in the United States, conducted by Louis Harris for *Time* magazine (published on March 30, 1970, in a special issue of *Time* which for the first time devoted virtually an entire issue to one subject) revealed that while "the vast majority want to work through the existing system" to further their position, 9 per cent of the black people across the country, more than two million black Americans, count themselves as "revolutionaries," and believe that only a "readiness to use violence will ever get them equality." The poll showed that the number of those who believe that the blacks "will probably have to resort to violence to win rights," had risen from 21 per cent in 1966 to 31 per cent in 1970. The finding also disclosed that while 75 per cent of blacks admired the NAACP "a great deal," 25 per cent had this view of the Black Panthers.

Another poll, of black Americans living in New York, San Francisco, Detroit, Baltimore, and Birmingham, Alabama, taken by Market Dynamics, Incorporated, for ABC-TV (broadcast on ABC-TV's "The Panthers," April 13, 1970), disclosed that of the best-known organizations, the NAACP is regarded as having done most for black people over the past two years; the late Martin Luther King's Southern Christian Leadership Conference came next, *with the Black Panthers showing up in third place.* But when it comes to the future, the Panthers are rated the *only* black group which will increase its effectiveness if only in a small way, while both the NAACP and SCLC contributions to the black cause are expected to diminish. *Sixty-two per cent of the people polled admire what the Black Panthers are doing.*

Never before in the history of black Americans has an admittedly revolutionary party won such support in the leading black communities of this country. Yet the Black Panther Party has been in existence less than four years.

In 1896 the National Association of Colored Men declared that "the American Negro has at no time in the past been either unmindful or indifferent to or failed to assert and contend for his own rights." What was true prior to 1896 has also been true since that year. The history of black Americans from 1619 to the present has been a history of protest. This protest reached a climax in the decade of the 1960's—the decade of the Civil Rights demonstrations, of the freedom rides and the sit-ins, of the Black Power movement, of the rebellions in Watts, Newark, and Detroit. New protest movements arose in black communities, and older ones increased their militancy. Since the assassination of Malcolm X on February 21, 1965, the most militant and effective leadership in the black community has been that of the Black Panthers—a name chosen because the panther is reputed never to make an unprovoked attack but to defend itself ferociously whenever it is attacked.[2]

The Black Panther Party for Self-Defense was organized in Oakland, California, in the fall of 1966 by two black militants: Huey P. Newton and Bobby G. Seale. (Seale was Chairman and Newton Minister of Defense.) Newton was born in Louisiana in 1942; when he was a year old, his family moved to California. Although he was graduated from high school, he became literate by "self determination," attended Merritt Junior College and went to law school for six months. He also attended a music conservatory and mastered the concert piano. Seale, a musician, carpenter, journeyman sheet metal mechanic and a mechanical draftsman, was born in Dallas, Texas, in 1936. He moved with his family to California, and was graduated from Oakland High School after a stint in the Air Force.

Newton and Seale met at Merritt College and worked together to initiate courses in Black History and lay the groundwork for hiring more black instructors. They also worked at the North Oakland Poverty Center, and both joined the Afro-American Association—a black nationalist group at Merritt—early in 1965. They left within a year, dissatisfied with the group's emphasis on cultural nationalism [3] and its middle-class composition. Not content to remain classroom theoreticians, they began working in the black community, knocking on doors and asking the residents of Oakland's ghetto what they needed and wanted. From the answers they received, they developed, after forming the Black Panther Party, its ten-point program. (See page 2 below.) "We're going to draw up a basic platform," Newton, who wrote the program, explained, "that the mothers who struggled hard to raise us, that the fathers who worked hard to feed us, that the young brothers in school who come out of school semi-illiterate, saying and reading broken words, and all of these, can read. . . ."

During all this time, Newton and Seale had been reading Malcolm X and Frantz Fanon, and they were deeply influenced by these black revolutionaries. (Later, they were to read and study the writings

---

[2] The "Black Panther" was originally the emblem of the Lowndes County Freedom Party in Alabama, organized in 1965. The Panther, symbol of black militancy, was hailed and copied at other points across the nation.

[3] Cultural nationalists see the white man as the oppressor, and make no distinction between racist whites and nonracist whites. They also emphasize that a black man cannot be the enemy of the black people. Apart from questioning the validity of this thesis, Newton and Seale were irritated by the fact that the cultural nationalists mainly met and talked and did nothing concrete to end the oppression in the black ghetto.

of Marx, Engels, Lenin, Mao Tse-tung, Ho Chi Minh, and Che Guevara.) Both knew that Malcolm had consistently denounced white oppressors, but after his visit to the Near East and Africa, he had no longer based his philosophy on hatred of whites alone. Rather, he chose to stress the beauty of black culture, its historic contributions, the joy of black brotherhood and community, and the wisdom of working with whites whenever it would be useful for black people to do so—provided that the power to decide policy and action alternatives lay in black hands. Modeling themselves on Malcolm's philosophy—Newton viewed himself as Malcolm's heir and the Black Panther Party as the successor to his Organization of Afro-American Unity—the founders of the BPP expressed belief in black nationalism and black culture, but they did not believe either would lead to black liberation.

It was the martyred Malcolm X's emphasis on self-defense and his effort to lead the struggle for freedom "by any means necessary" that most deeply impressed Newton and Seale, and they frequently quoted his famous statement: "We should be peaceful, law-abiding, but the time has come to fight back in self-defense whenever and wherever the black man is being unjustly and unlawfully attacked. If the government thinks I am wrong for saying this, then let the government start doing its job." Newton and Seale read and reread Fanon's *The Wretched of the Earth*, and they were impressed by the black psychiatrist's thesis that revolutionary violence was necessary in order for the oppressed to get the oppressors' boot off their neck and that it was essential in order to achieve the transformation or rebirth of the black personality. By fighting back, the black man would assert his dignity as a man.[4] The Black Panthers repeatedly reminded black Americans that their future was linked to their past, to the experience of such slave rebels as Toussaint L'Ouverture, Gabriel Prosser, Denmark Vesey, and Nat Turner, who did not hesitate to use revolutionary violence in their efforts to free their people from slavery.

In its early phase, the BPP emphasized Point No. 7 of its ten-point program: "We want an immediate end to police brutality and murder of black people.' In its relations with the police as in all

---

[4] It is interesting to note that the personality of Frederick Douglass was transformed when as a slave he fought back, risking death, against Edward Covey, the slave breaker. After having been flogged daily until he was "broken in body, soul and spirit," he found the courage one day to turn on his tormentor and soundly thrashed the slave breaker. The result was that Covey abandoned the whip and ignored Douglass for the four remaining months of hire. "The battle with Mr. Covey was the turning-point in my career," Douglass wrote later. "I was a changed being after that fight. I was nothing before, I was a man now . . . with a renewed determination to be a free man. . . . I now resolved that, however long I might remain a slave in form, the day had passed forever when I could be a slave in fact. . . ."

other aspects, Oakland was a typical black ghetto. What this means was graphically spelled out by the National Commission on the Causes and Prevention of Violence, set up under the chairmanship of Milton S. Eisenhower at the Center for the Study of Law and Society in Berkeley, California, August 28, 1968. In its report submitted March 21, 1969, the Commission said:

> . . . for the black citizen, the policeman has long since ceased to be —if indeed he ever was—a neutral symbol of law and order. Studies of the police emphasize that their attitudes and behavior towards blacks differ vastly from those taken toward whites. Similar studies show that blacks perceive the police as hostile, prejudiced, and corrupt. In the ghetto disorders of the past few years, blacks have often been exposed to indiscriminate police assaults and, not infrequently, to gratuitous brutality. . . . Many ghetto blacks see the police as an occupying army. . . .
> In view of these facts, the adoption of the idea of self-defense is not surprising. . . .

The Commission might have added, first, that black Americans had taken up guns and practiced self-defense in the struggle against slavery, kidnappers of fugitive slaves, anti-Negro rioters, and lynchers, and, secondly, that organized white and black workers had also armed themselves and used guns in self-defense against armed vigilantes, Pinkerton Detectives, militias, and police serving the interests of antiunion employers.

"The readiness of police to use their weapons is a tenet of blacktown life," W. H. Ferry has observed. "The cop's trigger-finger is the gavel of justice in blacktown.' To meet this ever-pressing problem facing the black people of Oakland, the Black Panther Party began to operate as an armed association for community protection against the police. (Carrying rifles and other unconcealed weapons was then legal in California.) Newton, a meticulous student of every legal aspect of the right of citizens to arm themselves, instructed all party members in the basic constitutional rights governing arrests and gun laws. He pointed to the second amendment of the Constitution of the United States and read the words—"the right of the people to keep and bear arms shall not be infringed." Newton went to great lengths to stress two points about armed self-defense: first, they were operating within the law as defined by gun regulations and the constitutional right to bear arms; second, the arms were to serve a political purpose and were not to be viewed in purely military terms.

The Party established a system of armed patrol cars, completely legal, carrying both guns and lawbooks. The Panthers trailed police cars through the slums of Oakland with guns and a lawbook, to halt police brutality. Whenever black men or women were stopped by the police, armed Panthers would be on the scene, making sure that their constitutional rights were not violated. The Oakland police were outraged, but the black community was impressed, especially after Newton, Seale and a half dozen other young Panthers calmly faced down a carload of police outside their Oakland headquarters. More important, the brutality and harassment directed against black men and women tapered off. Little wonder then that news of the Party's existence spread rapidly, and the armed and disciplined groups of Panthers in the Bay Area began to be the talk of black communities on the Coast.

Just how the Party operated in its early phase was shown in the action taken around the death of Denzil Dowell at the beginning of 1967. Dowell, a black youth living in North Richmond, California, had been shot and killed by the police, whose official account of the slaying contradicted dozens of black eyewitnesses. The Dowell family called in the Panthers to investigate, and the Party decided to hold a street-corner rally in the neighborhood to expose the facts of the slaying and the political importance of self-defense. The Panthers, assuming the police would try to stop the rally, decided to demonstrate their point on the spot and set up armed guards around the rally site.

Hundreds of black people turned out, many carrying their own weapons. The police who came to stop the rally quickly turned away, except for one, caught in the middle of the crowd, who sat quietly and listened to the speeches. Several Panthers addressed the crowd, explaining the Party's program. Then Huey Newton spoke. "The masses of the people want peace. The masses of the people do not want war. The Black Panther Party advocates the abolition of war. But at the same time, we realize that the only way you can get rid of war, many times, is through a process of war. Therefore, the only way you can get rid of guns is to get rid of the guns of the oppressor. The people must be able to pick up guns, to defend themselves. . . ."

At that point a police helicopter began buzzing over the crowd. Newton pointed up and shouted, "And always remember that the spirit of the people is greater than the man's technology." The crowds cheered, and hundreds signed up to work for the Party that day.

After the meeting, the first number of *The Black Panther*, the official organ of the Party, was issued. It was two sheets of legal-sized mimeographed paper, printed on both sides. The headline was WHY WAS DENZIL DOWELL KILLED? (See page 9 below.) About five to six thousand copies were printed and distributed in the black community of Richmond.

Early in 1967 the Party dropped "for Self Defense" from its title. William L. Patterson, a veteran black Communist and a longtime figure in the struggle for civil rights and for the legal defense of

black people, explains that the dropping of "for Self Defense" resulted from the understanding on the part of the Panther leaders
"that a broader political offensive was necessary to realize the self-
defense they sought. It [the BPP] took a political and organizational
leap forward that carried it beyond the positions occupied by any
of the other organizations of the black liberation movement. It began
to measure the strength of capitalism in the United States and to
analyze the position and weight of the forces aligned against the
blacks." Patterson points out that the Panther leadership challenged
the "illusion that the black people, of historical necessity, had to go
it alone . . . and began to see that the unity of the oppressed
was something for which a desperate fight had to be made." He also
observes that the Black Panther Party not only "repudiated the anti-
white abstraction," but rejected anti-Communism. "The Panthers,"
he notes, "are the first black-led organization to understand the
menace of anti-Communism and unqualifiedly to express opposition
to it."

To this, one should add that the Black Panthers, while by no
means the first blacks in the United States to oppose the capitalist
system and espouse the cause of Socialism, were the first to do so
as a separate organization. Heretofore, blacks who favored a Socialist
solution for the evils of capitalist society—and there have been many
since the end of the Civil War—did so either through the Socialist
Party, the Socialist Labor Party, or the Communist Party. Here they
became members of parties made up mainly of whites. The Black
Panthers, though favoring Socialism and coalitions with other oppressed groups, retain their separate identity as a revolutionary
movement.

While the Black Panthers were receiving attention for their self-
defense activities, by 1967 they were already deeply involved in a
wide variety of other work. The Party was protesting rent eviction,
informing welfare recipients of their legal rights, teaching classes in
Black History, and demanding and winning school traffic lights. The
installation of a street light at 55th and Market Streets is an important event in the Party's early history. Several black children
had been killed coming home from school, and the community was
enraged at the indifference of the authorities. Newton and Seale told
Oakland's power structure that if the light was not installed, the Party
would come down with its guns and block traffic so the children
could cross in safety. The traffic light was installed.

At this time, the Panthers had about seventy-five members, and
were based primarily in the Bay Area. But the Party was attracting
statewide attention, and new recruits were joining every day. One
of them was Eldridge Cleaver, who had spent nine years in prison
and was out on parole; he was writing for Ramparts, a radical, anti-

war, muckraking magazine published in San Francisco. Early in 1967 Cleaver got his first sight of an armed guard of Black Panthers, organized to escort Betty Shabazz (Malcolm X's widow) on her appearance at Black House, San Francisco. Here is how he was affected:

> The most beautiful sight I had ever seen. Four Black men wearing black berets, powder-blue shirts, black leather jackets, black trousers, shiny black shoes—and each with a gun! In front was Huey P. Newton. Beside him was Bobby Seale. A few steps behind him was Bobby Hutton. Where was my mind at? Blown.

Cleaver joined the Party and became Minister of Information. Later, the publication of his widely acclaimed *Soul on Ice*, written in prison, gave the Party nationwide publicity. Kathleen Cleaver, Eldridge's wife, also joined the Party and became Communications Secretary.

"We're the other half, the equal half," explained Artie Seale [Mrs. Bobby Seale, who also became a member of the Party]. "At first, when Bobby and Huey were just starting the organization, the women hung back. They felt they belonged at home in their kitchens because that had always been their role. But we began to find out that the pigs[5] don't care that we were women. So we had to change our way of looking at ourselves."

The Party's initial successes had already reverberated to the state legislature in Sacramento, where California Assemblyman Don Mulford introduced a gun-control bill designed as an attack on the Panthers. Huey Newton developed a plan to protest the state assembly's attempt to pass a bill infringing on the Panthers' right to bear arms as guaranteed by the second amendment to the Constitution. Although it was decided that he should not go to Sacramento,

---

5 The expression "pig," originally signifying the police and later extended to all elements in the capitalist power structure, was first popularized by the Black Panthers and later adopted by other radical groups, including many student protesters. It is interesting to note that the Panthers were not the first to use the concept of the "pig" to denote evil forces in American society. In *The New Flag*, an anti-imperialist poem by Henry Blake Fuller, published in 1899, American imperialism is depicted as a "hog." In the introduction to his poem, Fuller presented the following "Picture of the Great Expansion Argument."

In view of the militant stand taken by the Black Panthers against imperialism as a worldwide system whose center is in the United States, it is worth noting that leading black Americans, such as W. E. B. Du Bois, Kelly Miller, and Lewis H. Douglass, son of Frederick Douglass, were members of the American Anti-Imperialist League, founded in 1898.

thirty members of the Party went, carrying firearms. On May 2, 1967, while the gun bill was being debated, the armed Panthers, twenty-four men and six women, walked up the steps of the Capitol building, and Bobby Seale read a statement, written by Newton, asserting the Party's principles (see page 40 below). Then the Panthers walked into the visitors' gallery of the legislative Chambers.

When the police, press and TV cameramen arrived, creating a flurry of excitement, the Panthers left the building, read the statement again, and started to leave. At this point they were all arrested on a charge of conspiring to disturb the peace and held for several days until bailed out.

Newton had planned the action carefully and had taken every precaution to make sure it was legal at every step. But while members of the "gun lobby" who were also present registering opposition to the new law went unnoticed in the press, the specter of "blacks-with-guns-invading-the legislature"—as the headlines the following day read—was too much for the Establishment, and the news media reported the awesome event across the nation. None of this was entirely unexpected by the Panthers. "I'm going to show you how smart brother Huey was when he planned Sacramento," Bobby Seale stated. "He said, 'Now the papers are going to call us thugs and hoodlums. . . . But the brothers on the block, who the man's been calling thugs and hoodlums for 100 years, they're going to say, "Them's some out of sight thugs and hoodlums up there." ' . . . Who is these thugs and hoodlums? Huey was smart enough to know that the black people were going to say, 'Well, they've been calling us niggers, thugs and hoodlums for 400 years, that ain't gon' hurt me, I'm going to check out what these brothers is doing!' "

To be sure, Bobby Seale and several others served a six-month prison sentence as a result of the action and the gun restrictions were passed. But the Panthers were now nationally known, and within a few months branches had been established in Los Angeles, Tennessee, Georgia, New York and Detroit. Hundreds of black ghetto youth were attracted to the party and its program.

But Sacramento initiated a campaign of hysteria against the Panthers on a nationwide scale, and most white Americans recoiled in fear and horror at the sight of armed blacks. To the Panthers this reaction was to be expected. In time, the Panther program would win allies among whites who would understand that they, too, were victimized by the system. "We feel there are two things happening in this country," said Eldridge Cleaver. "You have a black colony and you have the white mother country and you have two different sets of political dynamics involved in these two relationships. What's called for in the mother country is a revolution and there's a black liberation called for in the black colony."

Following the Sacramento action and the legal defense they had built around it, the Panthers continued their operations in the Oakland black community. The police patrols functioned, as did the Party's educational work, around its ten-point program, and the circulation of the weekly Party newspaper grew. Newton made it clear that the Party was "the people's party," and was "like an oxen, to be ridden by the people and serve the needs of the people." If black children were being harassed in the schools, the Panthers organized mothers to patrol the halls while armed Party members stood guard outside.

As the Party's community activities increased and its successes grew, so did the intensity of police harassment. Police bulletin boards featured descriptions of Party members and their cars. On foot or driving around, Panthers would be stopped and arrested on charges ranging from petty traffic violations to spitting on the sidewalk. Newton was stopped almost daily by the police intent on arresting him.

Early in the morning of October 28, 1967, an Oakland police car reported over the radio that one of the occupants was asking for a license check on a tan VW and that he planned to stop it at Seventh and Willow. "It's a known Panther vehicle," Officer John Frey radioed.

The driver of the VW was Huey Newton, and the car was registered in the name of LaVerne Williams, his fiancée. The car was stopped, and Frey began to write out a citation before any information on the license check came over the radio. Newton, who had identified himself, was ordered out of the car. As he walked to the police cars parked behind it, shooting was said to have started. A few moments later Officer Frey was dead, another was wounded, and Huey Newton was under arrest with four bullet wounds in his stomach. When he recovered, he was charged with murder and kidnapping, and locked in Alameda County jail without bail.

Newton immediately proclaimed his innocence, and the Black Panther Party mobilized its forces for a "Free Huey" defense campaign. A number of blacks insisted that the Party hire a black lawyer to defend their leader, but the Panthers argued for a man with sufficient experience to win, especially with experience in defense of dissenters. Although it aroused considerable resentment among cultural nationalists and caused a number of blacks to abandon the campaign to "Free Huey," the Party engaged the services of Charles R. Garry, a white lawyer with a background of successfully defending radicals and trade unionists. When asked what fee his firm would charge, Garry replied, "Let's not worry about that. Let's worry about the fact that we want to free Huey."

While Newton was in prison awaiting his trial, thousands, black and white, rallied to his defense. During the same period, the Peace and Freedom Party emerged as a political force, first in California, and then across the country. The PFP was a coalition mainly of white left-liberals and radicals organized as a third-party electoral alternative in opposition to the war in Vietnam and in support of black liberation. The Panthers saw, in the emergence of the PFP and its campaign machinery, a chance for a wider campaign in Newton's defense. They indicated a willingness to join forces with the PFP, but insisted that any "functional coalition" with whites could be formed only on the basis of support for the demand to "Free Huey."

Because of fear of the liberal element that association with the Panthers would antagonize potential "respectable" voters, the PFP at first hesitated to join forces with the Black Panther Party. But as the time approached for the PFP to file its ballot petitions at the end of 1967, a shortage of signatures brought the issue to the fore. The radicals, who had favored the coalition from the beginning, won out and the alliance was formed. The Panthers took the petitions into the black community and put the PFP on the ballot. Huey Newton, Bobby Seale and Kathleen Cleaver ran as candidates for state offices on the PFP ticket, but on the basis of the Panther ten-point program. Eldridge Cleaver was to be the California PFP's presidential candidate, and later he won the national PFP nomination. Even though his name was kept off several state ballots (including California) because of his youth, the official election tallies gave him almost 200,000 votes. Moreover, his candidacy had enabled him to bring the program of the Black Panthers and the significance of the "Free Huey" campaign to thousands around the country, especially to scores of college campuses.

The basis of the coalition with the PFP was that the Panthers would set the PFP line on all issues related to the black community. As Cleaver summed it up: "We approached the whole thing from the point of view of international relations. We feel that our coalition is part of our foreign policy. . . ." Representatives of the "black colony" and the "white mother country" had joined in an alliance which respected the rights of black people to self-determination.

But a number of black radicals who were exponents of the doctrine of Black Power and of the necessity for blacks to form independent all-black political movements viewed the alliance with whites with considerable dismay, and some even charged a betrayal. The issue was complicated by the fact that precisely at this time, the Panthers were in the process of forming a "merger" with SNCC, which was formally announced at an Oakland "Free Huey" rally on February 17, 1968—Newton's birthday—and which was unusual not only for the size of the gathering, but for the fact that it was policed not by the police of Oakland but by the blacks themselves

—the Panthers. At the meeting, the principal leaders of SNCC—Stokely Carmichael, James Forman, and H. Rap Brown—were named to prominent positions in the Black Panther Party, with the leaders of both groups announcing a plan to form a mass black political party.

The "merger" was short-lived and began to crumble as soon as it was formed. Basically, the reason was the difference in outlook on the question of forming alliances with nonblacks. The Panthers would not accept the view of the SNCC leaders that all whites were evil and only blacks were worthy of being considered for inclusion in any struggle which had black liberation as its goal. "We know that you don't have to be white to be a pig," the Panthers put it. "The pig comes in all colors." By the same token, the victims of the "pigs," while primarily the black people, were also men and women of other colors who faced exploitation, poverty and repression.[6]

Soon after the PFP campaign and the defense of Newton got under way, the anticipated police repression began. On January 16, 1968, the police raided the Cleavers' home. "From then on," said Kathleen Cleaver, "the harassment of the Party intensified." A month later, following a raid on his home, Seale was arrested and charged with conspiracy to commit murder. Newly formed Party branches were raided across the country. On April 3, a public Party meeting was broken up by armed searches by Oakland police.

On April 4, 1968, Martin Luther King, Jr., was assassinated, and in the next few days riots exploded in the black ghettos of over one hundred cities in the United States. But Oakland was not among them. It was the Black Panther Party, pictured daily in the press as "gun-toting crazies who shriek and practice violence," which was responsible. In his report for the National Commission on the Causes and Prevention of Violence, Jerome H. Skolnick acknowledged that the Black Panther Party had to be "given credit for keeping Oakland cool after the assassination of Martin Luther King." He noted, correctly, that "this has not stemmed from any desire on their [the Panthers] part to suppress black protest in the community. Rather it stemmed from a sense that the police are waiting for a chance to shoot down blacks in the street."

Two days after the King assassination, dozens of police opened fire on a home where a Panther meeting was taking place. Bobby Hutton, the first member of the Party to join after Newton and Seale, was murdered while trying to surrender and Eldridge Cleaver was wounded and placed under arrest.

The trial of Huey Newton lasted from July 15 to September 8, and marked a high point both in Panther and Black History. The public attention given to the trial, resulting in large part from the

6 *See* Eldridge Cleaver's letter to Stokely Carmichael, page 104 below.

defense efforts and the PFP campaign, provided the Panthers with an excellent opportunity not only to defend Newton but to expose the racist character of the entire legal system.

The testimony during the trial—over four thousand pages—includes urban sociology, black history and the Declaration of Independence. At one point early in the proceedings, Superior Court Judge Monroe Friedman said, "I feel like I've taken a course in sociology the last few days." Viewing Newton as a "political prisoner" and the trial as a "political trial," Charles R. Garry, his attorney, made it a practice to enable those in the courtroom and thousands on the outside to learn the racist nature of court procedure in the United States: that black people are virtually excluded from jury panels, often cannot afford bail or are rejected by bondsmen, tried by juries not of their peers and under laws they did not participate in making, and that they receive consistently heavier sentences. All of this aside from the police harassment described so fully by the Kerner Commission. In his address to the jury, Garry pleaded: "White America, listen. The answer is not to put Huey Newton in the gas chamber. The answer is to listen to him so that black brothers and sisters can walk down the street with dignity."

In his own testimony Newton had denied having fired any shot. He had been wounded almost immediately after the car was stopped; he said that he had slumped to the ground unconscious, and that "I don't know what happened." He did not have a gun when he left his car. Doctors testified at the trial that, indeed, Newton's wound was compatible with his claim that he had been unconscious. Garry asked that the jury be given instructions that unconsciousness, if proved, constituted a complete defense to a charge of criminal homicide. But Judge Friedman refused to give such instructions. After deliberating for twenty-eight hours and fifty minutes, the jury handed down a contradictory verdict. It found Newton guilty of "voluntary manslaughter" in the death of policeman John Frey, and innocent of shooting patrolman Herbert Heanes. (Garry had already won an acquittal of the kidnapping charge.) As Garry noted immediately after the verdict: "It makes no sense on legal or evidentiary grounds. . . . He either had a gun or he didn't." But he was a Black Panther, and he had to be put away.

Newton was sentenced to two to fifteen years. On May 29, 1970, the California Court of Appeals, in a fifty-one-page opinion, reversed the conviction. It ruled that the trial judge had erred in not instructing the jury that if it accepted Newton's contention that he was unconscious at the time of the shooting, this would have constituted a complete defense and would have resulted in a verdict of acquittal. The court also cited other errors it noted had occurred during Newton's eight-week trial. Although Newton had already served over two years in prison, and although it agreed that he should have been acquitted, the Court still refused him bail pending the state's appeal to a higher court. The Oakland police had expected Newton to die in the gas chamber, and they were enraged by the verdict of manslaughter. Only hours after it was announced, the Panther office was riddled with bullets. On September 27, the day Newton was sentenced, the courts reversed the decision on Cleaver's parole and gave him sixty days to return to prison. In November, Cleaver went into foreign exile rather than return to prison, where he believed he would be killed.

But this was only the beginning of a deliberate campaign to destroy the Black Panther Party. Late in November, 1968, Seale publicly stated that the Party had been heavily infiltrated by police agents. By December, Party branches everywhere were under attack by local police, with clear indications that the attacks were directed from Washington. On February 7, 1970, Mayor Wes Uhlman of Seattle disclosed that he had turned down a Federal proposal for a raid on Black Panther headquarters. His statement confirmed the widely reported information that Treasury Department Agents have been largely responsible for provoking and organizing nationwide raids against the Black Panther Party.

On December 5, 1969, Charles R. Garry told newsmen that since January 1, 1969, twenty-eight members of the Black Panther Party had been killed by the police.[7] At a press interview on December 19, the Executive Director of the American Civil Liberties Union declared: "The record of police actions across the nation against the Black Panther Party forms a prima facie case for the conclusion that law enforcement officials are waging a drive against the black militant organization resulting in various civil liberties violations . . . [and that] high national officials, by their statements and actions, have helped to create the climate of oppression and have encouraged local police to institute the crackdown." The ACLU released a list of forty-eight major police-Panther "incidents."

The whole world knows of the murder of Fred Hampton and Mark Clark, killed by an invasion of Chicago police as they slept. As usual the police claimed that they had been attacked by the Panthers, but so flimsy was the claim that a Federal Grand Jury investigation labeled it false, and the case against the seven Panthers who survived the raid has been dismissed. (No action, however, was taken to bring the guilty police to justice.) In an editorial entitled "Panthers and the Law," *The New York Times* (May 18, 1970), while engaging in the typical anti-Panther diatribes, accusing them

[7] The entire issue of *The Black Panther* of February 21, 1970, is devoted to listing the victims of government harassment from May 2, 1967, to December, 1969. The "Special Issue" is entitled "Evidence and Intimidation of Fascist Crimes by U.S.A."

of having "committed unlawful and coercive acts, often against the black community itself," declared:

The story unfolded by the Chicago grand jury makes it appear that the law-enforcement agencies, more than the .Panthers, were acting out a conspiracy. The police, following Federal tips, sprayed the Panthers' lodging with massive gunfire, even though no more than one shot was found to have been fired from the inside. Chicago officials subsequently engaged in a deliberate publicity campaign to depict the Panthers as the aggressors. Police laboratories, lacking either in competence or integrity, provided erroneous findings to serve the same purpose.

Against a background of doctored evidence and coached police witnesses, it is not surprising that the State's Attorney, who initially had played a leading role in building the public case against the Panthers, finally dropped all charges against them. A more pertinent question now is whether a case which left two men dead can properly be closed with the mere demotion of three police officers.

Another "pertinent question" is whether *The New York Times* will report how an organization which it accuses of having committed "unlawful and coercive acts" against "the black community itself," how the Black Panther Party, while compelled to devote a large part of its time to defense activities, is carrying out the Party's original "serve the people" program in the black communities. Four programs have been launched: free breakfast for children, free health clinics, liberation schools and petition campaigns for community control of the police. (See page 168 below.) Every branch has moved to implement at least the breakfast program and the police petitions.

The Black Panthers have felt the type of repression that has been experienced by radical and labor groups throughout our history, but in addition, they are black and they are experiencing the type of repression that only black revolutionaries can experience in a racist society. Yet the evidence points to the conclusion that the Panthers are continuing to grow and to advance their program, and that they are gaining wide support among increasing numbers of people—black, brown, yellow, red, and white. There already is a Black Panther Party in England.

On June 19, 1970, the Panthers and their supporters gathered on the steps of the Lincoln Memorial in Washington, D.C., to hear the Black Panther Party issue a call for a "revolutionary people's constitutional convention" to be convened on September 7, Labor Day, in Philadelphia. The gathering was in observance of the anniversary of the Emancipation Proclamation, officially dated January 1, 1863, but actually delivered on June 19. The statement of the BPP, read by Chief of Staff David Hilliard, declared, "The end result of the Emancipation Proclamation was supposed to be the freedom and liberation of the black people from the cruel shackles of slavery;

yet one hundred and seven years later black people still are not free. Where is that freedom?" The statement documented the "unbroken chain of abuse" committed against black people by the ruling class, including the murder of Malcolm X, Martin Luther King, Jr., and hundreds of ordinary black citizens. (For the full text of the manifesto, see page 267.)

In February, 1969, Mayor of San Francisco Joseph Alioto told a Presbyterian convention that the Black Panthers "encouraged violence." Challenged from the audience by the Director of the Commission on Religion and Race, the Mayor retorted: "Have you ever read the ten commandments of the Black Panther Party? . . . Did you like that section about robbing and raping?" The reference (a perfect example of the "big lie") was actually to the "8 Points of Attention" which the Panthers print in every issue of their weekly newspaper, and, as the reader will see if he turns to page 6, these "commandments" actually encourage the opposite of what the Mayor of San Francisco charged. But how many in the audience had ever read *The Black Panther* and how many who listened to him over the air or read the account in the next morning's newspaper had ever seen the actual text of the "8 Points of Attention"? In his interview with Eldridge Cleaver in Algiers, late in June, 1969, Lee Lockwood asked the Minister of Information for the Black Panther Party: "But is it a Panther policy to tell somebody to take a gun and hold up a store?" Cleaver replied: "If you listen, you will not hear anyone saying that it is a Panther policy except those who are saying it at the behest of the pigs and to help the pigs. So just listen to what the Panthers are saying. . . ."

What the Black Panthers have been saying has been public information since the first issue of its weekly paper was published on April 25, 1967, a year after the Party was organized in Oakland, California. Each week thereafter *The Black Panther* made its appearance, carrying the Ten-Point Program and Rules and Regulations of the Party, editorials, speeches by leading Black Panthers, interviews with a number of them, poetry, art, letters and dispatches from various parts of the Third World. In addition, many of the leading radical journals such as *The Guardian*, the *Daily World*, and the *People's World*, and the less radical weekly, *Village Voice*, the chief underground papers, among them *The Movement, Rat, Nickel Review*, and *Quicksilver*, and student newspapers like *The Rag* of the University of Texas, have featured articles about the program and interviews with leaders of the Black Panthers.

In short, there has been no lack of information as to the program, policies and objectives of the Black Panther Party. Unfortunately, it has been easier to read distortions in the mass media than to obtain copies of the Party's weekly, radical journals, and the underground and student papers. It is the purpose of this volume to correct this situation. Here in their own words are the views, the policies and objectives of the black men and women who have in a short time built one of the most significant movements in the entire history of black Americans, as well as those of men and women of other races and colors—Puerto Ricans, Mexican-Americans, Chinese-Americans, and Poor Whites—who have been influenced by the Panthers to build a similar movement in their own communities. One does not necessarily have to agree with their philosophy or the solution they hold out for the evils of our society. But every American owes it to himself at least to understand what the Black Panthers are saying.

It may be argued by some that the present volume may derive its significance from the fact that it appears at a time when the Black Panther Party is doomed to extinction because of the nationwide repression against its leaders and members. David Hilliard, the Party's national chief of staff, and, at the time this is written (July, 1970), its highest ranking officer out of jail, rejected this viewpoint. "I don't think that we can say," he wrote in *The Black Panther* of January 3, 1970, "the organized attempt to destroy the B.P.P. was successful. What it has done, is that it brought to the attention of the American people the atrociousness of the American Government, in terms of its subjects. . . . But as far as their successfulness is concerned, they're not successful. They can never exterminate the Black Panther Party because the Black Panther Party is not just a party for itself but rather it's a party for the people." While I am aware of the effectiveness of government and vigilante repression in destroying a large number of past radical and labor movements which seemed to pose a threat to the established order in America, I am inclined to agree with David Hilliard. I am confident that the Black Panthers will continue to speak for a long time to come.

# Black Panther National Anthem

*by Elaine*

Yes—He turned and he walked
Past the eyes of my life.
And, he nodded and sang without sound.
And his face had the look
Of a man who knew strife
And a feeling familiarly came around.

REFRAIN:

> I said,
> Man, where have you been for all these years
> Man, where were you when I sought you
> Man, do you know me as I know you
> Man, am I coming through

And, he spoke in a voice
That was centuries old.
And, he smiled in a way that was strange.
And, his full lips of night
Spoke about our people's plight
And a feeling familiarly came around.

REFRAIN:

> And, we sat and we talked
> About freedom and things.
> And, he told me about what he dreamed.
> But I knew of that dream
> Long before he had spoke
> And a feeling familiarly came around.

REFRAIN

—*The Black Panther*, April 27, 1969

# 1.

# BLACK PANTHER
# PARTY PLATFORM
# AND PROGRAM
# RULES OF THE
# BLACK PANTHER PARTY

Between October 1 and October 15, 1966, in North Oakland, California, Huey P. Newton and Bobby Seale prepared the ten-point platform and program of the Black Panther Party. Seale made suggestions, but the platform and program were actually written by Newton, who divided them into "What We Want" and "What We Believe." The Rules of the Party were set down later and added to as more were required. Today there are twenty-six rules: some for members of the Party and others for office and Party functionaries.

October 1966 Black Panther
Party Platform and Program

# What We Want
# What We Believe

*1. We want freedom. We want power to determine the destiny of
our Black Community.*

We believe that black people will not be free until we are able
to determine our destiny.

*2. We want full employment for our people.*

We believe that the federal government is responsible and obligated to give every man employment or a guaranteed income. We
believe that if the white American businessmen will not give full
employment, then the means of production should be taken from
the businessmen and placed in the community so that the people
of the community can organize and employ all of its people and
give a high standard of living.

*3. We want an end to the robbery by the white man of our Black
Community.*

, We believe that this racist government has robbed us and now
we are demanding the overdue debt of forty acres and two mules.
Forty acres and two mules was promised 100 years ago as restitution
for slave labor and mass murder of black people. We will accept the
payment in currency which will be distributed to our many communities. The Germans are now aiding the Jews in Israel for the
genocide of the Jewish people. The Germans murdered six million
Jews. The American racist has taken part in the slaughter of over
fifty million black people; therefore, we feel that this is a modest
demand that we make.

*4. We want decent housing, fit for shelter of human beings.*

We believe that if the white landlords will not give decent housing
to our black community, then the housing and the land should be
made into cooperatives so that our community, with government aid,
can build and make decent housing for its people.

*5. We want education for our people that exposes the true nature
of this decadent American society. We want education that teaches
us our true history and our role in the present-day society.*

We believe in an educational system that will give to our people a knowledge of self. If a man does not have knowledge of himself and his position in society and the world, then he has little chance to relate to anything else.

6. *We want all black men to be exempt from military service.*

We believe that Black people should not be forced to fight in the military service to defend a racist government that does not protect us. We will not fight and kill other people of color in the world who, like black people, are being victimized by the white racist government of America. We will protect ourselves from the force and violence of the racist police and the racist military, by whatever means necessary.

7. *We want an immediate end to POLICE BRUTALITY and MURDER of black people.*

We believe we can end police brutality in our black community by organizing black self-defense groups that are dedicated to defending our black community from racist police oppression and brutality. The Second Amendment to the Constitution of the United States gives a right to bear arms. We therefore believe that all black people should arm themselves for self-defense.

8. *We want freedom for all black men held in federal, state, county and city prisons and jails.*

We believe that all black people should be released from the many jails and prisons because they have not received a fair and impartial trial.

9. *We want all black people when brought to trial to be tried in court by a jury of their peer group or people from their black communities, as defined by the Constitution of the United States.*

We believe that the courts should follow the United States Constitution so that black people will receive fair trials. The 14th Amendment of the U.S. Constitution gives a man a right to be tried by his peer group. A peer is a person from a similar economic, social, religious, geographical, environmental, historical and racial background. To do this the court will be forced to select a jury from the black community from which the black defendant came. We have been, and are being tried by all-white juries that have no understanding of the "average reasoning man" of the black community.

10. *We want land, bread, housing, education, clothing, justice and peace. And as our major political objective, a United Nations-supervised plebiscite to be held throughout the black colony in*

*which only black colonial subjects will be allowed to participate, for the purpose of determining the will of black people as to their national destiny.*

When, in the course of human events, it becomes necessary for one people to dissolve the political bands which have connected them with another, and to assume, among the powers of the earth, the separate and equal station to which the laws of nature and nature's God entitle them, a decent respect to the opinions of mankind requires that they should declare the causes which impel them to the separation.

We hold these truths to be self-evident, that all men are created equal; that they are endowed by their Creator with certain unalienable rights; that among these are life, liberty, and the pursuit of happiness. *That, to secure these rights, governments are instituted among men, deriving their just powers from the consent of the governed; that, whenever any form of government becomes destructive of these ends, it is the right of the people to alter or to abolish it, and to institute a new government, laying its foundation on such principles, and organizing its powers in such form, as to them shall seem most likely to effect their safety and happiness.* Prudence, indeed, will dictate that governments long established should not be changed for light and transient causes; and, accordingly, all experience hath shown, that mankind are more disposed to suffer, while evils are sufferable, than to right themselves by abolishing the forms to which they are accustomed. *But, when a long train of abuses and usurpations, pursuing invariably the same object, evinces a design to reduce them under absolute despotism, it is their right, it is their duty, to throw off such government, and to provide new guards for their future security.*


## Rules of the Black Panther Party

CENTRAL HEADQUARTERS, OAKLAND, CALIFORNIA


Every member of the BLACK PANTHER ·PARTY throughout this country of racist America must abide by these rules as functional members of this party. CENTRAL COMMITTEE members, CENTRAL STAFFS, and LOCAL STAFFS, including all captains subordinate to either national, state, and local leadership of the BLACK PANTHER PARTY will enforce these rules. Length of suspension or other disciplinary action necessary for violation of these rules will depend on national decisions by national, state or state area, and local committees and staffs where said rule or rules of the BLACK PANTHER PARTY WERE VIOLATED. Every member of the party must know these verbatim by heart. And apply them daily. Each member must report any violation of these rules to their leadership or they are counter-revolutionary and are also subjected to suspension by the BLACK PANTHER PARTY.

**The rules are:**

1. No party member can have narcotics or weed in his possession while doing party work.

2. Any party member found shooting narcotics will be expelled from this party.

3. No party member can be DRUNK while doing daily party work.

4. No party member will violate rules relating to office work, general meetings of the BLACK PANTHER PARTY, and meetings of the BLACK PANTHER PARTY ANYWHERE.

5. No party member will USE, POINT, or FIRE a weapon of any kind unnecessarily or accidentally at anyone.

6. No party member can join any other army force other than the BLACK LIBERATION ARMY.

7. No party member can have a weapon in his possession while DRUNK or loaded off narcotics or weed.

8. No party member will commit any crimes against other party members or BLACK people at all, and cannot steal or take from the people, not even a needle or a piece of thread.

9. When arrested BLACK PANTHER MEMBERS will give only name, address, and will sign nothing. Legal first aid must be understood by all Party members.

10. The Ten-Point Program and platform of the BLACK PANTHER PARTY must be known and understood by each Party member.

11. Party Communications must be National and Local.

12. The 10-10-10-program should be known by all members and also understood by all members.

13. All Finance officers will operate under the jurisdiction of the Ministry of Finance.

14. Each person will submit a report of daily work.

15. Each Sub-Section Leaders, Section Leaders, and Lieutenants, Captains must submit Daily reports of work.

16. All Panthers must learn to operate and service weapons correctly.

17. All Leadership personnel who expel a member must submit

this information to the Editor of the Newspaper, so that it will be published in the paper and will be known by all chapters and branches.

18. Political Education Classes are mandatory for general membership.

19. Only office personnel assigned to respective offices each day should be there. All others are to sell papers and do Political work out in the community, including Captains, Section Leaders, etc.

20. COMMUNICATIONS—all chapters must submit weekly reports in writing to the National Headquarters.

21. All Branches must implement First Aid and/or Medical Cadres.

22. All Chapters, Branches, and components of the BLACK PANTHER PARTY must submit a monthly Financial Report to the Ministry of Finance, and also the Central Committee.

23. Everyone in a leadership position must read no less than two hours per day to keep abreast of the changing political situation.

24. No chapter or branch shall accept grants, poverty funds, money or any other aid from any government agency without contacting the National Headquarters.

25. All chapters must adhere to the policy and the ideology laid down by the CENTRAL COMMITTEE of the BLACK PANTHER PARTY.

26. All Branches must submit weekly reports in writing to their respective Chapters.

**8 Points of Attention**
1) Speak politely.
2) Pay fairly for what you buy.
3) Return everything you borrow.
4) Pay for anything you damage.
5) Do not hit or swear at people.
6) Do not damage property or crops of the poor, oppressed masses.
7) Do not take liberties with women.
8) If we ever have to take captives do not ill-treat them.

**3 Main Rules of Discipline**
1) Obey orders in all your actions
2) Do not take a single needle or a piece of thread from the poor and oppressed masses.
3) Turn in everything captured from the attacking enemy.

# 2.

# THE BLACK PANTHER: VOICE OF THE PARTY

Huey P. Newton often declared: "The newspaper is the Voice of the Party and the Voice of the Panther must be heard throughout the land. Because the Newspaper is one of the main tools for educating the masses of Black People." In this section the reader will find an estimate of the function and role of *The Black Panther*, and some typical editorials, comments and letters which have appeared in the newspaper. From its earliest issues, *The Black Panther* carried poetry by black poets, either members of the Party or sympathizers, and several of the poems will be found in this section.

# The Black Panther: Mirror of the People

Just what is the Black Panther Black Community News Service? Is it something like the bourgeois press, to be read once and then discarded in the nearest trash can, or is it something else—something more?

'The Black Panther Black Community News Service, is not just a newspaper in the traditional sense of the word, it's more than that. The Black Panther Black Community News Service is a living contemporary history of our people's struggle for liberation at the grass roots level. It's something to be studied and grasped, and saved for future generations to read, learn and understand.

The Black Panther Black Community News Service tells the story of our people's struggle in the streets. Its story unfolds far from the perfumed parlors of the petty bourgeoisie. It tells the true story of what happens in the concrete inner-city jungles of Babylon when brothers and sisters off the block, workers, and members of the petty bourgeoisie decide to cast aside their petty personal goals and aspirations, and begin to work unselfishly together with a common goal in mind: to serve the people and liberate the colony, by the only means necessary—the GUN.

The history of the Black Panther Black Community News Service, goes back to the first issue printed in 1967 (VOL. I NO. 1), back to the vicious murder of Denzil Dowell by fascist gestapo pigs in Richmond, Calif., and documents what happens when the people of the community say "This is enough," decide to arm themselves to put an end to exploitation and oppression and is an objective lesson in the art of self-defense, serving the people, national liberation, and revolution.

The Black Panther documents step by step the actions taken by, and programs instituted by the Black Panther Party in its unstoppable drive to serve the people; and documents before the whole world the repression and murders committed by Amerikkka's corrupt monopoly capital in its dastardly attempts to stop this move to institute people's power.

The Black Panther Black Community News Service, tells how our courageous Minister of Defense, Huey P. Newton, the baddest brother to ever step into history, stood up in the bowels of fascist Amerikkka with a shotgun in his hands and told those murderous mad dogs who occupy our community like a foreign army: "My name is Huey P. Newton, Minister of Defense of the Black Panther

# *The* BLACK PANTHER

**BLACK COMMUNITY NEWS SERVICE**

**VOLUME 1**    APRIL 25, 1967    **NUMBER 1**

P.O. BOX 8641  OAK. CALIF.  EMERYVILLE BRANCH

PUBLISHED BY THE BLACK PANTHER PARTY FOR SELF DEFENSE

# WHY WAS DENZIL DOWELL KILLED

APRIL FIRST 3:50 a.m.

## "I BELIEVE THE POLICE MURDERED MY SON" SAYS THE MOTHER OF DENZIL DOWELL.

Brothers and Sisters of the Richmond community, here is the view of the family's side of the death of Denzil Dowell as compiled by the Black Panther Party for Self Defense, concerned citizens, and the Dowell family. As you know, April 1st, 1967, Denzel Dowell (age 22), was shot and killed by an "officer of the Martinez Sheriff's Department", so read the newspaper.

But there are too many unanswered questions that have been raised by the Dowell family and other neighbors in the North Richmond community. Questions that don't meet the satisfaction of the killing of Denzil. The Richmond Police, the Martinez Sheriff's Department, and the Richmond Independent would have us black people believe some thing contrary to Mrs. Dowell's accusation. That is, her son was "unjustifiably" murdered by a racist cop.

There are too many questionable facts supporting the Dowell family's point of view.

These questionable facts are as follows:

1. Denzil Dowell was unarmed so how can six bullet holes and shot gun blasts be considered "justifiable homocide"?

(Con't Page 2)

WE BLACK PEOPLE ARE MEETING SATURDAY 1:30 AT 1717 SECOND STREET LET US SUPPORT THE DOWELL FAIMLY EVERY BLACK BROTHER AND SISTER MUST UNITE FOR REAL POLITICAL ACTION

2. Why did the newspaper and police say only three shots were fired when the coroner's report and surrounding neighbors established the fact that six to ten shots were used and heard?

3. The police and the newspaper stated that the time of the shooting was 4:49 A.M. to 5:01 A.M., yet Denzil Dowell's sister and neighbors in the area testified to hearing shots at 3:50 A.M.

4. Only Richmond police were first seen on the scene; not until later (an hour or so), around 4:50 A.M. were Martinez sheriffs seen on the scene where Denzil Dowell was murdered.

5. The police reported that Denzil Dowell was running and jumped a fence and ran to jump another when he was shot. The Dowell family knows that Denzil had been injured in the hip in a car accident some time ago and after leaving the hospital could not run much at all, let alone jump two fences with a hamer in his hand.

6. The lot that Denzil was supposed to have run across between the two fences is an old car junk yard loaded with grease and oil and why wasn't oil found on his shoes?

7. The coroner reported that Denzil Dowell bled to death. Where was the blood where Denzil Dowell lay? Denzil's sister remembers that night and says she saw very little blood. She said she never saw a pool of blood and yet the coroner said he bled to death after being shot ten times.

8. Denzil Dowell was found by his brother and friend and they noticed that no attempt had been made by police to summon a doctor or to save his life.

9. The family of Denzil Dowell has been denied the right to see or have the clothes that Denzil was murdered in. They want the clothes to see how many bullet holes the clothes have in them. The family was also denied the right to take pictures of his body so they could check for numerous bullet holes.

10. The newspaper came out with a statement of "justifiable homocide" 2 hours before the jury gave its verdict. The foreman on the jury could not read. A biased jury of 10 white people and two "Negroes" protected the racist cop who murdered Denzil Dowell.

11. The Dowell family also notes a very important fact. The cop who shot Denzil Dowell knew him by name and had stopped Denzil and hollered to him many times, "Denzil Dowell give me your identification." The cop had at other times threatened to kill him.

The Dowell family and concerned citizens have called for a Grand Jury investigation and are demanding that all law enforcement officers change their policy of killing people over property.

On April 18th a group of concerned citizens went to discuss this proposal with Sheriff Young of Martinez. The citizens enumerated the areas of doubt in the case of Denzil Dowell and requested that the officer who admitted doing the shooting be removed from duty pending an investigation. The Sheriff REFUSED to hear our request and we consider his action to be a racist disregard for the reasonable request of black taxpayers and citizens concerned with the survival of black people.

LET US ORGANIZE
TO DEFEND OURSELVES

"We believe we can end police brutality in our black community by organizing black self-defense groups that are dedicated to defending our black community from racist police oppression and brutality. The second Amendment of the Constitution of the United States gives a right to bear arms. We therefore believe that all black people should arm themselves for self defense." (from the program of the Black Panther Party for Self Defense, Point No. 7 of "What We Believe")

WHY MUST BLACK PEOPLE ORGANIZE?

--The murder of Denzil Dowell April 1, 1967 her in North Richmond;

--The murder of two black Brothers a week before last Christmas here in North Richmond;

--The brutal beating of a black woman here in Richmond;

--The killing of George Thompson in Hunters Point, San Francisco

(con't Page 3)

in September, 1966;

--The beating of a 14 year old girl in East Oakland in October 1966.

These are only a few of the murders and brutal beatings by racist cops that have happened and been reported in the newspaper and are known about in the black community.

BROTHERS AND SISTERS THESE RACIST MURDERS ARE HAPPENING EVERY DAY; THEY COULD HAPPEN TO ANY ONE OF US.

BROTHERS AND SISTERS WE MUST

UNITE. MANY OTHER MURDERS AND

BRUTAL BEATINGS HAVE TAKEN PLACE

WITHOUT US DOING MUCH OF ANYTHING.

BUT LET'S STOP IT NOW!

WITH
        SOME

            REAL.
                NITTY GRITTY

            POLITICAL ACTION

# ARMED BLACK BROTHERS IN RICHMOND COMMUNITY

15 Black Brothers, most of them armed; with Magnum 12 gauge shot guns, M-1 rifles, and side arms, held a street rally at the corner of Third and Chesley in North Richmond last Saturday afternoon about 5 P.M. The nice thing about these Bloods is that they had their arms to defend themselves and their Black Brothers and Sisters while they exercised their Constitutional Rights: Freedom of Speech, and the right to Peacefully Assemble. And while they exercised another Constitutional right: the right to bear arms to defend themselves.

The racist cops could only look on. The Dog Cops made no attempt to break up the meeting like they generally do when Black people get together to sound out their greviances against the white power structure. The point to get firmly into your mind is that both the Black Brothers and the racist cops had "POWER". They had righteous "GUN POWER", but the significant thing is that the Black Brothers had some of this POWER. In the

(con't page 4)

# MEETING APRIL 29TH
## EVERYBODY
## THIS COMMING SATURDAY
## SO WE'LL KNOW WHAT TO DO AND HOW TO DO IT NOW!
## 1717 SECOND STREET
### NORTH RICHMOND
## AT 1:30 P.M.

past, Black People have been at the mercy of cops who feel that their badges are a license to shoot, maim, and out-right murder any Black man, woman, or child who crosses their gun-sights. But there are now strong Black men and women on the scene who are willing to step out front and do what is necessary to bring peace, security, and justice to a people who have been denied all of these for four hundred years.

At this rally, the Brothers were uptight and knew exactly what they were doing at all times. They knew that they were acting strictly within their rights. These Brothers have become aware of something that the white racists have been trying to keep secret from Black people all the time: that a citizen has the right to protect himself. They were ready to insure that the rally went ahead as planned, without any interference from outlaw cops who wanted to suppress the meeting so that other Black People would not get the message.

Black People must realize that the time is short and growing shorter by the day. Check it out. People talk about "Power". There is White Power, Black Power, Yellow Power, Green Power, etc. but all Black People want out of all these different forms of Power is BLACK POWER. Black People want and need the power to stop the white racist power structure from grinding the life out of the Black Race through the daily operation of this system which is designed to exploit and oppress Black People.

The beautiful thing about the Brothers who held the rally is that they are organized, disciplined and politically aware of all the ins and outs of the problems facing Black People throughout the Bay Area in particular. When the cops came rolling up looking, the brothers spreaded out all across the street waiting for some fool cop to try and start something. The brothers were organized.

So, Brothers and Sisters everywhere: righteous BLACK POWER organized is where its at. The BLACK PANTHER PARTY FOR SELF-DEFENSE really has something going. These brothers are the cream of Black Manhood. They are there for the protection and defense of our Black Community. The Black Community owes it to itself, to the future of our people, to get behind these

brothers and to let the world know that black people are not stupid fools who are unable to recognize when someone is acting in the best interest of Black People. These Brothers have a political perspective. Most important, they are down here on the GRASS ROOTS LEVEL where the great majority of our people are. The BLACK PANTHER PARTY FOR SELF DEFENSE moves. The PARTY takes action. Everybody else just sits back and talk. All Black People know what needs to be done, but not all of them are willing to do it. The White man has instilled fear into the very hearts of our people. We must act to remove this fear. The only way to remove this fear is to stand up and look the white man in his blue eyes. Many Black People are able nowadays to look the white man in the eyes--but the line thins out when it comes to looking the white cops in the eye. But the white cop is the instrument sent into our community by the Power Structure to keep Black People quiet and under control. So it is not surprising that the action these days centers around the conduct of these white cops who come from way across town to patrol our communities for 8 hours a day. But Black People have to live in these communities 24 hours a day. So it is time that Black People start moving in a direction that will free our communities from this form of outright brutal oppression. The BLACK PANTHER PARTY FOR SELF DEFENSE has worked out a program that is carefully designed to cope with this situation.

BLACK MEN!!! It is your duty to your women and children, to your mothers and sisters, to investigate the program of the PARTY. There is no other way. We have tried everything else. This is the moment in history when Black People have no choice but to move and move rapidly to gain their freedom, justice, and all the other ingredients of civilized living that have been denied to us. This is where it is at. Check it out, Black Brothers and Sister! This is our Day!!!!!.

Party. I'm standing on my constitutional right to bear arms to defend my people. If you shoot at me pig, I'm shooting back." And thus his courageous example moved the struggle of our people to a higher level—from throwing rocks and bottles, to arming themselves for survival. The Black Panther teaches the people the strategic means for resisting the power structure.

The Black Panther Black Community News Service, tells how the correct examples of the Party, led by Huey P. Newton, spread like wildfire throughout fascist Amerikkka—as exemplified by Detroit and Newark—and how on the morning of October 28, 1967, two night-riding greasy Oakland pigs tried to murder our Minister of Defense from ambush. It also tells how that attempt failed and one pig, Frey went to the pig' sty in the sky, and the other one, Haines, somehow received three bullet holes.

The Black Panther documents for all humanity to see, how the wretched slaves of Amerikkka moved fearlessly to establish ALL POWER TO THE PEOPLE. It also shows how the forces of reaction perfected their ambushes and murdered Li'l Bobby, Robert, Tommy, Steve and other Party members in attempts to stop us. The weekly issues of The Black Panther also shows how people who will be free refuse to be either cowed or intimidated by death, imprisonment or exile, and continue to develop and expand. It is a lesson in the objective truth, that the spirit of the people is indeed greater than the man's technology. The best that humanity possesses will never yield to any oppressor.

Issue by issue the people's revolutionary struggle for national salvation unfolds in the pages of THE BLACK PANTHER COMMUNITY NEWS SERVICE, free from the distortion, bias, and lies of the oppressor controlled mass media. The People's paper tells how starting out with nothing, the People's Party, The Black Panther Party, moved with the people to implement Free Breakfast Programs to feed our hungry children, Free Health Clinics to care for the sick, Free Clothing Programs to clothe our needy, Liberation Schools to educate our youth, and Community Centers to keep the community informed; and how with each meal served, with each child clothed, and with each bandage applied, we were attacked wilder and wilder—Fred Hampton and Mark Clark murdered in their sleep by Chicago's thin blue line on December 4, 1969 and the L.A. office attacked by 400 crazed pigs on December 8, 1969 (VOL. IV NO. 2).

The Black Panther Black Community News Service, is not only a history of the people's growth, but also the pigs fanatical repression as they near total destruction. The Black Panther documents and indicts Amerikkka for the fascist police state that it is, attempting to crush all dissent by force.

The Black Panther Black Community News Service, when put together is a glorious living history, a testament to the fact that no matter how the pigs try to stop us, the people will be free; clearly points out that all the wild attacks by the pigs is like a fool picking up a rock only to drop it on his own foot; and gives proof of the objective truth that oppression only creates resistance.

The Black Panther Black Community News Service, is a living, breathing history that continues each and every day. Each new issue has its message, its lessons to be learned, its objective truth.

No! The Black Panther Black Community News Service, is not an ordinary newspaper. It is the flesh and blood, the sweat and tears of our people. It is a continuation of the story of the middle passage, of Denmark Vesey, of Nat Turner, of Harriet Tubman, of Malcolm X, and countless other oppressed people who put freedom and dignity beyond personal gain. The Black Panther Black Community News Service, is truly a mirror of the spirit of the people

ALL POWER TO THE PEOPLE
POW'S FOR PANTHERS

BLACK PANTHER PARTY
Political Prisoner, Denver Colorado
Landon Williams
—*The Black Panther*, January 17, 1970


# A Pig

A Pig is an ill-natured beast who has no respect for law and order, a foul traducer who's usually found masquerading as a victim of an unprovoked attack.
—*The Black Panther*, May, 1967


# Black Lawyers

Scottsboro boys and of Sacco and Vanzetti. The issue at stake was Huey's life, and the best legal skills and resources were needed. There was no basis to quibble about color. If the Minister of Defense had suffered a heart attack, and the best heart specialist were needed to save his life, I wonder if the same outcry would be raised, if the doctor turned out to be white?

The point has been made that for Huey P. Newton to go to court
with a white lawyer weakens the argument for black liberation.
Seeing as how the entire legal system is white, the logic of this
complaint escapes me. However, to reply to it, as it has become
an issue in the Bay Area, I would say first that black lawyers do
far more to weaken the argument for black power than the Black
Panthers' using the assistance of white lawyers, and that what is on
trial before a white court is first of all, the Minister of Defense of
the Black Panther Party and secondly, the entire vanguard of the
radical black movement in this country. What is at stake is first of all,
Huey's life, and secondly, the right of black people to self-defense
against armed aggression on the part of the police as the military
arm of the racist power structure. What is necessary is for Huey to
be set free. This demands the most competent and powerful legal
resources available.

Charles R. Garry has a record of 24 capital cases, all of which
he has won. He has taken the extreme expense of some of his cases
out of his own pocket to defend a client he believed was innocent.
Attorney Garry has assured the Newton family and the Black Panther Party that he will fight this case as far as it can be fought. His
determination and technical skill is not dependent upon the ability
of the Huey P. Newton Defense Fund to pay the entire cost of the
case, which will be quite a few thousand dollars. The resources of
the entire firm, Garry, Dreyfus, McTernan, and Brodsky, of which
one of the lawyers is black, are being dedicated to this case.

White power runs this country, white power is dispensed in its
courts, white power shot Huey Newton and put him in jail, and
white power is trying to gas him. Huey P. Newton is a brilliant
spokesman of black power, a living embodiment of black power.
Whether his attorney is white or black, black power is on trial.
White resources at the disposal of black people, a white legal firm
defending the Minister of Defense of the Black Panther Party is a
defense example of black power. Black skin is not—as our black
lawyers, politicians, doctors, teachers, and other professionals highly
attest in their mad scurry for white power, white values, white acceptance, and white hostility to black power.

Being deeply committed to the struggle for black liberation, and
not feeling compromised by the use of white lawyers, I wonder
how many of these people who complain about the white attorney
are really concerned about the black movement, really concerned
about Huey's life, really concerned about the Black Panther Party,
really concerned about putting an end to the racist exploitation of
black people, really concerned about putting an ending to the wanton
murder of black people by the police, and if they are so concerned,
what are they doing to show it? Are these the same people who

have contributed to the Huey P. Newton Defense Fund, helped the
Black Panther Party to grow, made constant personal sacrifices and
endured serious danger to see their commitment bear fruit? Or are
these people onlookers of a liberation struggle being waged for their
benefit who just generally dislike white people and don't like the
way it looks in court? Are these people black lawyers and their
friends who want to cash in on the prestige associated with this
historic case? Whose benefit are they concerned with, Huey P. Newton's or black lawyers?

—*The Black Panther*, November 23, 1967

# Revolutionary Art/Black Liberation

Besides fighting the enemy, the Black Panther Party is doing propaganda among the masses of black people—
The form of propaganda I'm about to refer to is called art, such
as painting, sketching, etc.—

### Art as Revolution
The Black Panther Party calls it revolutionary art—this kind of
art enlightens the party to continue its vigorous attack against the
enemy, as well as educate the masses of black people—we do this
by showing them through pictures—"The Correct Handling of the
Revolution."

### Bridges Blown Up
We, the Black Panther artists, draw deadly pictures of the enemy
—pictures that show him at his death door or dead—his bridges are
blown up in our pictures—his institutions destroyed—and in the
end he is lifeless—
We try to create an atmosphere for the vast majority of black
people—who aren't readers but activists—through their observation
of our work, they feel they have the right to destroy the enemy.
To give you an example of where revolutionary art began—we
must focus on a particular people, our brothers, the Vietnamese. In
the beginning stages of their struggle against U.S. Imperialism—so
as to determine the destiny of their own community—they had no
modern technical equipment, such as, tanks, automatic weapons or
semi-automatic weapons, etc.
In these days of struggle for Black Liberation, here in America,—
we have no modern technical equipment compared to that of our

A LIBERATED NATIONAL PUBLICATION/NEW YORK/MAY 1, 1970/25¢

# LIBERATED *Guardian*

# "REVOLUTION IN OUR LIFETIME"

oppressor—going back to Vietnam, as time progressed, the Vietnamese people have the same kind of technical equipment as the U.S. imperialists which also is made by the same manufacturer—

**One Bullet, 40 Pigs**

So, here is where we began to create our revolutionary art—we draw pictures of our brothers with stoner guns with one bullet going through forty pigs taking out their intestines along the way—another brother comes along, rips off their technical equipment; brothers in tanks guarding the black house and the black community—also launching rockets on U.S. military bases—Minister of Justice H. Rap Brown burning America down; he knows she plans to never come around; Prime Minister of Colonized Afro-America Stokely Carmichael with handgrenade in hand pointed at the Statue of Liberty; preaching we must have undying love for our people; LeRoi Jones asking, "Who will survive America?" "Black people will survive America"—taking what they want—Minister of Defense Huey P. Newton defending the black community—two pigs down two less to go.

**Standard Oil Molotovs**

We draw pictures that show Standard Oil in milk bottles launched at Rockefeller with the wicks made of cloth from I Magnin and J Magnin—pictures of Chinese fire works in gunpowder form aimed at the heart of the enemy—Bank of America—pictures of pigs hanging by their tongues wrapped with barbed wire connected to your local power plant.

This is revolutionary art—pigs lying in alley ways of the colony dead with their eyes gouged out—autopsy showing cause of death: "They fail to see that majority rules." Pictures we draw show them choking to death from their inhuman ways—these are the kinds of pictures revolutionary artists draw—.

The Viet Cong stabbing him in his brain—black people taking the hearts of the enemy and hanging the hearts on the wall (put one more notch on our knife) skin them alive and make rugs out of them—

We must draw pictures of Southern cracker Wallace with cancer of the mouth that he got from his dead witch's uterus—

Pictures that show black people kicking down prison gates—sniping bombers shooting down helicopters police mayors governors senators assemblymen congressmen firemen newsmen businessmen Americans—

"We shall conquer
without a doubt"—
revolutionary artist—Emory

—*The Black Panther*, May 18, 1968

# On Violence

Let us make one thing crystal clear: We do not claim the right to indiscriminate violence. We seek no bloodbath. We are not out to kill up white people. On the contrary, it is the cops who claim the right to indiscriminate violence and practice it everyday. It is the cops who have been bathing black people in blood and who seem bent on killing off black people. But black people, this day, this time, say HALT IN THE NAME OF HUMANITY! YOU SHALL MAKE NO MORE WAR ON UNARMED PEOPLE. YOU WILL NOT KILL ANOTHER BLACK PERSON AND WALK THE STREETS OF THE BLACK COMMUNITY TO GLOAT ABOUT IT AND SNEER AT THE DEFENSELESS RELATIVES OF YOUR VICTIMS. FROM NOW ON, WHEN YOU MURDER A BLACK PERSON IN THIS BABYLON OF BABYLONS, YOU MAY AS WELL GIVE IT UP BECAUSE WE WILL GET YOUR ASS AND GOD CAN'T HIDE YOU.

We call upon the people to rally to the support of Minister of Defense, Huey P. Newton. We call upon black people and white people who want to see the dawn of a new history in this land. We call upon people who want to see an end to the flow of blood. We call upon people who want to avoid a war in this land, who want to put an end to the war that is now going on in this land. We call upon people to take up the cry: HUEY MUST BE SET FREE!

Minister of Information
Black Panther Party for
Self-Defense

—*The Black Panther*, March 23, 1968

The Black Panther Party recognizes, as do all Marxist revolutionaries, that the only response to the violence of the ruling class is the revolutionary violence of the people. The Black Panther Party recognizes this truth not as some unspecified mechanistic Marxist-Leninist truism, but as the basic premise for relating to the colonial oppression of Black people in the heartland of Imperialism where the white ruling class, through its occupation police forces, agents and dope-peddlers, institutionally terrorizes the Black community. Revolutionary strategy for Black people in America begins with the defensive movement of picking up the Gun, as the condition for ending the pigs' reign of terror by the Gun. Black people picking up the gun for self-defense is the only basis in America for a revolutionary offensive against Imperialist state power.

—*The Black Panther*, April 25, 1970

As Jose Marti, the Cuban revolutionary, said, "The best way of telling is doing." This does not mean arbitrary confrontations, rampages through the streets, knocking down old women; we can't be anarchists and emotionalists, we have to be clear-headed and organized. An example of this type of cool-headedness is the fact that young students cut their hair and took the time to go into the White middle-class communities to rally support for this trial and for the cause of justice in the United States. Breaking windows, snatching pocketbooks will never lay a foundation for the long, hard struggle ahead. Politicizing and educating the various segments of the young, the open-minded, and the concerned will.

—From Collective Statement by the Connecticut 9, Political Prisoners, published in *The Black Panther*, May 2, 1970

For Huey, Bobby, Eldridge

# Free by Any Means Necessary

by Sarah Webster Fabio

The pen
is a weapon;
it can discharge
volleys of
meaning
hurled toward
the bull's eye
of truth;

it can deafen
the ear with
the roar of
a people's voice
clamoring for
justice.

It can kill
lies emitted

in ink from
oppressor's presses
making beasts
of holy men
justifying
their slaughters

Black people
righteous men,
throw away
those water pistols
what we need
are stoners to
riddle America's
bastions of
bigotry

which have

kept the black
man back
the poor people
poor
the dispossessed
and isolated
estranged from
the mainstream
of life.

The pen
has always
been a white
weapon; it
must be wrested
from the oppressor's
hands by
black power.

It must blast
forth the fire
of black
consciousness,
creating new images
of our people,
by our people,
for our people;

the black panthers
are the holy men

of our time;
they are the
last practitioners
of the judeo-christian
ethic—all others
have turned their
priesthoods into a mafia
protecting, not man
but status quo.

Free Huey
Free American justice

Free Leroi
Free creativity & art

Free Rap
Free free speech

Free Bobby
Free love, respect and power

Free Eldridge
Free our souls on ice

Free black panthers.
Free humanism
Free black men
Free goodness & honor
Free Huey, now,
and Free us all.

—*The Black Panther*, May 18, 1968

## Correcting Mistaken Ideas

by Capt. Crutch

There are numerous adverse ideas within the Black Panther Party. In the Black Liberation Army which greatly hinder the application of the Party's correct ideology. But unless these ideas are thoroughly corrected, the Black Liberation Army cannot possibly shoulder the tasks assigned to it Black America's great revolutionary struggle. The source of such incorrect ideas is that the party is composed largely of ghetto street niggers, together with elements of petty bourgeois niggers. The leaders of the party, however, fail to wage a concerted and determined struggle against these incorrect ideas, to educate (and re-educate) the members in the party's correct ideology—which is also an important cause of their existence and growth. Therefore, I shall attempt to help point out some of the manifestations of various incorrect ideology within the party. And I call upon all party members to help eliminate mistaken ideas and incorrect methods thoroughly.

1. The purely military viewpoint is highly developed among quite a few members.

a. Some party members regard military affairs and politics as opposed to each other and refuse to recognize that military affairs are only one means of accomplishing political tasks.

b. They don't understand that the Black Panther Party is an armed body for carrying out the political tasks of revolution. We should not confine ourselves merely to fighting. But we must also shoulder such important tasks as doing propaganda among the people, organizing the people, arming the people, and helping them to establish revolutionary political power for Black people. Without those objectives fighting loses its meaning and the Black Panther Party loses the reason for its existence.

c. At the same time in propaganda work they overlook the importance of propaganda teams. They also neglect the organizing of the masses. Therefore, both propaganda and organizational work are abandoned.

d. They become conceited when a battle is won and dispirited when a battle is lost.

e. Selfish departmentalism—they think only of the Black Panther Party and do not realize that it is an important task of the Black Liberation army to arm the local masses. This is cliquism in a magnified form.

f. Unable to see beyond their limited environment within the Black Panther Party. Such statements as 'us San Francisco Panthers,' 'us New York Panthers,' and etc. They have to realize Panthers are all one and the same. Also, a few Panthers believe that no other revolutionary forces exist. Hence their extreme addiction to the idea of conserving strength and avoiding action. This is a remnant of opportunism.

g. Some Panthers disregarding the subjective and objective conditions, suffer from the malady of revolutionary impetuosity; they will not take pains to do minute and detailed work among the masses. They do not want to distribute leaflets, sell newspapers, etc. These things seem small although they are very important. Yet they are riddled with illusions, and want only to do big things. This is a remnant of putschism.

The sources of the purely military viewpoint are
1. A low political level.
2. The mentality of mercenaries.
3. Over confidence in military strength and absence of confidence in the strength of the masses of the people. This arises from the preceding three.
The methods of correction are as follows.
1. Raise the political level in the party by means of education. At the same time, eliminate the remnants of opportunism and putschism, and break-down selfish departmentalism.
2. Intensify the political training of officers and men. Select workers and people experienced in struggle to join the party; thus, organizationally weakening or even eradicating the purely military viewpoint.
3. The party must actively attend to and discuss military work.
4. Draw up party rules and regulations which clearly define its tasks, the relationship between its military and its political apparatus, and the relationship between the party and the masses of the people.

—*The Black Panther*, October 26, 1968

# The Power of the People

The Black Panther Party (or any Black liberation force) cannot be successful without the complete support of the people. All power comes from the people. But we often hear that a certain segment of the general population has all of the power because it has the largest concentration of money or weapons. This is not true. Without people, both money and weapons are useless. Weapons are a source of power only if they are subject to the will of the people. If a group of 10 men had the only atomic bomb in existence, their power would still be limited by their number. They could not force the rest of the world to pay tribute to them simply because ownership of a destructive weapon does not make man invincible. Man is always susceptible to defeat.

The people of the world would not submit to a group of 10 men. People would fake submission; then destroy the 10 men at the first opportunity.

The example of 10 men possessing an atomic bomb is pure conjecture, although the same situation could be reduced to one man holding a pistol on 10 men. The man with the gun only has the power to destroy, but not the power to control. The 10 unarmed men could overpower the one man and take his weapon. Some of the unarmed men might die in the attempt, but death for a few is often the price of liberty for all.

Money too requires people for power. If people would refuse to accept the money of a country as payment for goods and services, that country would have to depend on the labor of its people as its only source of wealth and power. Such a situation can be compared to traveling around America with a checkbook but no cash. If no one accepts your check, all of the money that you might have in your bank account would be useless.

The people are the ultimate source of power. Let's unite and give more power to the Black Panthers, so that the Panthers will liberate all the power for "the people."

—*The Black Panther*, October 26, 1968

# Black Child's Pledge

by Shirley Williams
(Richmond Black Belt)

I pledge allegiance to my Black People.

I pledge to develop my mind and body to the greatest extent possible.

I will learn all that I can in order to give my best to my People in their struggle for liberation.

I will keep myself physically fit, building a strong body free from drugs and other substances which weaken me and make me less capable of protecting myself, my family and my Black brothers and sisters.

I will unselfishly share my knowledge and understanding with them in order to bring about change more quickly.

I will discipline myself to direct my energies thoughtfully and constructively rather than wasting them in idle hatred.

I will train myself never to hurt or allow others to harm my Black brothers and sisters for I recognize that we need every Black man, Woman, and child to be physically, mentally and psychologically strong. These principles I pledge to practice daily and to teach them to others in order to unite my People.

—*The Black Panther*, October 26, 1968

# In White America Today

by Evette Pearson

The descendants of the god-fearing racists who committed genocide against a race of red men (so they can have a place to worship
god freely) are trying to commit genocide against you, black man.
Your wife is jacked up on birth control pills. Your daughter is being
eaten away by syphilis. Your son is in Viet Nam, black man.
In white america today, god-fearing racists are buying guns, black
man. The guns are to blow your brains out after they pray to the
god that ordered black Adam out of the garden of eden. He'll whis-
per a prayer, give your wife a pill; deny your daughter medication,
put your son on the front lines, and piously blow your brains out.
Dig it, black man. He has the grace of god on his side:

Our father, (says white america)
which art in heaven
how I love this game.
Of all the blessings
you've given me—
this game of pain
is closest to my heart.
I said I'd pray and pray
you gave me the U.S.A.
I joined the Trustee Board
You let me kill the Injuns, lord.
You blessed me with slaves
You blessed me with fools—
Then the niggers started going to schools.
Integration! Freedom!
Now it's revolution!
But I know
the lord is good
Your grace is sufficient to silence niggers—
                                        for good.
                    AMEN!

Dig it. They left their mother country to worship their god. They
crossed the wicked seas with their hands cupped in prayer. They
wiped out your red brothers and took over the land, black man.
They brought you here to build their nation. Machines have now
taken over the work your black hands have done.

Shrewdly, cunningly, he starts to do you in. Genocide.
Planned Parenthood
   Birth Control
      Vietnamese War
         Prostitution
            Venereal disease
               Pigs, punks and
                  Tricky Dicky Nixon
Genocide. Dig it, black man.
It is time to deal with the situation. Educate your woman to stop
taking those pills. You and your woman—replenish the earth with
healthy black warriors. You and your woman can build the black
Liberation Army to end the god-fearing, god loving racist white dog
monster who is piously praying to his scurvy god to WIPE YOU
OUT!! . . . . . Panther Power . . .

—*The Black Panther*, January 4, 1969

## Editorial Statement

The Black Panther Party appreciates the contributions of all revolutionary people and will attempt to publish all relevant material
that is submitted to the Black Panther newspaper. THE BLACK
PANTHER is an instrument of political education and is published
with the intent of countering the misinformation that often appears
in the mass communication media.

THE BLACK PANTHER is not to be considered an outlet for
emotional outburst of irrevelant profanity. This is not to imply that
all profanity will be eliminated from THE BLACK PANTHER, but
to inform contributors that all material must correspond with the
primary purpose of the paper—to educate the oppressed.

—*The Black Panther*, February 2, 1969

## Revolutionary Letter #15

When you seize Columbia, when you
seize Paris, take
the media, tell the people what you're doing
what you're up to and why and how you mean

to do it, how they can help, keep the news
coming, steady, you have 70 years
of media conditioning to combat, it is a wall
you must get through, somehow, to reach
the instinctive man, who is struggling like a plant
for light, for air

when you seize a town, a campus, get hold of the power
stations, the water, the transportation,
forget to negotiate, forget how
to negotiate, don't wait for De Gaulle or Kirk
to abdicate, they won't, you are not
"demonstrating" you are fighting
a war, fight to win, don't wait for Johnson or
Humphrey or Rockefeller, to agree to your terms
because it's yours

—*The Black Panther*, January 1, 1969

# The Genius of Huey Newton

by Alprentice (Bunchy) Carter

But I want to try to explain something here. I want to try to say what Huey Newton is. The genius of Huey Newton is that he is the highest personification of what Malcolm ever talked about. The genius of Huey Newton and the relevance of the BLACK PAN-THER PARTY is that the Party has been engendered from the first generation of urban blacks on the West Coast. That either if we weren't ourselves, if the rank and file of the BLACK PANTHER PARTY itself was not born in the south, then our parents were, but that by and large we grew up on the West Coast. That what's significant is that this has happened. That where in the South, niggers, you know, like the white man, racist white power structure, is not only upon 'em, oppressing them, around them, surrounding them, within them, intimidating them, killing them, black people are very conscious of this happening, you know, and consequently they're like affected by it, molded by it. And their activities, their whole course of life is directed from the fact that they ARE oppressed, surrounded, behind, over and under, by this power structure, by racism.

On the West Coast, it has not been the case. Like the first genera-tion of urban blacks (and that's us, the BLACK PANTHER

PARTY), we've been pushed into corners, into ghettos, you dig it? And the only time that we come into contact with, I mean into visual, physical contact, is either through the businessman, the avaricious businessman, the insurance salesman, the milkman, or the occupying forces of the pigs, you dig it? That we have not, even though we haven't been educated, you dig it? (Like we haven't had no schoolin', because we didn't relate to that), but we was still, by and large, kinda free. I mean like we were able to produce a Huey Newton, a cat who could be free, who would say, "Well, motherfuck the police." you dig it? "Parker's sister, too." Who could say, "The racist dog policeman must withdraw immediately from the black community, cease the wanton murder and brutality of black people, or suffer the wrath of the armed people." He was free enough to realize this, and free enough to express this. This is the genius of Huey Newton, of being able to TAP this VAST RESERVOIR of revolutionary potential. I mean, street niggers, you dig it? Niggers who been BAD, niggers who weren't scared, because they ain't never knew what to be scared was, because they been down in these ghettos, and they knew to live they had to fight; and so they been able to do that. But I mean to really TAP it, to really TAP IT, to ORGANIZE it, and to direct it into an onslaught, a sortie against the power structure, this is the genius of Huey Newton, this is what Huey Newton did. Huey Newton was able to go down, and to take the nigger on the street and relate to him, understand what was going on inside of him, what he was thinking, and then implement that into an organization, into a PROGRAM and a PLATFORM, you dig it? Into the BLACK PANTHER PARTY—and then let it spread like wildfire across this country.

This is the genius of Huey Newton, the engendering, the establishing of the first vanguard party in the liberation struggle in the Western hemisphere. Huey Newton and the genius of it.

—*The Black Panther*, March 3, 1969


## by Eldridge Cleaver

One of the great contributions of Huey P. Newton is that he gave the Black Panther Party a firm ideological foundation that frees us from ideological flunkeyism and opens up the path to the future—a future in which we must provide new ideological formulations to fit our ever changing situation.

Essentially, what Huey did was to provide the ideology and the methodology for organizing the Black Urban Lumpenproletariat. Armed with this ideological perspective and method, Huey transformed the Black lumpenproletariat from the forgotten people at the bottom of society into the vanguard of the proletariat.

—From "On the Ideology of the Black Panther Party," *The Black Panther*, June 6, 1970

## Erica's Poem

by Erica Huggins

This is the dawning of the age of aquarius
the rise of the Black man
the liberation of the black woman
the year of the PANTHER
This is the beginning of the end of the beginning of
    Revolutionary struggle
This is the new world
the world of guns and political direction
and shouts of no more MURDER put an end to the terror
this dying has been done
for all of us—no crucifixion, no martyrdom
There is true understanding—no ignorance
but revolutionary arrogance
we will dare to struggle and dare to win
this head, this heart, this hand, this body
will clean itself of
this filth these morals, these ethics
This spirit will strike out against
Racism, Capitalism, Imperialism, oppression and brutality
Huey is free—he realizes—WE are jailed
this woman will fight to the end for Malcolm, for Bobby,
    Eldridge, for Huey, for Jon, for Bunchy
for Mai and for the anonymous
black man, black woman, black child
I am anonymous so I must FIGHT
This is the dawning of the age of
REV-O-LU-TION! GUNS! BLOODSHED?
BLOODSHED—No, this is the dawning of the age of JUST war
    against unjust degradation, humiliation, starvation, castration,
    unsurpation, abasement torture
If blood be shed for the future of our people, LET IT BE DONE
    Coldblooded—this is cold-blooded COLD BLOODED

Black man, can you hear me?
We are being murdered S.O.SS.O.S.
Black woman, your unborn baby is dying
LISTEN—somebody
I am screaming
I can hear my mind scream
  H * E * L * P
there is no other hope
there is no other generation
there are no more ways of looking at this problem
We must change this dawning of the age of permanent
  darkness
(dark except for the bark of riot 20 shotguns)
In the hands of Nixon's gestapo

Forget the pleasure you once had, it
Remains that we suffer
Even when we do not know it
Even when we smile

Hell awaits us, we will die
Unless we fight to the
End using political direction and
Your strength

—*The Black Panther*, May 25, 1969

# The revolutionary spirit of Antonio Maceo lives on today in the People's revolutionary vanguard, the Black Panther Party, and in our new revolutionary warrior named after him.

A new revolutionary warrior has been born into our midst. Our new little brother's name is Antonio Maceo Cleaver. He is the son of our Minister of Information, Eldridge Cleaver, and our Communications Secretary, Kathleen Cleaver.

He is named after the Black Cuban revolutionary, Antonio Maceo (1848–1896) who played a vital role in the struggle of the Cuban people for independence from Spain. He was one of the few leaders in the struggle that refused to agree with the phony Armistice Pact proposed in 1878 by the Spanish government after an armed struggle of the Cuban people against the Spanish rulers.[1] Unfortunately, the majority of the Cuban leaders accepted the Pact and the Cuban people were forced to suffer the consequences of continuing Spanish oppression, exploitation and brutality toward them. Antonio Maceo, (like our brother and leader Eldridge Cleaver), was forced to leave the country—into exile.

In 1892 Jose Marti who was the founder of the Cuban Revolutionary Party along with Antonio Maceo and other revolutionary leaders planned an uprising against the Spanish rule. On February 24, 1895, the call to war was heard all over Cuba. In April, Maceo landed in Cuba with a rebel group. Jose Marti was supreme chief; Maximo Gomez was Commander-in-Chief of the Liberation Army; Antonio Maceo was Lieutenant. The brilliant military strategy and tactics of Maceo and Gomez was called "the most daring military campaign of the century." This time around, Spain lost and the Cuban people gained their independence.

Antonio Maceo, the best warrior of the 1895 campaign was killed by the enemy on December 7, 1896.

All Power to the People
Right On Eldridge and Kathleen!

—*The Black Panther*, August 16, 1969

## A Black Panther Song

by Elaine Brown

Have you ever stood
In the darkness of night
screaming silently you're a man
Have you ever hoped
That a time would come
When your voice could be heard
In the noonday sun?
Have you waited so long
Till your unheard song
Has stripped away your very soul
well then believe it my friends
That the silence will end
We'll just have to get guns and
be men.

## To the Courageous Vietnamese People, Commemorating the Death of Ho Chi Minh

To die for the fascist imperialistic warmongers of the U.S. and others in the world; to die for the oppressive ruling circles of the bourgeoisie exploiters; to die for the capitalistic, aggressive, inhumane, atrocious, genocidal regimes is a death lighter than a feather which a destructive windstorm can blow about at random will.

But to die for the people; to die for the correct socialistic development of mankind; to die in the midst of socialistic revolutionary change for human survival; to die for your nation and peoples' right to self-determination in their land, home and community; to die for the freedom of all from oppression that the Black Panther Party has witnessed in the proletarian internationalism practiced by the Vietnamese peoples' revolutionary representatives that we have met; to die after all the great heroic and dedicated years of sacrifice to bring to the world and its people an end to the murderous, stormy winds of capitalism's fascist, aggressive imperialism; to die because he loved the people of his nation and humans of the world (and Brother Ho Chi Minh had practiced this all the days of his life); to die for all of this is a death heavier than the highest mountain in the world of which no, not any destructive fascist imperialistic storm can blow away at will.

Who can find the feather or feathers that were blown away by the destructive windstorm? I can't find any. Who can see the mountains since the windstorm is gone? I can see many, they still stand. There! That mountain will always stand and Ho Chi Minh is that mountain—a death heavier than Mt. Thai.

—*The Black Panther*, September 13, 1969

## The Chicago 8

by John Coleman

Anyone who has closely been following the trial in Chicago now must realize that Fascism is running rampant in courts where political prisoners are being tried. I have been following the trial closely and the proceedings of that kangaroo court under the direction of "Judge Magoo" has hardened my stand behind the Black Panther Party and I am quite certain it has also won the vanguard party increased support.

Chairman Bobby, has made evident by the treatment he has received, to the whole of America what has been known by many Black brothers who have come in contact with justice in a racist society, a fair impartial trial is impossible. Chairman Bobby asks for only what he is entitled to under the constitution, that being: the right to cross examine witnesses, the right to represent himself or have a lawyer of his own choice. All these have been denied, Judge Hoffman is truly a "blatant racist", for he has denied them to Bobby.

Judge Hoffman, merely Tricky Dick's "flunky", is trying to have the trial labeled a mistrial, drop all charges and prevent the inevitable, an appeal to the higher courts. They realize that if this so-called riot conspiracy law was ever tested for constitutionality it would not survive, it is an obvious denial of the free speech amendment.

The purpose of the trial as everyone knows, is to make it appear that the violence of last year's demonstration was planned by the eight now on trial, this is utterly ridiculous and completely unfounded. The denial of the eight, Bobby Seale in particular, the right to cross examine witnesses is an obvious attempt to cover up something. Whatever is trying to be hidden must be vital to the court because they are denying those on trial their constitutional rights.

A conspiracy does exist however, a governmental conspiracy of suppression of political activists Black and White who are hell bent on kicking the racists, the capitalists and others who would not grant self-determination to people, out of places of power. The eyes of the world are on this court thanks to Chairman Bobby's undaunted cry for justice, credit must also be given to Judge Magoo, for his inability to cope with Bobby's cry, he has shed much light on the suppressive policy of Tricky Dick and his running dog flunkies. People are not going for all the bulls--t America preaches, the inconsistencies are becoming clearer and the people of the U.S. (oppressed peoples) are forming a proletarian internationalistic force that will rise and crush the pig power structure.

ALL POWER TO THE PEOPLE!!

—*The Black Panther*, November 15, 1969

## Pigs—Panthers

by Candy

It is undeniably true, that in the cities of "Babylon" fortunate enough to have a branch of the Black Panther Party, a day does not pass where there isn't at least one instance of Police—Panther antagonism. To many people, I'm sure that this phenomenon must seem perplexing. Why is it that the police are always raiding Panther pads, vamping on their offices and harassing the Panthers in their various duties of serving the people? Do the police antagonize this group merely because they are Black men and women, and exhibit their pride of this in all of their actions? Or do they fear the Panthers because they represent certain threats to their security?

To understand this antagonism between the two groups, we have to examine objectively their purposes, tactics, and legitimacy. Their purpose would be why they exist; tactics would be the means they use to achieve the purpose; and legitimacy would answer whether their existence was valid or not.

On every police car, one can read the words, "To protect and to serve". The question that arises here is, "To protect and to serve who?" Well, if we remember that Babylon today is a racist, fascist oppressive state, we can begin to answer that question.

One aspect of American society consists of the oppressor-oppressed relationship. As we live in a capitalist environment, the masses of the public are exploited at the hands of a few individuals that control and hold all of this nation's wealth. More people are waking up to the facts of capitalism's true nature, and as these people do so, they see that capitalism is the oppressor. Once this is realized these aware segments of our communities then move to further the destruction of this capitalist state. That puts them in direct opposition to the government, which perpetrates and tries to spread capitalism and imperialism throughout the world.

As capitalism is very individualistic, the perpetrators of this system have no regard for the people. Their only interest is in making money, and they will use any means to achieve this goal. The capitalist has even gone so far as to distort the Constitution. Some people actually believe that we are living in a country that follows the doctrine: "Government of the people, for the people, and by the people". The system of today comes no where near this. Do you think that the people would exploit themselves? Obviously there is some discrepancy here between the way this country is supposed to be run, and the way it is being run.

No, there are no limits to the means the capitalist will employ to increase his wealth. He's pit different racial groups against one another, so that the people will be busy fighting and hating one another, rather than realizing that it is capitalism that they should fight and hate. He's enslaved one group of people, and tried to exterminate another (the Indians). The capitalist is completely unscrupulous in his quest for power and money.

From this basic understanding, we can see who the police are to "protect and serve". They are in our communities to protect and serve the interests of this capitalist, exploitative state. They have no conception of what it would be to protect and serve the people, because they are merely an extension of the state that exists to keep the minorities in a state of neo-colonialism, and all people oppressed and exploited. This means that they must not allow for any disturbances of the status quo, which would be detrimental to the interests of the capitalist state.

On the other hand, the Black Panther Party has seen through the screen of madness that the capitalists have created to keep our minds from dealing with why this society is in the situation that we find ourselves. The Panthers therefore, work to bring about a revolution that will free all peoples from the oppression of capitalism, racism and imperialism. They are working to establish a society in which every man will be free to determine his own destiny.

Here lies one antagonism between the two groups. Police, who represent this capitalist state, are working for, and in the interests of a few individuals. Panthers are working for, and in the interests of the people.

In the area of tactics, we have many examples of both groups. As the function of the police is to make sure that the people act according to the needs and wants of the state, their means of reaching this end is through facism. Terror, intimidation, brutality, and murder have become the order of the day as the police try to keep any progressive or dissenting elements from developing in our communities.

In sharp contrast to this are the tactics that the Panthers use. They feel that through setting correct examples for the people, and by educating the people, their purpose will be fulfilled. For example, after the Party initiated the Free Breakfast Programs, many communities realized the need and validity of such programs, and moved to establish their own Free Breakfast or Lunch Program. This can be attributed to the correct example set by the Black Panther Party.

Dealing with legitimacy, the Constitution is based upon the idea of the power of the people to enjoy certain "inalienable rights", and exercise these rights. Supposedly it is the people that direct the actions of the government and sanction its authority. Today, the Constitution has been distorted and we find "Government of a few, for a few, and by a few". In light of this, the police, in their present role, as arms of this type of government have no right in our communities. They are not, in these fascist times, living up to their motto, or the U.S. Constitution, and are therefore illegitimate bodies in our society.

The members of the Black Panther Party are of the people, for the people, and their actions, programs and direction is governed by the needs of the people. They see the police for what they are—oppressive forces that are keeping the American people in a repressed state. This is why they must fight the legitimacy of the police's presence in our communities. The move for decentralization of the police department is just one means of attacking the existence of the hostile occupying troops.

There could be nothing but antagonism between the police and the Panthers, as they serve different groups, with different interests. One (the police) functioning only to keep the people oppressed, exploited and mere pawns in the Man's game—and the other (Panthers) trying to free the people and move to a society where men individually, determine their own destiny, and collectively, their type of society.

Think about the phrase, "All Power to the People". The founding fathers realized the beauty of the essence of those words and based the Constitution upon them. We must all realize their beauty, and live to make them become a reality in this country.

ALL POWER TO THE PEOPLE

—*The Black Panther*, November 22, 1969

## On Criticism of Cuba

There are two types of criticism, revolutionary criticism and reactionary criticism. Revolutionary criticism is done on a principled basis, at the proper time, when the objective and subjective conditions are right, and it is given to reach a higher level of unity and to strengthen the revolutionary camp. Reactionary criticism generally takes the form of a personal attack because of some personal grievance. It is generally onesided criticism based on a subjective analysis not having looked at a situation on all sides and reactionary criticism only served the interest of the fascist and imperialist.

On the question of socialism and racism the Black Panther Party does not and never has said that if socialism is instituted that racism automatically ceases. Although some critics of the Black Panther Party have implied, namely Stokely Carmichael, that we have taken that position. What we say is that in a socialist society the conditions are more favorable for a people to begin to struggle to eliminate racism.

Cuba, 90 miles from Florida where they launch those Saturn rockets, with a U.S. naval base, Guantanamo, right on their island, is struggling for the defense of the Cuban people and their revolution under an economic blockade, and this is strangulating and threatening to get tighter. We see the Cuban revolution as a great achievement in the world revolution by establishing an island of socialism in an ocean, the western hemisphere, of capitalist exploitation, imperialist aggression and fascist suppression. We wish the Cuban people victory in their struggle against the blockade and may the Cuban people achieve their goal of 10,000,000 tons in the 1970 sugar cane harvest.

We were not born on Cuban soil. Some members of the Black Panther Party used Cuba as the means of escape from fascist suppression in Babylon and they are alive, well and free today. It would not be in the interest of Cuba or the world revolution to begin to launch attacks at Cuba because they have not been able to eliminate all forms of racism in the ten years since their revolution began.

The cardinal rule of the Black Panther Party says, Have Faith in the People, Have Faith in the Party. This principle is not to be applied just in Babylon but around the world. On this basis and relating to historical materialism we know that Cuba, the U.S. and the world will be free of racism and the last shall be first and the first shall be last.

ALL POWER TO THE PEOPLE

Los Ten Million Van [We're making the ten million tons.]

—*The Black Panther*, December 27, 1969

# 3.

# HUEY P. NEWTON SPEAKS

Black Panthers refer repeatedly to "The Genius of Huey P. Newton." Here are representative articles, interviews, and messages of the Minister of Defense of the Black Panther Party which clearly reveal why this characterization is used. Most of them were written or taped in prison at Los Padres, California, where Huey Newton is still imprisoned as of this writing.

# In Defense of Self-Defense:
# Executive Mandate Number One

In response to the Mulford Gun Bill, Minister of Defense Huey
Newton wrote a statement which Panther Chairman Bobby Seale
delivered on the steps of the Capitol in Sacramento on May 2, 1967.
The statement is as follows:

The Black Panther Party for Self-Defense calls upon the American
people in general and the Black people in particular to take careful
note of the racist California Legislature, which is now considering
legislation aimed at keeping the Black people disarmed and powerless at the very same time that racist police agencies throughout the
country are intensifying the terror, brutality, murder and repression
of Black people.

At the same time that the American government is waging a racist
war of genocide in Vietnam, the concentration camps in which
Japanese Americans were interned during World War II are being
renovated and expanded. Since America has historically reserved the
most barbaric treatment for nonwhite people, we are forced to conclude that these concentration camps are being prepared for Black
people, who are determined to gain their freedom by any means
necessary. The enslavement of Black people from the very beginning
of this country, the genocide practiced on the American Indians and
the confining of the survivors on reservations, the savage lynching of
thousands of Black men and women, the dropping of atomic bombs
on Hiroshima and Nagasaki, and now the cowardly massacre in Vietnam, all testify to the fact that towards people of color the racist
power structure of America has but one policy: repression, genocide,
terror and the big stick.

Black people have begged, prayed, petitioned, demonstrated and
everything else to get the racist power structure of America to right
the wrongs which have historically been perpetrated against Black
people. All of these efforts have been answered by more repression,
deceit, and hypocrisy. As the aggression of the racist American government escalates in Vietnam, the police agencies of America escalates the repression of Black people throughout the ghettos of America. Vicious police dogs, cattle prods and increased patrols have become familiar sights in Black communities. City Hall turns a deaf
ear to the pleas of Black people for relief from this increasing terror.

The Black Panther Party for Self-Defense believes that the time
has come for Black people to arm themselves against this terror
before it is too late. The pending Mulford Act brings the hour of

doom one step nearer. A people who have suffered so much for so long at the hands of a racist society, must draw the line somewhere. We believe that the Black communities of America must rise up as one man to halt the progression of a trend that leads inevitably to their total destruction.

—*The Black Panther*, June 2, 1967

## The Correct Handling of a Revolution

Most human behavior is learned behavior. Most things the human being learns are gained through an indirect relationship to the object. Humans do not act from instinct as lower animals do. Those things learned indirectly many times stimulate very effective responses to what might be later a direct experience. At this time the black masses are handling the resistance incorrectly. The brothers in East Oakland learned from Watts a means of resistance fighting by amassing the people in the streets, throwing bricks and molotov cocktails to destroy property and create disruption. The brothers and sisters in the streets were herded into a small area by the gestapo police and immediately contained by the brutal violence of the oppressor's storm troops. This manner of resistance is sporadic, short-lived, and costly in violence against the people. This method has been transmitted to all the ghettos of the black nation across the country. The first man who threw a molotov cocktail is not personally known by the masses, but yet the action was respected and followed by the people.

The Vanguard Party must provide leadership for the people. It must teach the correct strategic methods of prolonged resistance through literature and activities. If the activities of the party are respected by the people, the people will follow the example. This is the primary job of the party. This knowledge will probably be gained secondhand by the masses just as the above mentioned was gained indirectly. When the people learn that it is no longer advantageous for them to resist by going into the streets in large numbers, and when they see the advantage in the activities of the guerrilla warfare method, they will quickly follow this example.

But first, they must respect the party which is transmitting this message. When the Vanguard group destroys the machinery of the oppressor by dealing with him in small groups of three and four, and then escapes the might of the oppressor, the masses will be overjoyed and will adhere to this correct strategy. When the masses hear that a gestapo policeman has been executed while sipping coffee at a counter, and the revolutionary executioners fled without being traced, the masses will see the validity of this type of approach to resistance. It is not necessary to organize thirty million Black people in primary groups of two's and three's but it is important for the party to show the people how to go about revolution. During slavery, in which no vanguard party existed and forms of communication were severely restricted and insufficient, many slave revolts occurred.

There are basically three ways one can learn: through study, through observation, and through actual experience. The black community is basically composed of activists. The community learns through activity, either through observation of or participation in the activity. To study and learn is good but the actual experience is the best means of learning. The party must engage in activities that will teach the people. The black community is basically not a reading community. Therefore it is very significant that the vanguard group first be activists. Without this knowledge of the black community one could not gain the fundamental knowledge of the black revolution in racist America.

The main function of the party is to awaken the people and to teach them the strategic method of resisting the power structure, which is prepared not only to combat the resistance of the people with massive brutality, but to totally annihilate the black community, the black population.

If it is learned by the power structure that black people have "x" amount of guns in their possession, this will not stimulate the power structure to prepare itself with guns, because it is already more than prepared.

The result of this education will be positive for Black people in their resistance and negative for the power structure in its oppression, because the party always exemplifies revolutionary defiance. If the party is not going to make the people aware of the tools of liberation and the strategic method that is to be used, there will be no means by which the people will be mobilized properly.

The relationship between the vanguard party and the masses is a secondary relationship. The relationship between the members of the vanguard party is a primary relationship. It is important that the members of the vanguard group maintain a face-to-face relationship with each other. This is important if the party machinery is to be effective. It is impossible to put together functional party machinery or programs without this direct relationship. The members of the vanguard group should be tested revolutionaries. This will minimize the danger of Uncle Tom informers and opportunists.

The main purpose of a vanguard group should be to raise the consciousness of the masses through educational programs and certain physical activities the party will participate in. The sleeping masses must be bombarded with the correct approach to struggle through the activities of the vanguard party. Therefore, the masses must know that the party exists. The party must use all means available to get this information across to the masses. If the masses do not have knowledge of the party, it will be impossible for the masses to follow the program of the party.

The vanguard party is never underground in the beginning of its existence, because this would limit its effectiveness and educational processes. How can you teach people if the people do not know and respect you? The party must exist above ground as long as the dog power structure will allow, and hopefully when the party is forced to go underground the message of the party will already have been put across to the people. The vanguard party's activities on the surface will necessarily be shortlived.

This is why it is so important that the party make a tremendous impact upon the people before it is driven into secrecy.

At this time, the people know the party exists, and they will seek out further information on the activities of this underground party.

Many would-be revolutionaries work under the fallacious illusion that the vanguard party is to be a secret organization that the power structure knows nothing about, and the masses know nothing about, except for occasional letters that come to their homes by night. Underground parties cannot distribute leaflets announcing an underground meeting. These are contradictions and inconsistencies of the so-called revolutionaries. The so-called revolutionaries are in fact afraid of the very danger that they are advocating for the people. These so-called revolutionaries want the people to say what they themselves are afraid to say, and the people to do what they themselves are afraid to do. This makes the so-called revolutionary, a coward and a hypocrite.

If these imposters would investigate the history of revolution, they would see that the vanguard group always starts out above ground and is later driven underground by the aggressor. The Cuban Revolution exemplifies this fact; when Fidel Castro started to resist the butcher Batista and the American running dogs, he started by speaking on the campus of the University of Havana in public. He was later driven to the hills. His impact upon the dispossessed people of Cuba was very great and received with much respect. When he went into secrecy, Cuban people searched him out. People went to the hills to find him and his band of twelve. Castro handled the revolutionary struggle correctly. If the Chinese Revolution is investigated, it will be seen that the Communist Party was quiet on the surface so that they would be able to muster support from the masses. There are many areas one can read about to learn the correct approach, such as the revolution in Kenya, the Algerian Revolution, Fanon's THE WRETCHED OF THE EARTH, the Russian Revolution, the works of Chairman Mao Tse-tung, and a host of others.

A revolutionary must realize that if he is sincere, death is imminent due to the fact that the things he is saying and doing are extremely dangerous. Without this realization, it is impossible to proceed as a revolutionary. The masses are constantly looking for a guide, a Messiah, to liberate them from the hands of the oppressor. The vanguard party must exemplify the characteristics of worthy leadership. Millions and millions of oppressed people might not know members of the vanguard party personally or directly, but they will gain through an indirect acquaintance the proper strategy for liberation via the mass media and the physical activities of the party. It is of prime importance that the vanguard party develop a political organ, such as a newspaper produced by the party, as well as employ strategically revolutionary art and destruction of the oppressor's machinery. For example, Watts. The economy and property of the oppressor was destroyed to such an extent that no matter how the oppressor tried to whitewash the activities of the black brothers, the real nature and the real cause of the activity was communicated to every black community. For further example, no matter how the oppressor tries to distort and confuse the message of Brother Malcolm X, Black people all over the country understand it perfectly and welcome it.

The Black Panther Party for Self Defense teaches that in the final analysis, the amount of guns and defense weapons, such as hand grenades, bazookas, and other necessary equipment, will be supplied by taking these weapons from the power structure, as exemplified by the Viet Cong. Therefore, the greater the military preparation on the part of the oppressor, the greater is the availability of weapons for the black community. It is believed by some hypocrites that when the people are taught by the vanguard group to prepare for resistance, this only brings the man down on them with increasing violence and brutality; but the fact of the matter is that when the man becomes more oppressive, this only heightens the revolutionary fervor. The people never make revolution. The oppressors by their brutal actions cause the resistance by the people. The Vanguard Party only teaches the correct methods of resistance. So, if things can get worse for oppressed people, then they will feel no need for revolution or resistance. The complaint of the hypocrites that the Black Panther Party for Self Defense is exposing the people to deeper suffering is an incorrect observation. People have proved that they will not tolerate any more oppression by the racist dog police through their rebellions in the black communities across the country. The people are looking now for guidance to extend and strengthen their resistance struggle.

—*The Black Panther*, May 18, 1968

## Functional Definition of Politics

/ Politics is war without bloodshed. War is politics with bloodshed. Politics has its particular characteristics which differentiate it from war./ When the peaceful means of politics are exhausted and the people do not get what they want, politics are continued. Usually it ends up in physical conflict which is called war, which is also political.

Because we lack political power, Black people are not free. Black reconstruction failed because Black people did not have political and military power. The masses of Black people at the time were very clear on the definition of political power. It was evident in the songs of Black people at that time. In the songs it was stated that on the Day of Jubilee we'd have forty acres and two mules. This was promised Black people by the Freedman's Bureau. This was freedom as far as the Black masses were concerned.

The Talented Tenth at the time viewed freedom as operative in the political arena. Black people did operate in the political arena during reconstruction. They were more educated than most of the whites in the south. They had been educated in France, Canada and England and were very qualified to serve in the political arena. But yet, Black Reconstruction failed.

/When one operates in the political arena, it is assumed that he has power or represents power; he is symbolic of a powerful force. There are approximately three areas of power in the political arena: economic power, land power (feudal power) and military power. If Black people at the time had received 40 acres and 2 mules, we would have developed a powerful force. Then we would have chosen a representative to represent us in this political arena. Because Black people did not receive the 40 acres and 2 mules, it was absurd to have a representative in the political arena.

When White people send a representative into the political arena, they have a power force or power base that they represent. When

White people, through their representatives, do not get what they want, there is always a political consequence. This is evident in the fact that when the farmers are not given an adequate price for their crops the economy will receive a political consequence. They will let their crops rot in the field; they will not cooperate with other sectors of the economy. To be political, you must have a political consequence when you do not receive your desires—otherwise you are non-political.

When Black people send a representative, he is somewhat absurd because he represents no political power. He does not represent land power because we do not own any land. He does not represent economic or industrial power because Black people do not own the means of production. The only way he can become political is to represent what is commonly called a military power—which the BLACK PANTHER PARTY FOR SELF-DEFENSE calls Self-Defense Power. Black people can develop Self-Defense Power by arming themselves from house to house, block to block, community to community, throughout the nation. Then we will choose a political representative and he will state to the power structure the desires of the Black masses. If the desires are not met, the power structure will receive a political consequence. We will make it economically non-profitable for the power structure to go on with its oppressive ways. We will then negotiate as equals. There will be a balance between the people who are economically powerful and the people who are potentially economically destructive.

The White racist oppresses Black people not only for racist reasons, but because it is also economically profitable to do so. Black people must develop a power that will make it non-profitable for racists to go on oppressing us. If the White racist imperialists in America continue to wage war against all people of color throughout the world and also wage a civil war against Blacks here in America, it will be economically impossible for him to survive. We must develop a strategy that will make his war campaigns non-profitable. This racist United States operates with the motive of profit. He lifts the gun and escalates the war for profit reasons. We will make him lower the guns because they will no longer serve his profit motive.

Every man is born, therefore he has a right to live, a right to share in the wealth. If he is denied the right to work, then he is denied the right to live. If he can't work, he deserves a high standard of living, regardless of his education or skill. It should be up to the administrators of the economic system to design a program for providing work or livelihood for his people. To deny a man this is to deny him life. The controllers of the economic system are obligated to furnish each man with a livelihood. If they cannot do this or if they will not do this, they do not deserve the position of administrators. The means of production should be taken away from them and placed in the people's hands, so that the people can organize them in such a way as to provide themselves with a livelihood. The people will choose capable administrators, motivated by their sincere interest in the people's welfare and not the interest of private property. The people will choose managers to control the means of production and the land that is rightfully theirs. Until the people control the land and the means of production, there will be no peace. Black people must control the destiny of their community.

Because Black people desire to determine their own destiny, they are constantly inflicted with brutality from the occupying army, embodied in the police department. There is a great similarity between the occupying army in Southeast Asia and the occupation of our communities by the racist police. The armies are there not to protect the people of South Vietnam, but to brutalize and oppress them for the interests of the selfish imperial power.

The police should be the people of the community in uniform. There should be no division or conflict of interest between the people and the police. Once there is a division, then the police become the enemy of the people. The police should serve the interest of the people and be one and the same. When this principle breaks down, then the police become an occupying army. When historically one race has oppressed another and policemen are recruited from the oppressor race to patrol the communities of the oppressed people, an intolerable contradiction exists.

THE RACIST DOG POLICEMEN MUST WITHDRAW IMMEDIATELY FROM OUR COMMUNITIES, CEASE THEIR WANTON MURDER AND BRUTALITY AND TORTURE OF BLACK PEOPLE, OR FACE THE WRATH OF THE ARMED PEOPLE.

—*The Black Panther*, January 17, 1969

## Message to "Free Huey Rally," Oakland Auditorium, February 17, 1968

**"Taped in Prison"**
REVOLUTIONARY BROTHERS AND SISTERS, WHITE RADICALS WHO ARE BECOMING BROTHERS AND SISTERS:

I'm very happy that we are all here together today, not because it's my birthday, but because we should be together on any and every occasion that we possibly can in the name of solidarity.

February 17th fortunately is also the Tet of the lunar new year. So we're celebrating the lunar new year with our brothers in Viet Nam. We're daily making the people more and more aware of the need for unity among all revolutionary people and also that it's impossible for us to overcome the treacherous bureaucratic class without an organized force.

The students at the many universities across the nation are challenging the reactionary authority of the schools and are also pointing out very vividly that it's impossible to have a free university, free schools, or a free society, in a society that's ruled by a fascist military-industrial complex. The community is now seeing that our fight on the campuses is more than just a fight for "freedom of speech" on the campus, or Blacks gaining a knowledge of our heritage; it's also showing the direct relationship between the reactionary government and the agencies and institutions that are only an arm of these reactionaries. Until we penetrate the community and make them aware, and plant the seed of revolution, we will never have freedom at our schools. The community now is being mobilized by the Black revolutionary forces and along with them are our white revolutionary comrades.

It seems that the time has come for an escalation of our offensive. Just as our brothers in Viet Nam had the Tet offensive last year, this celebration today will only be a prelude or celebration to the offensive that we are going to wage in the not-too-far future. "In the near future a colossal event will occur where the masses of the people will rise up like a mighty storm and a hurricane, sweeping all evil gentry and corrupt officials into their graves." Brother Mao put that quite well, and we will follow the pattern and follow the thoughts of Chairman Mao.

Today it should mark a new time for the TWO-REVOLUTIONARY force in the country: the alienated white group and the masses of Blacks in the ghettos, who for years sought freedom and liberation from a racist, reaction-system. After approximately three years now that the Panthers have been organized, we have gained even closer relationship with our Latin American brothers, our Chicano brothers in the United States, and the Cuban people, and every other people who are striving for freedom.

I would like to thank everyone very much for coming, and we must remember that we must never make excuses for such gatherings as this. Today we'll use the excuse of my birthday; but the real issue is the need to come together in unity and brotherhood.

Our Minister of Information Eldridge Cleaver is with us in spirit, and I'm very sure that this decadent fascist society wasn't worthy of him and couldn't tolerate his presence because he acted as a guide flag for the people. So we must make a society that will welcome people like our Minister of Information.

The Oakland Seven are now standing trial for resisting the fascist system, and we would like to let them know and would like to rally the community for support. They have a very able representative in court with them, Charles Garry, who is very capable and truly a revolutionary. Brother Eldridge Cleaver has said on more than one occasion that he would go into any court in the world with an attorney like Charles Garry. I would like to bear witness to that from a personal experience. With a representative like Charles Garry we're sure that we would have victory as long as the community supports us. We have, with the support of the community and with the fine attorney such as Charles Garry, we have nothing to fear.

A short time ago we suffered a very tragic experience in that two of our very talented and gifted and dedicated brothers were assassinated in L.A.: Brother "Bunchy" and Brother Huggins. This was only an escalation of the oppression against us. The assassins were agents of the establishment, and they took the occasion to eliminate the people's fighters, or fighters for the people. Knowing that the people have no recourse, the institutions and the court institutions give us no recourse because they're only representatives of the reactionary system. The community will have to erect revolutionary courts and also a community militia to protect the community and see that the community gets justice.

Brother Ruben has suffered many investigations, and now he's under investigation. He's going to trial on or about four or five different alleged crimes, and the crimes are SEEKING JUSTICE. The society views any person who's striving after justice and freedom and to end exploitation as a "criminal." We know that if we are criminals, the criminals have received their ultimate revenge when Karl Marx indicted the bourgeoisie of grand theft. We realize that it's they who are criminals and it's they who will have to be brought to justice. We will have to go on fighting in spite of the losses and in spite of the hardships that we're bound to suffer, until the final downfall of the reactionary power structure.

SO, POWER TO THE PEOPLE, BLACK POWER TO BLACK PEOPLE, AND PANTHER POWER TO THE VANGUARD!
Huey P. Newton
Minister of Defense
Black Panther Party

—*The Black Panther*, March 3, 1969

# Huey Newton Talks to the Movement About the Black Panther Party, Cultural Nationalism, SNCC, Liberals and White Revolutionaries

THE MOVEMENT: The question of nationalism is a vital one in the black movement today. Some have made a distinction between cultural nationalism and revolutionary nationalism. Would you comment on the differences and give us your views?

HUEY P. NEWTON: There are two kinds of nationalism, revolutionary nationalism and reactionary nationalism. Revolutionary nationalism is first dependent upon a people's revolution with the end goal being the people in power. Therefore to be a revolutionary nationalist you would by necessity have to be a socialist. If you are a reactionary nationalist you are not a socialist and your end goal is the oppression of the people.

Cultural nationalism, or pork chop nationalism, as I sometimes call it, is basically a problem of having the wrong political perspective. It seems to be a reaction instead of responding to political oppression. The cultural nationalists are concerned with returning to the old African culture and thereby regaining their identity and freedom. In other words, they feel that the African culture will automatically bring political freedom. Many times cultural nationalists fall into line as reactionary nationalists.

Papa Doc in Haiti is an excellent example of reactionary nationalism. He oppresses the people but he does promote the African culture. He's against anything other than black, which on the surface seems very good, but for him it is only to mislead the people. He merely kicked out the racists and replaced them with himself as the oppressor. Many of the nationalists in this country seem to desire the same ends.

The Black Panther Party, which is a revolutionary group of black people, realizes that we have to have an identity. We have to realize our black heritage in order to give us strength to move on and progress. But as far as returning to the old African culture, it's unnecessary and it's not advantageous in many respects. We believe that culture itself will not liberate us. We're going to need some stronger stuff.

### Revolutionary Nationalism

A good example of revolutionary nationalism was the revolution in Algeria when Ben Bella took over. The French were kicked out but it was a people's revolution because the people ended up in power. The leaders that took over were not interested in the profit motive where they could exploit the people and keep them in a state of slavery. They nationalized the industry and plowed the would-be profits into the community. That's what socialism is all about in a nutshell. The people's representatives are in office strictly on the leave of the people. The wealth of the country is controlled by the people and they are considered whenever modifications in the industries are made.

The Black Panther Party is a revolutionary Nationalist group and we see a major contradiction between capitalism in this country and our interests. We realize that this country became very rich upon slavery and that slavery is capitalism in the extreme. We have two evils to fight, capitalism and racism. We must destroy both racism and capitalism.

MOVEMENT: Directly related to the question of nationalism is the question of unity within the black community. There has been some question about this since the Black Panther Party has run candidates against other black candidates in recent California elections. What is your position on this matter?

HUEY: Well a very peculiar thing has happened. Historically you got what Malcolm X calls the field nigger and the house nigger. The house nigger had some privileges, a little more. He got the worn-out clothes of the master and he didn't have to work as hard as the field black. He came to respect the master to such an extent until he identified with the master because he got a few of the leftovers that the field blacks did not get. And through this identity with him, he saw the slavemaster's interest as being his interest. Sometimes he would even protect the slavemaster more than the slavemaster would protect himself. Malcolm makes the point that if the master's house happened to catch on fire the house Negro will work harder than the master to put the fire out and save the master's house, while the field Negro, the field blacks was praying that the house burned down. The house black identified with the master so much that when the master would get sick the house Negro would say, "Master, we's sick!"

### Black Bourgeoisie

The Black Panther Party are the field blacks, we're hoping the master dies if he gets sick. The Black bourgeoisie seem to be acting in the role of the house Negro. They are pro-administration. They would like a few concessions made, but as far as the overall setup, they have a little more material goods, a little more advantage, a few more privileges than the black have-nots; the lower class. And so they identify with the power structure and they see their interests as the power structure's interest. In fact, it's against their interest.

The Black Panther Party was forced to draw a line of demarcation. We are for all of those who are for the promotion of the interests of the black have-nots, which represents about 98% of blacks here in America. We're not controlled by the white mother country radicals nor are we controlled by the black bourgeoisie. We have a mind of our own and if the black bourgeoisie cannot align itself with our complete program, then the black bourgeoisie sets itself up as our enemy. And they will be attacked and treated as such.

MOVEMENT: The Black Panther Party has had considerable contact with white radicals since its earliest days. What do you see as the role of these white radicals?

HUEY: The white mother country radical is the off-spring of the children of the beast that has plundered the world exploiting all people, concentrating on the people of color. These are children of the beast that seek now to be redeemed because they realize that their former heroes, who were slave masters and murderers, put forth ideas that were only facades to hide the treachery they inflicted upon the world. They are turning their backs on their fathers.

The white mother country radical, in resisting the system, becomes somewhat of an abstract thing because he's not oppressed as much as black people are. As a matter of fact his oppression is somewhat abstract simply because he doesn't have to live in a reality of oppression.

Black people in America and colored people throughout the world suffer not only from exploitation, but they suffer from racism. Black people here in America, in the black colony, are oppressed because we're black and we're exploited. The whites are rebels, many of them from the middle class and as far as any overt oppression this is not the case. So therefore I call their rejection of the system somewhat of an abstract thing. They're looking for new heroes. They're looking to wash away the hypocrisy that their fathers have presented to the world. In doing this they see the people who are really fighting for freedom. They see the people who are really standing for justice and equality and peace, throughout the world. They are the people of Vietnam, the people of Latin America, the people of Asia, the people of Africa, and the black people in the black colony here in America.

### White Revolutionaries

This presents somewhat of a problem in many ways to the black revolutionary especially to the cultural nationalist. The cultural nationalist doesn't understand the white revolutionaries because he can't see why anyone white would turn on the system. So they think that maybe this is some more hypocrisy being planted by white people.

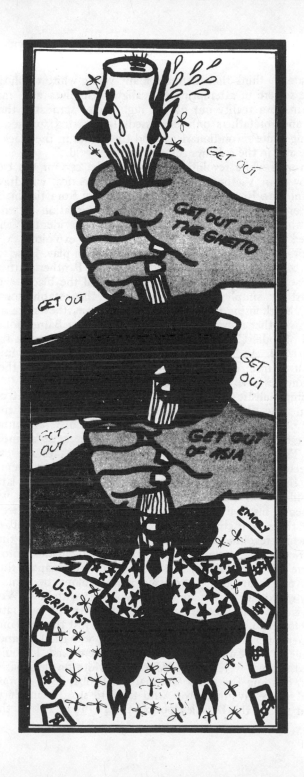

I personally think that there are many young white revolutionaries who are sincere in attempting to realign themselves with mankind, and to make a reality out of the high moral standards that their fathers and forefathers only expressed. In pressing for new heroes the young white revolutionaries found the heroes in the black colony at home and in the colonies throughout the world.

The young white revolutionaries raised the cry for the troops to withdraw from Vietnam, hands off Latin America, withdraw from the Dominican Republic and also to withdraw from the black community or the black colony. So you have a situation in which the young white revolutionaries are attempting to identify with the oppressed people of the colonies and against the exploiter.

The problem arises then in what part they can play. How can they aid the colony? How can they aid the Black Panther Party or any other black revolutionary group? They can aid the black revolutionaries first by simply turning away from the establishment, and secondly by choosing their friends. For instance, they have a choice between whether they will be a friend of Lyndon Baines Johnson or a friend of Fidel Castro. A friend of Robert Kennedy or a friend of Ho Chi Minh. And these are direct opposites. A friend of mine or a friend of Johnson's. After they make this choice then the white revolutionaries have a duty and a responsibility to act.

The imperialistic or capitalistic system occupies areas. It occupies Vietnam now. They occupy them by sending soldiers there, by sending policemen there. The policemen or soldiers are only a gun in the establishment's hand. They make the racist secure in his racism. The gun in the establishment's hand makes the establishment secure in its exploitation. The first problem it seems is to remove the gun from the establishment's hand. Until lately the white radical has seen no reason to come into conflict with the policemen in his own community. The reason I said until recently is because there is friction now in the mother country between the young white revolutionaries and the police. Because now the white revolutionaries are attempting to put some of their ideas into action, and there's the rub. We say that it should be a permanent thing.

Black people are being oppressed in the colony by white policemen, by white racists. We are saying they must withdraw. We realize that it is not only the Oakland police department but rather the security forces in general. On April 6 it wasn't just the Oakland police department who ambushed the Panthers. It was the Oakland police department, the Emeryville police department and I wouldn't be surprised if there were others. When the white revolutionaries went down to close up the Army terminal in October 1965 it wasn't the Oakland police by themselves who tried to stop them. It was the Oakland police, the Berkeley police, the Highway Patrol, the Sheriff's Department and the national guard was standing by. So we see that they're all part of the security force to protect the status quo; to make sure that the institutions carry out their goals. They're here to protect the system.

As far as I'm concerned the only reasonable conclusion would be to first realize the enemy, realize the plan, and then when something happens in the black colony—when we're attacked and ambushed in the black colony—then the white revolutionary students and intellectuals and all the other whites who support the colony should respond by defending us, by attacking the enemy in their community. Every time that we're attacked in our community there should be a reaction by the white revolutionaries; they should respond by defending us, by attacking part of the security force. Part of that security force that is determined to carry out the racist ends of the American institutions.

As far as our party is concerned, the Black Panther Party is an all black party, because we feel as Malcolm X felt that there can be no black-white unity until there first is black unity. We have a problem in the black colony that is particular to the colony, but we're willing to accept aid from the mother country as long as the mother country radicals realize that we have, as Eldridge Cleaver says in SOUL ON ICE, a mind of our own. We've regained our mind that was taken away from us and we will decide the political as well as the practical stand that we'll take. We'll make the theory and we'll carry out the practice. It's the duty of the white revolutionary to aid us in this.

So the role of the mother country radical, and he does have a role, is to first choose his friend and his enemy and after doing this, which it seems he's already done, then to not only articulate his desires to regain his moral standard and align himself with humanity, but also to put this into practice by attacking the protectors of the institutions.

MOVEMENT: You have spoken a lot about dealing with the protectors of the system, the armed forces. Would you like to elaborate on why you place so much emphasis on this?

HUEY: The reasons that I feel very strongly about dealing with the protectors of the system is simply because without this protection from the army, the police and the military, the institutions could not go on in their racism and exploitation. For instance, as the Vietnamese are driving the American imperialist troops out of Vietnam, it automatically stops the racist imperialist institutions of America from oppressing that particular country. The country cannot implement its racist program without the guns. And the guns are the military and the police. If the military were disarmed in Vietnam then the Vietnamese would be victorious.

We are in the same situation here in America. Whenever we attack the system the first thing the administrators do is to send out their strongarm men. If it's a rent strike, because of the indecent housing we have, they will send out the police to throw the furniture out the window. They don't come themselves. They send their protectors. So to deal with the corrupt exploiter you are going to have to deal with his protector, which is the police who take orders from him. This is a must.

MOVEMENT: Would you like to be more specific on the conditions which must exist before an alliance or coalition can be formed with predominantly white groups? Would you comment specifically on your alliance with the California Peace and Freedom Party?

HUEY: We have an alliance with the Peace and Freedom Party. The Peace and Freedom Party has supported our program in full and this is the criterion for a coalition with the black revolutionary group. If they had not supported our program in full, then we would not have seen any reason to make an alliance with them, because we are the reality of the oppression. They are not. They are only oppressed in an abstract way; we are oppressed in the real way. We are the real slaves! So it's a problem that we suffer from more than anyone else and it's our problem of liberation. Therefore we should decide what measures and what tools and what programs to use to become liberated. Many of the young white revolutionaries realize this and I see no reason not to have a coalition with them.

MOVEMENT: Other black groups seem to feel that from past experience it is impossible for them to work with whites and impossible for them to form alliances. What do you see as the reasons for this and do you think that the history of the Black Panther Party makes this less of a problem?

### SNCC and Liberals

HUEY: There was somewhat of an unhealthy relationship in the past with the white liberals supporting the black people who were trying to gain their freedom. I think that a good example of this would be the relationship that SNCC had with its white liberals. I call them white liberals because they differ strictly from the white radicals. The relationship was that the whites controlled SNCC for a very long time. From the very start of SNCC until here recently whites were the mind of SNCC. They controlled the program of SNCC with money and they controlled the ideology, or the stands SNCC would take. The blacks in SNCC were completely controlled program-wise; they couldn't do any more than these white liberals wanted them to do, which wasn't very much. So the white liberals were not working for self-determination for the black community. They were interested in a few concessions from the power structure. They undermined SNCC's program.

Stokely Carmichael came along and realizing this started to follow

Malcolm X's program of Black Power. This frightened many of the white liberals who were supporting SNCC. Whites were afraid when Stokely came along with Black Power and said that black people have a mind of their own and that SNCC would be an all-black organization and that SNCC would seek self-determination for the black community. The white liberals withdrew their support leaving the organization financially bankrupt. The blacks who were in the organization, Stokely and H. Rap Brown, were left very angry with the white liberals who had been aiding them under the disguise of being sincere. They weren't sincere.

The result was that the leadership of SNCC turned away from the white liberal, which was very good. I don't think they distinguished between the white liberal and the white revolutionary, because the white revolutionary is white also and they are very much afraid to have any contact whatsoever with white people. Even to the point of denying that the white revolutionaries could give support, by supporting the programs of SNCC in the mother country. Not by making any programs, not by being a member of the organization, but simply by resisting. Just as the Vietnamese people realize that they are supported whenever other oppressed people throughout the world resist. Because it helps divide the troops. It drains the country militarily and economically. If the mother country radicals are sincere then this will definitely add to the attack that we are making on the power structure. The Black Panther Party's program is a program where we recognize that the revolution in the mother country will definitely aid us in our freedom and has everything to do with our struggle!

### Hate the Oppressor

I think that one of SNCC's great problems is that they were controlled by the traditional administrator: the omnipotent administrator, the white person. He was the mind of SNCC. And so SNCC regained its mind, but I believe that it lost its political perspective. I think that this was a reaction rather than a response. The Black Panther Party has NEVER been controlled by white people. The Black Panther Party has always been a black group. We have always had an integration of mind and body. We have never been controlled by whites and therefore we don't fear the white mother country radicals. Our alliance is one of organized black groups with organized white groups. As soon as the organized white groups do not do the things that would benefit us in our struggle for liberation, that will be our departure point. So we don't suffer in the hangup of a skin color. We don't hate white people; we hate the oppressor. And if the oppressor happens to be white then we hate him. When he stops oppressing us then we no longer hate him. And right now in

America you have the slave-master being a white group. We are pushing him out of office through revolution in this country. I think the responsibility of the white revolutionary will be to aid us in this. And when we are attacked by the police or by the military then it will be up to the white mother country radicals to attack the murderers and to respond as we respond, to follow our program.

### Slave Masters

MOVEMENT: You indicate that there is a psychological process that has historically existed in white-black relations in the U.S. that must change in the course of revolutionary struggle. Would you like to comment on this?

HUEY: Yes. The historical relationship between black and white here in America has been the relationship between the slave and the master; the master being the mind and the slave the body. The slave would carry out the orders that the mind demanded him to carry out. By doing this the master took the manhood from the slave because he stripped him of a mind. He stripped black people of their mind. In the process the slave-master stripped himself of a body. As Eldridge puts it the slave-master became the omnipotent administrator and the slave became the supermasculine menial. This puts the omnipotent administrator into the controlling position or the front office and the supermasculine menial into the field.

The whole relationship developed so that the omnipotent administrator and the supermasculine menial became opposites. The slave being a very strong body doing all the practical things, all of the work becomes very masculine. The omnipotent administrator in the process of removing himself from all body functions realizes later that he has emasculated himself. And this is very disturbing to him. So the slave lost his mind and the slave-master his body.

### Penis Envy

This caused the slave-master to become very envious of the slave because he pictured the slave as being more of a man, being superior sexually, because the penis is part of the body. The omnipotent administrator laid down a decree when he realized that his plan to enslave the black man had a flaw, when he discovered that he had emasculated himself. He attempted to bind the penis of the slave. He attempted to show that his penis could reach further than the supermasculine menial's penis. He said "I, the omnipotent administrator can have access to the black woman." The supermasculine menial then had a psychological attraction to the white woman (the ultra feminine freak) for the simple reason that it was forbidden fruit. The omnipotent administrator decreed that this kind of contact would be punished by death. At the same time in order to reinforce his sexual desire, to confirm, to assert his manhood, he would go into the slave quarters and have sexual relations with the black woman (the self-reliant Amazon). Not to be satisfied but simply to confirm his manhood. Because if he can only satisfy the self-reliant Amazon then he would be sure that he was a man. Because he doesn't have a body, he doesn't have a penis, he psychologically wants to castrate the black man. The slave was constantly seeking unity within himself: a mind and a body. He always wanted to be able to decide, to gain respect from his woman. Because women want one who can control. I give this outline to fit into a framework of what is happening now. The white power structure today in America defines itself as the mind. They want to control the world. They go off and plunder the world. They are the policemen of the world exercising control especially over people of color.

**Re-capture the Mind**
The white man cannot gain his manhood, cannot unite with the body because the body is black. The body is symbolic of slavery and strength. It's a biological thing as he views it. The slave is in a much better situation because his not being a full man has always been viewed psychologically. And it's always easier to make a psychological transition than a biological one. If he can only recapture his mind, recapture his balls, then he will lose all fear and will be free to deter-mine his destiny. This is what is happening at this time with the rebellion of the world's oppressed people against the controller. They are regaining their mind and they're saying that we have a mind of our own. They're saying that we want freedom to determine the destiny of our people, thereby uniting the mind with their bodies. They are taking the mind back from the omnipotent administrator, the controller, the exploiter.

In America black people are also chanting that we have a mind of our own. We must have freedom to determine our destiny. It's almost a spiritual thing, this unity, this harmony. This unity of the mind and of the body, this unity of man within himself. Certain slogans of Chairman Mao I think demonstrate this theory of uniting the mind with the body within the man. An example is his call to the intellectuals to go to the countryside. The peasants in the countryside are all bodies; they're the workers. And he sent the intellectuals there because the dictatorship of the proletariat has no room for the omnipotent administrator; there's no room for the exploiter. So therefore he must go to the countryside to regain his body; he must work. He is really done a favor, because the people force him to unite his mind with his body by putting them both to work. At the same time the intellectual teaches the people political ideology, he educates them, thus uniting the mind and the body in the peasant.

Their minds and bodies are united and they control their country. I think this is a very good example of this unity and it is my idea of the perfect man.

### The Guerrilla

MOVEMENT: You mentioned at another point that the guerrilla was the perfect man and this kind of formulation seems to fit in directly with the guerrilla as a political man. Would you like to comment on this?

HUEY: Yes. The guerrilla is a very unique man. This is in contrast to Marxist-Leninist orthodox theories where the party controls the military. The guerrilla is not only the warrior, the military fighter; he is also the military commander as well as the political theoretician. Debray says "poor the pen without the guns, poor the gun without the pen".[2] The pen being just an extension of the mind, a tool to write down concepts, ideas. The gun is only an extension of the body, the extension of our fanged teeth that we lost through evolution. It's the weapon, it's the claws that we lost, it's the body. The guerrilla is the military commander and the political theoretician all in one.

In Bolivia Che said that he got very little help from the Communist Party there. The Communist Party wanted to be the mind, the Communist Party wanted to have full control of the guerrilla activity. But yet weren't taking part in the practical work of the guerrillas. The guerrilla on the other hand is not only united within himself, but he also attempts to spread this to the people by educating the villagers, giving them political perspective, pointing out things, educating them politically, and arming the people. Therefore the guerrilla is giving the peasants and workers a mind. Because they've already got the body you get a unity of the mind and the body. Black people here in America, who have long been the workers, have regained our minds and we now have a unity of mind and body.

MOVEMENT: Would you be willing to extend this formula in terms of white radicals; to say that one of their struggles today is to get back their bodies.

HUEY: Yes. I thought I made that clear. The white mother country radical by becoming an activist is attempting to regain his body. By being an activist and not the traditional theoretician who outlines the plan, as the Communist Party has been trying to do for ever so long, the white mother country radical is regaining his body. The resistance by white radicals in Berkeley during the past three nights is a good indication that the white radicals are on the way home. They have identified their enemies. The white radicals have integrated theory with practice. They realize the American system is the real enemy but in order to attack the American system they must attack the ordinary cop. In order to attack the educational system they must attack the ordinary teacher. Just as the Vietnamese people to attack the American system must attack the ordinary soldier. The white mother country radicals now are regaining their bodies and they're also recognizing that the black man has a mind and that he is a man.

MOVEMENT: Would you comment on how this psychological understanding aids in the revolutionary struggle?

HUEY: You can see that in statements until recently black people who haven't been enlightened have defined the white man by calling him "the MAN". "The Man" is making this decision, "The Man" this and "The Man" that. The black woman found it difficult to respect the black man because he didn't even define himself as a man! Because he didn't have a mind, because the decision maker was outside of himself. But the vanguard group, the Black Panther Party along with all revolutionary black groups have regained our mind and our manhood. Therefore we no longer define the omnipotent administrator as "the Man" . . . or the authority as "the MAN". Matter of fact the omnipotent administrator along with his security agents are less than a man because WE define them as pigs! I think that this is a revolutionary thing in itself. That's political power. That's power itself. Matter of fact what is power other than the ability to define phenomenon and then make it act in a desired manner? When black people start defining things and making it act in a desired manner, then we call this Black Power!

MOVEMENT: Would you comment further on what you mean by Black Power?

HUEY: Black Power is really people's power. The Black Panther Program, Panther Power as we call it, will implement this people's power. We have respect for all of humanity and we realize that the people should rule and determine their destiny. Wipe out the controller. To have Black Power doesn't humble or subjugate anyone to slavery or oppression. Black Power is giving power to people who have not had power to determine their destiny. We advocate and we aid any people who are struggling to determine their destiny. This is regardless of color. The Vietnamese say Vietnam should be able to determine its own destiny. Power of the Vietnamese people. We also chant power of the Vietnamese people. The Latins are talking about Latin America for the Latin Americans. Cuba Si and Yanqui, Non. It's not that they don't want the Yankees to have any power they just don't want them to have power over them. They can have power over themselves. We in the black colony in America want to be able to have power over our destiny and that's black power.

MOVEMENT: A lot of white radicals are romantic about what Che said: "In a revolution one wins or dies . . ." For most of us it is really an abstract or theoretical question. It's a real question for you and we'd like you to rap about how you feel about it.

HUEY: Yes. The revolutionary sees no compromise. We will not compromise because the issue is so basic. If we compromise one iota we will be selling our freedom out. We will be selling the revolution out. And we refuse to remain slaves. As Eldridge says in SOUL ON ICE "a slave who dies of natural causes will not balance two dead flies on the scales of eternity." As far as we're concerned we would rather be dead than to go on with the slavery that we're in. Once we compromise we will be compromising not only our freedom, but also our manhood. We realize that we're going up against a highly technical country, and we realize that they are not only paper tigers, as Mao says, but real tigers too because they have the ability to slaughter many people. But in the long run, they will prove themselves paper tigers because they're not in line with humanity; they are divorced from the people. We know that the enemy is very powerful and that our manhood is at stake, but we feel it necessary to be victorious in regaining ourselves, regaining our manhood. And this is the basic point. So either we will do this or we won't have any freedom. Either we will win or we will die trying to win.

**Mood of Black People**

MOVEMENT: How would you characterize the mood of black people in America today? Are they disenchanted, wanting a larger slice of the pie, or alienated, not wanting to integrate into a burning house, not wanting to integrate into Babylon? What do you think it will take for them to become alienated and revolutionary?

HUEY: I was going to say disillusioned, but I don't think we were ever under the illusion that we had freedom in this country. This society is definitely a decadent one and we realize it. Black people are realizing it more and more. We cannot gain our freedom under the present system; the system that is carrying out its plans of institutionalized racism. Your question is what will have to be done to stimulate them to revolution. I think it's already being done. It's a matter of time now for us to educate them to a program and show them the way to liberation. The Black Panther Party is the beacon light to show black people the way to liberation.

You notice the insurrections that have been going on throughout the country, in Watts, in Newark, in Detroit. They were all responses of the people demanding that they have freedom to determine their destiny, rejecting exploitation. Now the Black Panther Party does not think that the traditional riots, or insurrections that have taken place are the answer. It is true they have been against the Establishment, they have been against authority and oppression within their community, but they have been unorganized. However, black people learned from each of these insurrections.

They learned from Watts. I'm sure the people in Detroit were educated by what happened in Watts. Perhaps this was wrong education. It sort of missed the mark. It wasn't quite the correct activity, but the people were educated through the activity. The people of Detroit followed the example of the people in Watts, only they added a little scrutiny to it. The people in Detroit learned that the way to put a hurt on the administration is to make Molotov cocktails and to go into the street in mass numbers. So this was a matter of learning. The slogan went up "Burn, baby, burn". People were educated through the activity and it spread throughout the country. The people were educated on how to resist, but perhaps incorrectly.

### Educate Through Activity

What we have to do as a vanguard of the revolution is to correct this through activity. The large majority of black people are either illiterate or semi-literate. They don't read. They need activity to follow. This is true of any colonized people. The same thing happened in Cuba where it was necessary for twelve men with a leadership of Che and Fidel to take to the hills and then attack the corrupt administration; to attack the army who were the protectors of the exploiters in Cuba. They could have leafleted the community and they could have written books, but the people would not respond. They had to act and the people could see and hear about it and therefore become educated on how to respond to oppression.

In this country black revolutionaries have to set an example. We can't do the same things that were done in Cuba because Cuba is Cuba and the U.S. is the U.S. Cuba has many terrains to protect the guerrilla. This country is mainly urban. We have to work out new solutions to offset the power of the country's technology and communication; its ability to communicate very rapidly by telephone and teletype and so forth. We do have solutions to these problems and they will be put into effect. I wouldn't want to go into the ways and means of this, but we will educate through action. We have to engage in action to make the people want to read our literature. Because they are not attracted to all the writing in this country; there's too much writing. Many books makes one weary.

### Threat from Reformers

MOVEMENT: Kennedy before his death, and to a lesser extent Rockefeller and Lindsay and other establishment liberals have been talking about making reforms to give black people a greater share in

the pie and thus stop any developing revolutionary movement.
Would you comment on this?

HUEY: I would say this: If a Kennedy or Lindsay or anyone else can
give decent housing to all of our people; if they can give full employment to our people with a high standard; if they can give full
control to black people to determine the destiny of their community; if they can give fair trials in the court system by turning over
the structure to the community; if they can end their exploitation
of people throughout the world; if they can do all of these things
they would have solved the problems. But I don't believe that under
this present system, under capitalism, that they will be able to solve
these problems.

**People Must Control**

I don't think black people should be fooled by their come-ons
because every one who gets in office promises the same thing. They
promise full employment and decent housing; the Great Society, the
New Frontier. All of these names, but no real benefits. No effects are
felt in the black community, and black people are tired of being deceived and duped. The people must have full control of the means of
production. Small black businesses cannot compete with General
Motors. That's just out of the question. General Motors robbed us
and worked us for nothing for a couple hundred years and took
our money and set up factories and became fat and rich and then
talks about giving us some of the crumbs. We want full control.
We're not interested in anyone promising that the private owners
are going to all of a sudden become human beings and give these
things to our community. It hasn't ever happened and, based on
empirical evidence, we don't expect them to become Buddhists over
night.

MOVEMENT: We raised this question not because we feel that
these reforms are possible, but rather to get your ideas on what
effects such attempted reforms might have on the development of a
revolutionary struggle.

HUEY: I think that reforms pose no real threat. The revolution has
always been in the hands of the young. The young always inherit the
revolution. The young population is growing at a very rapid rate and
they are very displeased with the authorities. They want control. I
doubt that under the present system any kind of program can be
launched that will be able to buy off all these young people. They
have not been able to do it with the poverty program, the great
society, etc. This country has never been able to employ all of its
people simply because it's too interested in private property and the
profit motive. A bigger poverty program is just what it says it is, a

program to keep people in poverty. So I don't think that there is any real threat from the reforms.

MOVEMENT: Would you like to say something about the Panther's organizing especially in terms of the youth?

HUEY: The Panthers represent a cross section of the black community. We have older people as well as younger people. The younger people of course are the ones who are seen on the streets. They are the activists. They are the real vanguard of change because they haven't been indoctrinated and they haven't submitted. They haven't been beaten into line as some of the older people have. But many of the older people realize that we're waging a just fight against the oppressor. They are aiding us and they are taking a part in the program.

### Jail

MOVEMENT: Tell us something about your relations with the prisoners in the jail.

HUEY: The black prisoners as well as many of the white prisoners identify with the program of the Panthers. Of course by the very nature of their being prisoners they can see the oppression and they've suffered at the hands of the Gestapo. They have reacted to it. The black prisoners have all joined the Panthers, about 95% of them. Now the jail is all Panther and the police are very worried about this. The white prisoners can identify with us because they realize that they are not in control. They realize there's someone controlling them and the rest of the world with guns. They want some control over their lives also. The Panthers in jail have been educating them and so we are going along with the revolution inside of the jail.

MOVEMENT: What has been the effect of the demonstrations outside the jail calling for "Free Huey"?

HUEY: Very positive reactions. One demonstration, I don't remember which one, a couple of trustees, white trustees, held a cardboard sign out the laundry window reading "Free Huey". They say people saw it and responded to it. They were very enthusiastic about the demonstrators because they too suffer from being treated unfairly by the parole authorities and by the police here in the jail.

### Open or Underground

MOVEMENT: The Panthers' organizing efforts have been very open up until this point. Would you like to comment about the question of an underground political organization versus an open organization at this point in the struggle?

HUEY: Yeah. Some of the black nationalist groups feel that they have to be underground because they'll be attacked. But we don't feel that you can romanticize being underground. They say we're romantic because we're trying to live revolutionary lives, and we are not taking precautions. But we say that the only way we would go underground is if we're driven underground. All real revolutionary movements are driven underground. Take the revolution in Cuba. The agitation that was going on while Fidel was in law school was very much above ground. Even his existence in the hills was, so to speak, an above the ground affair because he was letting it be known who was doing the damage and why he was doing the damage. To catch him was a different story. The only way we can educate the people is by setting an example for them. We feel that this is very necessary.

This is a pre-revolutionary period and we feel it is very necessary to educate the people while we can. So we're very open about this education. We have been attacked and we will be attacked even more in the future but we're not going to go underground until we get ready to go underground because we have a mind of our own. We're not going to let anyone force us to do anything. We're going to go underground after we educate all of the black people and not before that time. Then it won't really be necessary for us to go underground because you can see black anywhere. We will just have the stuff to protect ourselves and the strategy to offset the great power that the strong-arm men of the establishment have and are planning to use against us.

### White Organizing

MOVEMENT: Your comments about the white prisoners seemed encouraging. Do you see the possibility of organizing a white Panther Party in opposition to the establishment possibly among poor and working whites?

HUEY: Well as I put it before Black Power is people's power and as far as organizing white people we give white people the privilege of having a mind and we want them to get a body. They can organize themselves. We can tell them what they should do, what their responsibility is if they're going to claim to be white revolutionaries or white mother country radicals, and that is to arm themselves and support the colonies around the world in their just struggle against imperialism. But anything more than that they will have to do on their own.

—Pamphlet published by *The Movement*

# Message on the Peace Movement

The Peace Movement is extremely important, more important than I thought it was, say, two years ago. Matter of fact, it's one of the most important movements that's going on at this time. Because a person is in the Peace Movement and he works with the Peace Movement, the Peace Movement is not necessarily a pacifist movement. I think that the reason I place so much emphasis now upon the Peace Movement I see that if peace were to come about this would force a re-evaluation and a revolution in the basic economic composition of the country.

I'll explain that further. For instance, we all know now this is a garrison state, the warfare state. And this is not by accident. After capitalism reaches a point where it can no longer expand, it looks for other avenues, other deposits, other places to expand the Capitalistic interest. And at this time super-capitalists (we know people like General Motors, Chrysler, General Dynamics, and all the SUPER COMPANIES—I understand there's about 76 that control the whole economy of this country) and these companies, including the automobile companies that I just named are the prime people, or they are the military contractors. They run the defense plants as far as getting the contracts from the Pentagon. Chrysler made that batch of tanks that wouldn't fire, (you probably saw in the paper) through a contract with the government and with the Pentagon. In other words, super-capitalists are now putting their over-expanded capitalistic surplus into military equipment. And this military equipment is then placed in foreign countries, which is the final depository for expendable goods, such as Viet Nam, such as what happened in the Dominican Republic some years ago.[3] In other words, with the wedding of the industry with the Pentagon, they have a new avenue to invest. And they invest in military equipment. And this equipment is expendable, because this is the purpose of it: To explode it and then build new ones, you see. So it's a perpetual type of process.

We know now that the U.S. has a secret pact with Thailand. These things are not by accident, are not by chance; but it's all part of a super-plan in order to keep the economy going. What would happen then, if peace were to come about? If peace were to come about then you wouldn't have that final depository for expendable goods and the surplus would then be turned back into the country. The military plants and the related defense plants, industrial plants would be brought to a grinding halt.

And this is why you have some of the union representatives supporting the war effort. This is why the AFL-CIO supported the invasion of the Dominican Republic. It forced out Juan Bosch for the simple reason, they know that as long as war goes on, then they can exploit the people through taxation and also exploit the people through human lives, because we sent soldiers, you see brothers, because they're expendable too; people are expendable. So, this is to keep it going, to keep getting the contracts.

So what happens is that one of the favored arguments of the capitalists is that America is not an imperialistic country because the traditional ways and means of imperialists is to go into a developing country and rape the country of its raw materials and refine them in the colony, in the developing country or send them to the mother country to be refined or refine them and sell them back at a high price to the colonized people. And the argument is that "America is not doing that. We don't need what's in Vietnam; we don't need any equipment, and the raw materials out of Vietnam." And this is very true. This sort of puzzled me for a while; and I couldn't really answer it, and so I just talked around it. But now I understand that something new has happened; that with the wedding of science with industry, with the industrial plants, that America has solved the basic problem of raw materials through synthetics and through knowing how to use raw materials that are already here and using them in a variety of ways, therefore keeping the plants going. So, therefore this is the favored argument of the capitalist: "So, we must be there to stop communism or wars of subversion, you see, subversive wars." But what's overlooked is the fact that the super-capitalists know we don't need to rape the country. I think Cuba was the turning point where it was sort of the traditional colonized country. And I'll inject this and that is that.

Another argument is that we need the positions, their strategic military positions, which we know that the U.S. does not need any strategic military positions because they already have enough equipment to defend this country from any point in the world if we were attacked. So they could only be there to use this developing country as depository for expendable goods. And in traditional imperialism, people from the mother country usually go to the colony, set up government there and the government heads and also the leaders of the military.

And this is not so at this point, see. In Vietnam, people from the mother country have not gone to the colonized country and jockeyed for position, but it's all been turned back into America.

The defense contractors jockey for position now in the mother country, you see, for the defense contracts. And then they set up a puppet government or a military regime so that they can supply these developing countries with military equipment. And they really don't want to be in Vietnam or any of the developing countries, because they feel (and they have done this) they've bought off the militaries in these various developing countries so that they will only be an arm of the Pentagon, for instance, the military regime in Greece. So therefore, they have full control of the military officers, through buying them off, paying them high salaries and so forth so they feel that they won't have to send American troops, and therefore, they won't disturb or cause chaos in America and the mother country.

But what happens when one battalion of your military is defeated? Then you send in reinforcements to a defeated puppet army in that developing country. The whole government becomes subject to the army. And the army becomes suspicious of the civil government in these developing countries, because they are told by the Pentagon through indoctrination and money that the civil government is communist or a threat to the nation. So then you have military coups, and this is what happens over and over with the support of the U.S.

So what we have, we have really an imperialistic variation of imperialism. And I said before, the jockeying for position of power is inside of the mother country now. So, in fact, the American people have become colonized.

At one time I thought that only Blacks were colonized. But I think we have to change our rhetoric to an extent because the whole American people have been colonized, if you view exploitation as a colonized effect, now they're exploited. They support the super-capitalist through taxation. And (through taxation) with tax to support the super-capitalist, or these 76 companies.

So, therefore, the whole American people are colonized people and even more so than the people in these developing countries where the militaries operate. And these are the points that we have to get across to the people to show them that we are a colonized people and lift their consciousness to a point to have a successful revolution.

Well, anyway, I won't go on with that. But I hope you get the point, and I hope I'm clear enough. But, this is why the Peace Movement is so important. If the Peace Movement is successful, then the revolution will be successful. If the Peace Movement fails, then the revolution in the mother country fails. In other words the people will be pushed so up-tight once they found war were to stop, but then the whole economy would go down the drain because you would have to have a planned economy to combat the chaos that would be caused by the absence of any incentive for the factories to go. Now war is the incentive for the military contractors.

So this is why it is very important that we have communications with, not only communications with, we should engage in writing in our paper that we support the Peace Movement, actually get out and support it in various ways through literature and demonstrations in all the ways that the people struggle against the antagonistic ruling capitalist class in order to bring about change, because we realize that waging the struggles of antagonistic forces are the elements and the essence of all change. So at this point we're just involved in a struggle by antagonistic forces, and that is the people who work for a living and the people who own and exploit for their well-being.

So we have to realize our position and we have to know ourselves and know our enemies. A thousand wars and a thousand victories. And until we know who the enemy is and what the situation is we will only be marking time. Even the Peace Movement doesn't compromise our defense principles. We still will defend ourselves against attack and against agression. But overall, we're advocating the end to all wars. But, yet, we support the self-defense of the Vietnamese people and all the people who are struggling.

ALL POWER TO THE PEOPLE
Huey P. Newton
Minister of Defense,
Black Panther Party

—*The Black Panther*, September 27, 1969

# To the R.N.A.

This is Huey P. Newton, at Los Padres, California 1969, September 13.

Greetings to the Republic of New Africa and President Robert Williams. I'm very happy to be able to welcome you back home.[4] I might add that this is perfect timing. And we need you very much, the people need you very much. And now that the consciousness of the people is at such a high level, perhaps they will be able to appreciate your leadership, and also be ready to move in a very revolutionary fashion.

Some time ago I received a message from the Republic of New Africa with a series of questions concerning the philosophy of the Black Panther Party; and very detailed questions on certain stands, and our thinking on these positions. At that time I wasn't prepared to send a message out. I've had to think about many of the questions, and due to the situation here it's very difficult for me to communicate, so that explains this lapse in time between question and answer. I won't be able to expound on all the questions, but I would like to give some general explanations to the Black Panther Party's position, as related to the Republic of New Africa.

The Black Panther Party's position is that the Black people in the country are definitely colonized, and suffer from the colonial plight more than any ethnic group in the country. Perhaps with the exception of the Indian, but surely as much even as the Indian population. We too, realize that the American people in general are colonized. And they're colonized simply because they're under a capitalistic society, with a small clique of rulers who are the owners of the means of production in control of decision making, they're the decision making body. Therefore, that takes the freedom from the American people in general. And they simply work for the enrichment of this ruling class. As far as Blacks are concerned, of course, we're at the very bottom of this ladder, we're exploited not only by the small group of ruling class, we're oppressed, and repressed by even the working class Whites in the country. And this is simply because the ruling class, the White ruling class uses the old Roman policy of divide and conquer. In other words, the White working class is used as pawns or tools of the ruling class, but they too are enslaved. So it's with that historical thing of dividing and ruling, that the ruling class can effectively and successfully keep the majority of the people in an oppressed position; because they're divided in certain interest groups, even though these interests that the lower class groups carry doesn't necessarily serve as beneficial to them.

As far as our stand on separation, we've demanded, as you very well know, a plebiscite of the U.N. to supervise, so that Blacks can decide whether they want to secede the union, or what position they'll take on it. As far as the Black Panther Party is concerned we're subject to the will of the majority of the people, but we feel that the people should have this choice, and we feel that the Republic of New Africa is perfectly justified in demanding and declaring the right to secede the union. So we don't have any contradiction between the Black Panther Party's position and the Republic of New Africa's position that I know, it's simply a matter of timing. We feel that certain conditions will have to exist before we're even given the right to make that choice. We also take into consideration the fact that if Blacks at this very minute were able to secede from the union, and say have five states, or six states, it would be impossible to function in freedom side by side with a capitalistic imperialistic country. We all know that mother Africa is not free simply because of imperialism, because of Western domination. And there's no indication that it would be any different if we were to have a separate country, here in North America. As a matter of fact, by all logic we would suffer imperialism and colonialism even more so than the Third World is suffering it now. They are geographically better located, thousands of miles away, but yet they are not able to be free simply because of highly technological developments, the highest technological developments that the West has that makes the world so much smaller, one small neighborhood.

So taking all these things into consideration, we conclude that the only way that we're going to be free is to wipe out once and for all the oppressive structure of America. We realize we can't do this without a popular struggle, without many alliances and coalitions, and this is the reason that we're moving in the direction that we are to get as many alliances as possible of people that are equally dissatisfied with the system. And also we're carrying on, or attempting to carry on a political education campaign, so that the people will be aware of the conditions and therefore perhaps they will be able to take steps to controlling these conditions. We think this is the most important thing at this time; is to be able to organize in some fashion so that we'll have a formidable force to challenge the structure of the American empire.

So we invite the Republic of New Africa to struggle with us, because we know from people whom I've talked to, (I've talked to May Mallory, and other people familiar with the philosophy of the Republic of New Africa) they seem to be very aware that the whole structure of America will have to be changed, in order for the people of America to be free. And this is again with the full knowledge and the full view of the end goal of the Republic of New Africa to secede. In other words we're not really handling this question at this time because we feel that for us that it is somewhat premature, that I realize the physiological value of fighting for a territory. But at this time the Black Panther Party feels that we don't want to be in an enclave type situation where we would be more isolated than we already are now. We're isolated in the ghetto areas, and we think that this is a very good location as far as strategy is concerned, as far as waging a strong battle against the established order. And again I think that it would be perfectly justified if the Blacks decided that they wanted to secede the union, but I think the question should be left up to the popular masses, the popular majority. So this is it in a nutshell.

As I said before, I don't have the facilities here to carry on long discussions, I look forward to talking with Milton Henry in the near future (if it's possible, I know that he has his hands full now) or representatives of the Republic of New Africa. So we can talk these things over. There are many things that I don't know about the position of the Republic of New Africa, there are things I heard, things I read, I'm in total agreement with. I would like for the Republic of New Africa to know that we support Robert Williams and his plight at this time, that we support him one hundred per cent, and we're willing to give all services asked of us; and we would like to find out exactly what we can do that would be most helpful in the court proceedings coming up, what moral support we could give. Perhaps we could send some representatives, and we will publish in our paper, The Black Panther, articles educating people to Robert Williams' position on the criminal activities that he's been victim of for some eight or nine years. I would also like to request of the Republic of New Africa to give us some support in Bobby Seale, our Chairman of the Black Panther Party. Bobby Seale is now in prison as you know in San Francisco, he has a case coming up in Chicago, and one in Connecticut, and we invite the Republic of New Africa to come in support. We would like this very much, and whatever moral support they could possibly give, we would welcome it.

We should be working closer together than we are, and perhaps this would be an issue that we could work together on. The issue is the political prisoners of America, and people as one to stand for the release of all political prisoners. This might be a rallying point where all the Black revolutionary organizations and parties could rally around. Because I truly believe that some good comes out of every attack that the oppressor makes. It educates, it enlightens many people to his viciousness. So perhaps this will be a turning point in both our organizations and parties. So I would like to say, "ALL POWER TO THE PEOPLE, AND MORE POWER TO THE PRESIDENT OF THE REPUBLIC OF NEW AFRICA, ROBERT WILLIAMS."

—*The Black Panther*, December 6, 1969

# Prison, Where Is Thy Victory?

When a person studies mathematics, he learns that there are many mathematical laws which determine the approach he must take to solving the problems presented to him. In the study of geometry, one of the first laws a person learns is that "the whole is not greater than the sum of its parts". This means simply that one cannot have a geometrical figure such as a circle or a square which in its totality, contains more than it does when broken down into smaller parts. Therefore, if all the smaller parts add up to a certain amount, the entire figure cannot add up to a larger amount. The prison cannot have a victory over the prisoner, because those in charge take the same kind of approach to the prisoner and assume if they have the whole body in a cell that they have there all that makes up the person. But a prisoner is not a geometrical figure, and an approach which is successful in mathematics, is wholly unsuccessful when dealing with human beings.

In the case of the human, we are not dealing only with the single individual, we are also dealing with the ideas and beliefs which have motivated him and which sustain him, even when his body is confined. In the case of humanity the whole is much greater than its parts, because the whole includes the body which is measurable and confineable, and also the ideas which cannot be measured and which cannot be confined. The ideas are not only within the mind of the prisoner where they cannot be seen nor controlled, the ideas are also within the people. The ideas which can and will sustain our movement for total freedom and dignity of the people, cannot be imprisoned, for they are to be found in the people, all the people, wherever they are. As long as the people live by the ideas of freedom and dignity there will be no prison which can hold our movement down. Ideas move from one person to another in the association of brothers and sisters who recognize that a most evil system of capitalism has set us against each other, when our real enemy is the exploiter who profits from our poverty. When we realize such an idea then we come to love and appreciate our brothers and sisters who we may have seen as enemies, and those exploiters who we may have seen as friends are revealed for what they truly are to all oppressed people. The people are the idea; the respect and dignity of the people, as they move toward their freedom is the sustaining force which reaches into and out of the prison. The walls, the bars, the guns and the guards can never encircle or hold down the idea of the people. And the people must always carry forward the idea which is their dignity and their beauty.

The prison operates with the idea that when it has a person's body it has his entire being—since the whole cannot be greater than the sum of its parts. They put the body in a cell, and seem to get some sense of relief and security from that fact. The idea of prison victory then, is that when the person in jail begins to act, think, and believe the way they want him to, then they have won the battle and the person is then "rehabilitated". But this cannot be the case, because those who operate the prisons, have failed to examine their own beliefs thoroughly, and they fail to understand the types of people they attempt to control. Therefore, even when the prison thinks it has won the victory, there is no victory.

There are two types of prisoners. The largest number are those who accept the legitimacy of the assumptions upon which the society is based. They wish to acquire the same goals as everybody else, money, power, greed, and conspicuous consumption. In order to do so, however, they adopt techniques and methods which the society has defined as illegitimate. When this is discovered such people are put in jail. They may be called "illegitimate capitalists" since their aim is to acquire everything this capitalistic society defines as legitimate. The second type of prisoner, is the one who rejects the legitimacy of the assumptions upon which the society is based. He argues that the people at the bottom of the society are exploited for the profit and advantage of those at the top. Thus, the oppressed exist, and will always be used to maintain the privileged status of the exploiters. There is no sacredness, there is no dignity in either exploiting or being exploited. Although this system may make the society function at a high level of technological efficiency, it is an illegitimate system, since it rests upon the suffering of humans who are as worthy and as dignified as those who do not suffer. Thus, the second type of prisoner says that the society is corrupt and illegitimate and must be overthrown. This second type of prisoner is the political prisoner. They do not accept the legitimacy of the society and cannot participate in its corrupting exploitation, whether they are in the prison or on the block.

The prison cannot gain a victory over either type of prisoner no matter how hard it tries. The "Illegitimate capitalist" recognizes that if he plays the game the prison wants him to play, he will have his time reduced and be released to continue his activities. Therefore, he is willing to go through the prison programs and do the things he is told. He is willing to say the things the prison authorities want to hear. The prison assumes he is "rehabilitated" and ready for the society. The prisoner has really played the prison's game so that he can be released to resume pursuit of his capitalistic goals. There is no victory, for the prisoner from the beginning accepted the idea of the society. He pretends to accept the idea of the prison as a part of the game he has always played.

The prison cannot gain a victory over the political prisoner because he has nothing to be rehabilitated from or to. He refuses to accept the legitimacy of the system and refuses to participate. To participate is to admit that the society is legitimate because of its exploitation of the oppressed. This is the idea which the political prisoner does not accept, this is the idea for which he has been imprisoned, and this is the reason why he cannot cooperate with the system. The political prisoner will, in fact, serve his time just as will the "illegitimate capitalist". Yet the idea which motivated and sustained the political prisoner rests in the people, all the prison has is a body.

The dignity and beauty of man rests in the human spirit which makes him more than simply a physical being. This spirit must never be suppressed for exploitation by others. As long as the people recognize the beauty of their human spirits and move against suppression and exploitation, they will be carrying out one of the most beautiful ideas of all time. Because the human whole is much greater than the sum of its parts, the ideas will always be among the people. The prison cannot be victorious because walls, bars and guards cannot conquer or hold down an idea.

POWER TO THE PEOPLE:
Huey P. Newton
Minister of Defense
Black Panther Party

—*The Black Panther*, January 3, 1970

# 4.

# BOBBY SEALE SPEAKS

Bobby Seale, Chairman of the Black Panther Party, defendant in the Chicago Conspiracy cases, and one of the New Haven Panther 14, was cofounder with Huey P. Newton of the Black Panther Party. Here, in articles, messages, and an interview, Bobby Seale explains the ideology of the Black Panther Party.

# The Ten-Point Platform and Program of the Black Panther Party

"WE WANT LAND, BREAD, HOUSING, EDUCATION, CLOTHING, JUSTICE, AND PEACE. . . ." Today, that's only part of number 10 of the Black Panther Party's Ten Point Platform and Program of "What We Want." The exploited, laboring masses and poor, oppressed peoples throughout the world want and need these demands for basic human survival. The Black Panther Party began when Huey and I outlined the basic political desires and needs and put them into the form of a platform and program with ten points of "What We Want" and ten of "What We Believe." Huey and I sat there in the Poverty Office where we worked, one night in October 1966, and began a revolutionary political party, knowing that the program was not just something we had thought up.' The program was an outline of the basic political desires and needs that went back into the history of Black people suffering under the exploitative oppression by the greedy, vicious, capitalistic ruling class of America. The Platform and Program is nothing more than the 400-year old crying demands of us Black Americans. They are basic demands of 'What We Want' and 'What We Believe'.

Naturally these demands have a very international proletarian likeness to those of any people who are struggling against the three levels of oppression: the greedy, exploiting, rich, avaricious businessmen; the misleading, lying, tricky, demagogic politician, and the atrocious, murdering, brutalizing, intimidating, fascist, pig cops. These three levels of oppression exist in virtually every country where there is overt capitalistic exploitation and the minority, but oppressive ruling class circles of America are in the head of it all. They lead it with their imperialistic, fascist, aggressive, colonialistic war mongering, not only abroad, but right here at home in America (Babylon), where hundreds of years of subtle and maniacal racism has been organized and developed by the greedy rich, organized and developed into domestic imperialism—fascism.

Community imperialism is manifested or is readily seen with respect to the domestic colonialization of Black, Chicano, Indian, and other non-White peoples being cooped up in wretched ghettos and/or on Southern plantations and reservations with the murdering, fascist, brutalizing pig, occupying the communities and areas just like a foreign troop occupies territory. Domestic imperialism of this sort is not limited to Black, Brown, and Red peoples, especially nowadays when the masses of Americans take time to remember fascist suppression by thousands of cops and National Guardsmen at the Democratic Convention last November. Also, in the last few years, on every major college campus, murderous, brutal fascism in America made its appearance against White, Black, and Brown students and other students who attempted to use their basic "democratic rights" to change racist administrations and protest the war in Vietnam and brutality and poverty in the ghettos in America.

Fascism in America has existed for so many more years before the recent forms of repression came about. And every American (and Black people in particular) CAN identify it for exactly what it is. Racism plus capitalism breeds fascism when the avaricious businessmen refuse to give control to the unemployed workers and their unions. And history has testified to this from the years of repression and unemployment in the thirties to the present day, when the union people will work and strike and peoples will demand right before our eyes that they be allowed to work too. And brutal cops will come about and tricky politicians will come about to trick and mislead the people, to oppress the people and repress their actions, to take over the very factories where they have to produce goods and wealth that they never receive back.

Fascism breeds when the lazy, tricking, demagogic politicians lie and mislead people about the suffering that Black people are subjected to, that Brown peoples are subjected to, that any color peoples or minority group peoples, or any poor White peoples are subjected to. When the people move to demonstrate or protest and these human rights workers and civil rights workers are murdered and killed; when babies are bombed in the church as back in 1963 in Birmingham, thousands of demonstrators are clubbed and brutalized such as in Birmingham, Alabama back in 1963. This in itself begins to prove the demagogic politicians for what they are—with promises of ending poverty, with promises of a "Great Society", the promises of "looking into the matter," etc., etc., etc.

Because of the basic Ten Point Platform and Program that was put together that deals with the need for full employment for our people, that spells it out; that deals with a need for decent housing, fit for shelter of human beings; that deals with a decent education that teaches us our history and our place in the world and in society; that deals with the need to have fair trials by our peer groups or people from our Black communities or the districts where we live—because of a program that talks about land, bread, housing, education, clothing, justice, and peace; because of a program that talked about a United Nations supervised plebiscite to be held throughout the

Black colony where the colonial subjects would participate and determine our will and our destiny; because of a program that stated in it that we wanted Black men to be exempt from military services because of all the injustices we have suffered after fighting in wars in the past for the fascist ruling class (and we refuse to continue dying for them); because our Ten Point Platform and Program had in it point number seven that says, "We want an immediate end to police brutality and murder of Black people"; because Huey P. Newton put this program together and founded this organization with this Ten Point Platform and Program that outlined the basic political desires and needs of the people; because of that; because we began to implement it; because we went to the streets to begin to teach the people and educate the people to the strategic methods to have these political desires and needs answered; because of that, Bobby Hutton was murdered by fascist Oakland pigs. Because of that, we had Alprentice "Bunchy" Carter and brother John Huggins also murdered at UCLA by jealous, egotistical, piggish dogs who worked for the pigs of the ruling class. Because of that and because of this Ten Point Platform and Program that's there for the basic political desires and needs of Black people here in America and any other people and any other proletarian struggles going on throughout the world—because of that we've had two more brothers murdered by these Black nationalist, cultural nationalist pigs.

Because of this program, we have political prisoners. We have dead members. We have a war going on. The war started 400 years ago, and the war must be ended. And only by us continually going forth to implement the Ten Point Platform and Program; by us hanging to the fact that we will receive, through all the struggle, some kind of freedom and dignity and justice, will point number ten be realized. We say in number ten, we want some land, some bread, some housing, some education, some clothing, some justice, and some peace. Because of that, it seems that we'll die; it seems that we'll be in exile; and it seems we'll have political prisoners.

So let's free all the political prisoners, because of the Ten Point Platform and Program. Because that's the idea; that's the idea that can never be stopped. And as our Minister of Defense so eloquently explained to us in "Prison—Where Is Thy Victory?" and idea belongs to the people.

POWER TO THE PEOPLE
Chairman, Bobby Seale
Black Panther Party

—*The Black Panther*, October 18, 1969

# Bobby Seale Explains Panther Politics: An Interview

*You have been in jail since August. Could you give some details on your treatment in jail since then.*
Well I've been in a number of jails since I was arrested Aug. 19 —S.F. County and Cook County [Chicago] and a number of other jails across the country. In S.F. County jail I was thrown in the hole for having a Black Panther party newspaper that one of the guards here actually let me have after my lawyer, Charles Garry, requested that I have it based on the fact that I had to make some notes and outlines on some speeches that I had made, the content of which was to come up in court.
*Could you describe the hole?*
The hole itself is a box five feet wide and seven feet long. You have no bed, no bunk, no toilet. There is only a hole in the floor where one could defecate, urinate and this often overflows. This hole was ruled unconstitutional by state supreme court in 1966. The ruling stated that a man's supposed to have at least a mattress of some kind, full meals and a toilet. Recently there has been a grand jury investigation of county jail conditions, but every time a grand jury member comes around they take prisoners out of the hole until he has left; then they'll put him back in.
*What kind of reading are you allowed here?*
The only thing allowed is the daily newspaper and of course that's very limited in terms of any kind of black history or literature dealing with the revolutionary change that's going on in America. Even if I wanted to read about the history of Chicano people, Asian or African peoples, they won't allow those materials in the jails. They call it contraband here.
*Why were you charged in the Chicago 8 conspiracy case since your connection with the other seven was tenuous and you spent only some 12 hours in Chicago during the riot period?*
Well, I was one of the leaders in the Panther's contribution to the revolutionary struggle along with Huey Newton and Eldridge Cleaver. Huey was in jail and Cleaver was in political exile and I think they also saw the necessity to move on me. At the time I was charged I was on a speaking tour in the Scandinavian countries [5] so perhaps they were hoping I wouldn't come back. All in all, their reasons for moving against me are the same as the reasons they are

now moving against brother [David] Hilliard and other Panther leaders. They don't have any evidence against me. All I did was make a speech [in Chicago] about the right to self-defense against brutal, unjust attack. We've always made speeches like this, but they turned it around and said that I was advocating a riot. The Black Panther party shows that we don't believe in spontaneous riots because we've seen so many of our people killed due to the lack of proper organization. Another reason they included me in the conspiracy is that the power structure is beginning to realize that 30 million black people are beginning to listen to the Panther party. If we were black racists they could easily isolate us, but such is not the case.

*The Black Panther party has been criticized for its rhetoric. What is your reaction to this?*

When we use the term "pig," for example, we are referring to people who systematically violate peoples' constitutional rights— whether they be monopoly capitalists or police. The term is now being adopted by radicals, hippies and minority peoples. Even the workers, when the pigs supported strike-breakers like they did at Union Oil in Richmond where 100 local police came in and cracked strikers' heads, began to call them by their true name. But I think people, especially white people, have to come to understand that the language of the ghetto is a language of its own and as the party —whose members for the most part come from the ghetto—seeks to talk to the people, it must speak the people's language.

*Were you brought to trial in the conspiracy as a result of the continuing crackdown by Mayor Daley and Chicago authorities on the Black Panther party, which in December resulted in the deaths of Fred Hampton and Mark Clark? Were they afraid of the growing influence of the party on Chicago's West Side?*

Definitely. But I would not only localize this conspiratorial attempt to part of the avaricious demogogic ruling class, which extends from the Nixon regime on down. All are part and parcel of this attempt to wipe out the party. When we see what happened to brother Fred Hampton and brother Mark Clark in the pre-dawn raid. When we see this kind of action we see the smack of fascism. They think they can get away with what they're doing because they've fooled and misled the people. You see when they charge a person with a crime the mass media will tend to discredit a person completely. We see this happen in the Panther cases in Connecticut and New York . . . and in the case of brother Hilliard, there was no understanding in the press of the way he talks and the language in the ghetto. For example his remarks represented a gross criticism of Nixon and the power structure he represented. The media took his remarks out of this context and created a

climate of public opinion whereby he could be charged with threatening the President's life. (See page 130.) As a result of this type of media coverage, law enforcement felt that the people had been sufficiently misled to allow them to move on the Panthers.
*After they had effectively taken away the leadership they could then move on the rank and file membership of the Party?*
Exactly.
*Why do you think this backfired on them?*
They couldn't wipe the blood off their hands quick enough. They had done similar things in the past. A lot of brothers had been shot and killed. Before, the press would print the police reports and no one would be able to know what really happened. But in this case it was different. An estimated 80,000 people went through the house where Hampton was shot dead and actually saw the bullet holes in the wall. These people received a first-hand experience of genocidal tactics.
*In the case of the police attack in Los Angeles, a similar educational experience took place didn't it?*
Precisely. I assume that what the L.A. police hoped to do was pull off an early morning 10 or 15 minute raid and shoot up and kill whoever they wanted to and get out of there but the party was smart and a sister in the office got a phone call out before they cut the lines saying we need the people and press here, and they came to the shoot-out scene. So when the police version of the story came out in the press the people were able to compare that version with what they saw. . . .
*It is significant that in the L.A. case some 300 to 500 police equipped with the most advanced weaponry took five hours to overcome a force of 14 men and women Panthers.*
That's an important point. You know they had a tank ready on the scene. That's fascism—that's all that is. Despite police reports to the contrary that they knocked on the door and asked the brothers to come out, the brothers were sleeping when the police riddled the office with bullets and when they broke down the door and came in shooting the brothers had no choice but to defend themselves. Such tactics reveal the true nature of police intentions: one, to shoot up and kill as many Panthers as possible; two, to put the rest in jail on trumped up charges. In other words, law enforcement wants to wipe the Panthers out. They don't hide their conspiratorial intent. In the L.A. case it was in the papers how [Gov. Ronald] Reagan and [FBI head] Hoover were talking over the phone before the raid shows this. Then when the Justice Department claims that it has no intention of wiping out the Panthers we know its claims to be false and we know that they are bent on political repression.

*With regard to the Chicago conspiracy trial, defendant Rennie Davis has said that the single most important issue dramatized by the trial was racism, as symbolized by your gagging and chaining. How do you see that?*

Well, it's symbolic in the sense that judicial racism is as old as Dred Scott and it shows that very little has changed since 1857 in the courts. On the other hand, my chaining and gagging points out the fact that in America nobody has justice. I mean the white cats in that trial were treated similar to the way I was treated. The racist mentality can also be applied to people other than blacks. This is the most important point raised by my treatment in the trial. I mean the fact that they had black marshals in the trial didn't really stop the racism of the trial itself. The use of the black marshals was a diversionary tactic on the part of the court. The court could then claim as it did that the presence of black law enforcement in the courtroom made my claims of racism inapplicable. Well, I say that if a black judge was going to use the same fascist, racist tactics as Julius Hoffman, I would have acted no differently. You see an important thing to understand is that the system itself is white.

*It's evident lately that there has been a tactical change on the part of radicals with regard to the judicial system. Heretofore radicals, both white and black would sit back and allow the court to proceed in "orderly" fashion. Now radicals have decided to make their trials into political forums to expose the political nature of the prosecution and to publicize political ideas and life styles. Why has this change happened?*

We have all found that the process of the American judicial system, including trial procedure and jury makeup, presently violates the constitutional right to a fair trial by a jury of one's peers. It doesn't stop in the courtroom. Look at the ransom bails in the N.Y. 21 case, which amount to forcible detention. They do have bail—$100,000 each—but it can't be met. This is an outright violation of constitutional rights. In my case in Chicago, I wasn't allowed to even defend myself, whereas in Nazi Germany in 1933, a Bulgarian Communist [Dimitroff] accused of setting the Reichstag fire was allowed to. In L.A. recently, the Panthers accused of attempted murder in the Watts shootout brought rats to the courtroom which they had caught in their jail cells. Even jail conditions violate one's constitutional rights. In that same jail recently, one of the deputies tried to beat a brother up and the brothers had to defend themselves against the deputies, so one can see that the unconstitutionality of the judicial system applies to all levels, including the penal. The people who bear the blunt end of this system are now showing a willingness to stand up against it and recent trials point this out. They are willing to define a racist judge as a fascist and a pig—that's what the party means by pig, one who violates a person's constitutional rights. In any case the judicial branch of the government is the last area of appeal for a person whose rights have been violated by unjust laws and brutal enforcement, so when you get to a courtroom and find that the judge himself is a fascist at this point one doesn't have much choice but to expose his racism and fascism and stand up for his constitutional rights. All I did in Chicago was to exercise my legal right to speak in my own behalf and I was given four years in jail as a result. But I think the most serious injustice perpetrated by the court system in America is the inability of a black man to get a jury of his peers. In Huey Newton's trial there was one black on the jury and he was over 40. This happened in a city which is over 50% black. Now Huey had been a student in college. Why couldn't he have had some young people or students on that jury?

*What do you think about the recent revelation by the Mayor of Seattle that federal authorities attempted to influence him to raid the Panther headquarters in that city?*

It's no revelation. We have been talking about a federally-led conspiracy against the party for some time. In one sense it is a revelation that a government official would expose the attempt. But the man compared us to Minutemen and we're not Minutemen. We don't believe in building arsenals of weapons. If you were to go into a Panther office and find 10 Panthers you would probably find that each one of these people owns a gun for self-defense only. The party's rules are quite strict about this. I think it's important that this official didn't give in to the Gestapo tactics of federal law enforcement, but I think his conception of the party's attitude about self-defense is erroneous. This is a typical mistake: many people concentrate on the self-defense aspect of the party's program and don't take a look at other programs the party supports like free breakfast for children, community control of the police, free clothing programs, cooperative markets, cooperative housing, with an emphasis to unify all workers around the issue of a 30-hour work week in this country with the same pay, the issue of jobs for the poor and oppressed and the issue of who controls the means of production in this country. In other words, drastic social change through socialism. With this in mind, it is hard to accuse us of being Minutemen types.

*The self-defense aspect of the party does bother a lot of people in this country. Could you clarify the Panther position?*

First of all, no Panther can break a gun law unless his life is in danger and the party recognizes this. If he does so we will expel or suspend him depending on the seriousness of his offense. Panther party training in the area of self-defense includes a study of gun

laws, safe use of weapons and there is a strict rule that no party
member can use a weapon except in the case of an attack on his
life—whether the attacker be a police officer or any other person.
In the case of police harassment the party will merely print the
offending officer's picture in the newspaper so the officer can be
identified as an enemy of the people . . . no attempt on his life
will be made.

*What is the Black Panther party's position on male chauvinism?*

The fight against male chauvinism is a class struggle—that's hard
for people to understand. To understand male chauvinism one has
to understand that it is interlocked with racism. Male chauvinism is
directly related to male domination and it is perpetuated as such
by the ruling class in America. When we talk about women's liberation we're not talking so much about biological equality. There is
a basic biological difference between males and females just as there
are even more striking biological similarities between the sexes.
Though male and female differ with respect to the genitalia, all
human beings have an essential biological similarity—two arms, two
legs and what have you. But that is not what we're talking about
when we talk about equality for women. All people talk, think, feel
and human relationships have to be determined on that basis, not
on a sex basis. The same goes for racial differences. The puritanical
tradition also had a lot to do with male chauvinism. The taboo on
sex was absurd in the first place because three billion people got
on this earth that way. Looking back in history, it is easy to see
that women have received the blunt end of European prejudice
against sex. How is racism connected with this? A good part of
racism is the absurd psychological fears on the part of people who
think that the black man has a bigger penis than the white. Thus
male supremacy on the basis of sexual organs can be connected to
racial supremacy arrived at through the notion of sexual differences
by race. Cultural nationalists, like Ron Karenga, are male chauvinists
as well. What they do is oppress the black woman. Their black
racism leads them to theories of male domination as well. Thus
black racists come to the same conclusions that white racists do
with respect to their women. The party says no to this. Personally,
I don't think that women who want liberation want penises—they
just want to be treated as human beings on an equal basis, just as
blacks who demand the liberation of their people. Eldridge Cleaver
talked about this in "Soul on Ice." Superman never tries to relate
to Lois Lane, nor does he try to relate to the oppressed. Rather he
relates to superficial violence, throwing people halfway across the
ocean, etc. The concept I'm trying to establish is the cross-relation
of male chauvinism to any other form of chauvinism—including
racism. In other words the idea of saying "keep a woman in her

place" is only a short step away from saying "keep a nigger in his place." As Eldridge said in his book, the white woman is a symbol of freedom in this country. The white man took this chick and stuck her up on a pedestal and called her the Statue of Liberty and gave her a torch to hold. Well I say put a machine gun in her other hand.

*Recently Jerry Rubin remarked that although the judge in the conspiracy trial has complained about the language of the defendants, the real obscenity in the case was the willingness of the court to use violence in the courtroom to prevent the defendants from asserting their constitutional rights.*

That's typical. It shows the system's preoccupation with words rather than the more basic question of how people relate to one another. For example, in lower class terms, motherfucker doesn't necessarily mean a sexual taboo. It can be used five times in one sentence by a brother in the black ghetto and each time it will have a different meaning and connotation. In any case, research indicates that the origin of the term comes from the slave master's rape of a slave's mother. We see the taboo concept as being closely linked to racism. At the same time the party sees the need to stop using the term just so we can get a segment of the white population to understand the aims of the party. When we talk about obscenity in the courtroom, I think the most obscene thing is the ruling class' refusal to relate to the life, liberty and pursuit of happiness of those who culturally refuse to go along with its norms. We say human beings have a right to live and survive. The obscenity in the Chicago courtroom is the violation of human and constitutional rights.

*Much of the mass media has been playing up the circus aspect of the trial in Chicago and has been treating Hoffman as an exceptional case in a judicial system which is otherwise just and honorable. What do you think?*

People like Hoffman are the rule especially with respect to minority peoples. Murtagh, the judge in the New York Panther 21 case, is a notorious racist. It's just now that people like Murtagh and Hoffman are being exposed for what they are: fascist and racist.

*Do you expect any changes in the structure or direction of the Black Panther party in the future?*

Our objective is the education of the people. I don't think we'll make the same mistake that the Communist party made in the 1950s as a result of the repressive measures the government took during that time. You have to go out and fight the battle for the oppressed people—white, black, red, brown—wherever they may be. The party's recent formation of the National Committee to Combat Fascism represents a change, a good one, in that it creates an organ-

ization in which movement groups can come together and coalesce
to fight the oppressor. In any case I don't think there is any way
for the party to stop doing what it's doing and I don't think it will
undertake any significant policy change in the near future.

—*The Guardian*, February, 1970

## Black Soldiers as Revolutionaries
## to Overthrow the Ruling Class

This is the county jail, city prison, San Francisco, California.
And this is Bobby Seale, the Chairman of the Black Panther Party
of which Huey P. Newton is the Minister of Defense, and Eldridge
Cleaver is the Minister of Information. I am presently incarcerated
here as a political prisoner in the same manner that our Minister
of Defense, Huey P. Newton, is incarcerated in another prison here
in California known as C.M.C. (south of San Francisco 200 miles).
And I wanted to send a message from jail here as a political prisoner.

We are here in America, brothers, (Black G.I.'s, who this message
is to), trying to rid ourselves of the oppressive conditions that
we've been subjected to for 400 years. And now they have Black
brothers with their lives on the line, dying and fighting a people
who are only wanting for themselves, self-determination in their
own homeland and to unify their country and unify their people.
And the only reason that Black G.I.'s are over there, or Brown
G.I.'s, or Red (Indian-American) G.I.'s, Chicanos, and even white
G.I.'s, the only reason you're there is because the fascist, ruling
class circles of America (the avaricious, big-time, businessmen, the
big rich men; the demagogic, lying politicians, the misleading politicians who mislead and try to lie to the people) are the ones who
put you there and the ones who mean to keep you there. They're
the ones making fascists out of you brothers. And it's correct that
the Vietnamese should defend themselves and defend their land
and fight for the right to self-determination, because they have
NEVER oppressed us. They have NEVER called us "nigger". They
have NEVER done anything wrong to us. The leadership of the
Vietnamese is that of heroic people. This is also true of the Vietnamese people who are heroic people, fighting for their right to
self-determination.

And so, the same goes for Black people here in America living in
wretched ghettos and oppression. We have been struggling for 400

years, as many of you Black brothers are well aware. I know you dream about home. But when you come home, come home and realize that you have a fight here, that we have the right to control our destinies in our Black community; as the Chicano people have a right to control their destinies in their Chicano community or areas and places where they live; as the American Indians have a right to control their destiny; as the poor, oppressed white people have a right to control their destiny (many poor, oppressed white people must realize that it's the ruling class). The Indian-Americans, the Chicano-Americans, the Latino-Americans and Brown people, and Black people in America are beginning to move more and more in opposition to the oppressive conditions that the SAME avaricious businessmen and demagogic, lying politicians create and maintain—that exploitation. The workers of this country are beginning to move more and more, day by day, step by step from a lower to a higher level in opposing the ruling class circles, because they (the ruling class circles) are the ones who keep the racism going. They are the ones who keep people hating each other because of skin color, etc.

The Black Panther Party, brothers, does not fight racism with racism. There are no white people in the Black Panther Party but we do have alliances with white radical student groups who have stood up in protest against that war for your sake and for all the G.I.'s sake. We wanted them back home. We wanted to bring them back home as a means to end that war, demanding and protesting that the G.I.'s come back home and the war end.

The Black brothers, Vietnam Black G.I.'s, must understand and feel desire to oppose oppression right here at home domestically. Oppose fascism. The cops occupy our community just like a foreign troop occupies territory. Just like, you are a foreign troop there in Vietnam, occupying territory at the directions of the fascist ruling class and their military leaders who are also a part of the fascist ruling class. Not at the will of the people of America are you there. You're there because the imperialist U.S. aggressors (and that's exactly what they are) have sent you there. And we'll be glad when you come back, because here you must fight the pigs who occupy our community. In every major city and metropolis throughout America police forces have been doubled, tripled, and quadrupled wherever Black people live; where the large populations of Chicano people live; where the large populations of people who are protesting and opposing war, are protesting and opposing the poverty and the murder and brutality that's committed against Black people in the Black community. Wherever the case, these police forces have been tripled and quadrupled with machine guns, AR-15s (the same kinds of guns you brothers got and are carrying over there) .357

magnums (you can stand up and shoot 10 demonstrators with one bullet with a .357 or a .44 magnum) that these cops carry here.

They're not solving the problems of the people, the U.S. government, the local government, the federal government, and the city governments. All they're doing is putting money out for more arms. And now a state of DOMESTIC imperialism exists here to the extent that genocide can begin to be committed tomorrow, if they decide.

We'll be glad when you come home. We oppose the war here, we say, "Power to the People." We want all the people to move to have proletarian democracy—workers democracy (a real people's democracy), and not capitalistic, exploiting democracy for the minority ruling class. There are only 800 big, rich businessmen who control this imperialistic regime in America. There are numerous demagogic politicians, from the local government to the federal government. There are approximately half a million or more local police, some more millions of national guardsmen. But they are used against, not to protect the people. They're used to murder and to brutalize the people, such as at the National Democratic Convention back in August of 1968.

The numerous amounts of brutality that are going on, and you brothers haven't even heard about them. The political prisoners that Black Panther Party members have been made (We have over 50 political prisoners here.) all because the Ten Point Platform and Program of the Black Panther Party began to be implemented. And what was the Ten Point Platform and Program of the Black Panther Party?

From the very beginning of the Party the Ten Point Platform has always read: We want freedom. We want the right to determine our destiny in our own Black community. Number two: We want full employment for our people. Number three: We want the end to oppression and the exploitation of the Black community by the capitalists in our communities. Number four: We want decent housing fit for shelter of human beings. Five says: We want a decent education. It says we want decent education that teaches us about the true nature of this decadent American society, an education that teaches us our true history and our role in the present day society. And number six says: We want all Black men to be exempt from military service. That's what we demand here of this government. (We really want you home, brothers). Number seven says: We want an immediate end to police brutality and murder of Black people. The last two points of the Program covers our right to fair trial by peers as it says in the Constitution of the United States.

It's important Black brothers that we understand the need to come home. It's important that we understand that the Vietnamese people are only fighting for the right to self-determination in their land. It's important, brothers, that we understand it's the fascist ruling class circle who have you there, who got you fighting there. It's important, brothers, that you understand that your fight is really right here at home in America. So when you come back, you'll be fighting against the oppression that we've been subjected to for 400 years. So I will wind this statement up and probably, hopefully, send some more. Better yet, I think I should say a few more things concerning Black G.I.'s and the history of this country.

In the Civil War when there was a fight between the North and the South, in that Civil War, 186,000 Black people enlisted in the military service. We were promised freedom, justice, and equality; and we never received it. During World War I there were over 350,000 Black Americans in World War I. And we were promised freedom, justice, and equality; and we never received it. In World War II some 850,000 almost a million Black Americans fought in that war as Black G.I.'s. And we were promised freedom, justice, and equality; and we never received it. Then there was the Korean War the fascist ruling class aggressors put together. And we fought there. Now, here it is again—another war against a people who are trying to fight for the right of their self-determination. They don't even promise you "freedom, justice, and equality" anymore. Kinda bad now, brothers.

If we would only begin to realize the necessity of not being a tool for the fascist aggressor! And that doesn't only go for Black G.I.'s. That goes for Mexican-American G.I.'s, Chicano brothers, rather; that goes for the Indian American G.I.'s and Chinese-American G.I.'s; and that goes for even the poor white American G.I.'s who have to understand. That goes for even the G.I.'s who have some humanistic understanding about a people's right to survive and a right to determine their own destiny in their own land, like the average human being who can understand that Black people have been oppressed for 400 years here in America—all G.I.'s. And the Chicano people are oppressed, and the Indian-Americans are oppressed.

You guys know that. Every last one of you know that. You cats come from off the block, you Black brothers. And I know you. You know me just as well as I know you. The many times we use to break off into parties and be fighting and carrying on. Some of you would be blowing joints, and drinking and carrying on and being sharp, trying to get you some clean clothes, and chasing them sisters out there. You ain't no different from other brothers; only we just turned political. We just turned political. We're being made political prisoners because we're standing up out there against this fascist ruling class, against those fascist, racist pigs who occupy our community like a foreign troop occupies territory. We're the same, but we're just in two different places. We should be here fighting here at home. They protest over here for the freedom of political prisoners. You should all be closer at protesting over there for the freedom of political prisoners in America.

Power to the people. Power to the people; that's what we say. Power to all the people. And get rid of the power, take the power away from the minority ruling class circles, the imperialists and fascists here in America. The same thing they're doing over there to the Vietnamese people, they're getting ready to upstep and do to Black American people. The same thing; the same kind of weapons, vicious weapons. They have tanks; they have nerve gas and everything else prepared. And it's time that we understand and realize this. All the masses of the people and the G.I.'s and the people at home are the ones who have to protest the war, are the ones who have to protest the injustices right here at home.

So you brothers who are dreaming about coming back home, when you get back home, you're going to see that same oppression. They're going to promise you a job; but you're going to be out of a job. In some cases they're going to try to give some of you dishonorable discharges for one reason or another and tell you that you can't get a job when you get back. But all you have to do is tell him it wasn't no jobs here when you left. And that's why you got off into that thing anyway. You went into the service for the same reason I went into it at one time over 10 years ago, some fourteen years, now; 'cause it wasn't no jobs, it wasn't nothing to do, and you didn't have any money in your pocket and you was frustrated with your surroundings and basically your environment. That's the reason most of you brothers went in there. It was a way to get a chance to do something. And you feel you'd go in the Army and some guy'd sell you some insidious notion about being a man, and all that kind of crap. And you were already a man. You're a human being. That's the first basis for being a man; it's being a human being, and not going out trying to prove how many colored peoples you can kill in a foreign land. That's not being a man; that's being a fascist. And that's what the fascist power structure does.

So to ALL Black American G.I.'s, it's very important that you understand the need to come home; the need to relate to the struggle here; the need for the people and us to get mobilized and to amass together to free the political prisoners; the need to fight for community control of police where the people will have control, not of the same police, but fire those in now and set up community control operations. The Breakfast for Children Programs. Understand that the demagogic politicians are lying. They're lying on the Party. They've attacked the Party; they've attacked our offices. And in some cases we've had to defend ourselves with weapons because we vowed that we would stand and defend ourselves, to defend our people and teach our people the correct methods to resist the pig power structure here in America, the fascist ruling class, the exploiters. That's what they are—oppressors.

So, power to the people, brothers. And please come on home, brothers. And when you get home, we'll be waiting for you.

BOBBY SEALE
CHAIRMAN
BLACK PANTHER PARTY

—*The Black Panther*, September 20, 1969

## Bring It Home

Editor's Note: On November 5, 1969, over half a million Americans gathered in Washington, D.C., to demand immediate total withdrawal from Vietnam. They marched, sang songs, and listened to speeches by Coretta King, Dr. Benjamin Spock, Dave Dellinger, and others. One speech was read to the audience because the man who was to deliver it was in jail. Seale was one of eight defendants in the Chicago Conspiracy trial, and he sent the following message from prison.

This is Bobby Seale in the San Francisco County Jail. I just arrived back here today, November 10th, Monday. And there's a word to be said to the progressive forces in America, about imperialism abroad, and domestic imperialism (fascism) here at home.

It's correct that many millions of people, 55–60 percent of the nation or more, are fed up with this unjust, aggressive war against the Vietnamese people. It's understood that the Vietnamese people are fighting for their right to self determination, their right to determine their own destiny in their own land, country, in their communities. It's good that progressive forces (organizations and people) can come forth and mass and demonstrate and redress their grievances against the government for waging such a war against people unjustly, not only in Vietnam, but anywhere else in the world. But it's got to be understood that if there is imperialism abroad, if there is a war going on in the part of the fascist ruling class circles that are infested inside the U.S. government, if there is a war going on that they perpetrate and put together there, it must be understood that they're not waging that war for those peoples' right to self determination, that they're waging that war for some inequality and unjustness against those people. And it's evident that it is being waged for this reason on their part because of the fact that there is no equality and there's no justice at home for people right here in America, like Black people in particular who've suffered under racism and brutality and murder for 400 years right here in America. It's evident and it's clear that if there is genocide in a country as in Germany during World War II, then anything that ruling class fascist government does outside is also unjust and is also aggression and is also out to deny and murder and kill people.

What we have to understand is that right here at home in America we have to oppose imperialism, also. That you can't just fight imperialism, the acts of imperialism abroad, without understanding and recognizing community imperialism abroad, without recognizing community imperialism here of Black people, Brown people, Red people and even to the point of protesting students and radicals and progressive peoples here, in America.

Domestic imperialism at home is in fact fascism. But what in essence is it? I think Black people if we go over the concrete experiences that we've had in America and what's going on now against us we can understand exactly what it is—to be corralled in wretched ghettoes in America and look up one day and see numerous policemen occupying our community, and brutalizing us, killing brother Linthcombe, murdering young Bobby Hutton. The fact that much brutality goes on to the extent that all the fascist press and all the demagogic politicians say it and the only thing that the courts put out is that it's supposedly "justifiable homicide" on the part of policemen who occupy our community.

The police state that exists here in America right now is in fact fascism right before our eyes. There are numerous examples of the police state activities. Only last week, I hear and understand, that a young Black brother was allegedly or supposedly cashing a so-called fictitious check in a bank here in San Francisco and was walking out of the bank amongst a crowd of people and this police guard runs out of the bank and he's only walking and the brother is shot dead in the mid-section of his back. He's dead and killed. Black brothers and Black people who have experienced and know these fascist tactics and know of too many cases and too many situations where young brothers and Black people have been gunned down and murdered by these cops, and it's becoming more and more out of hand. It's becoming out of hand because in every major city, in every major metropolis where Black people live, police forces have been doubled, tripled, and quadrupled.

Also, the racist courts of America are justifying the police brutality
and murder of Black people and any people. The democratic convention as EVERYBODY knows, as everybody saw on the T.V.
and read in the papers was nothing more than pigs, cops running
rampant, brutalizing, murdering and bashing skulls. And many Black
people looked on and said, "Look at those White people getting
beaten", because we knew we had been beaten and brutalized for
many years and still are.

They dragged me into this case. They put me as one of the
defendants there, and they literally, overtly, fascisticly, piggishly, and
racistly denied me my basic constitutional rights. Charles R. Garry,
the most beautiful lawyer in the world, a revolutionary lawyer, was
here at home going through an operation. He's a beautiful brother.
He's 60 years old and had to have an operation for his health and
couldn't come to the court. Dr. Goodlett explained it to the court
a month before the court even convened that Charles would be
risking his life, and I made motion after motion, request after request, and argued those requests and those motions on my behalf
in my attempts to defend myself there and was literally denied,
(literally denied) my constitutional rights to be able to defend
myself, after it was clear that my lawyer wouldn't be able to be there
to assist me. For a man to stand up and demand his constitutional
rights and in turn the court looks at him and denies him that is
to say he's not intelligent enough to see what's going on. But in fact
we Black people, we people, all people, American people, know that
to deny people their constitutional rights, their right to defend
themselves, their right to council, or any constitutional right is
nothing more than to justify the brutal tactics, murderous fascist
tactics of the police running rampant in the communities of America,
and in particular the Black communities of America.

To the Peace Forces, the progressive forces in America, the pro-
testors, those who know the war in Vietnam is unjust, those who
are going to the streets and demonstrating, those who think they're
really, really doing something—what they're doing in trying to end
the war in Vietnam, is not meaningful at all, yet. It's not meaningful
at all and will not become meaningful at all if you really want to
stop the war in Vietnam, until you take some action here in America against the fascist brutal forces against Black people here in
America. The very fact that the North Vietnamese government has
announced that they are willing to release prisoners of war, for the
release and dropping of all charges and trumped-up charges against
the Minister of Defense Huey P. Newton, and myself, this should
be demanded also. This is directly relating to the very fact that we
have to end police brutality and murder of Black people right here
at home. Because the Black Panther Party itself has moved in this

direction from its very inception to get rid of those fascist forces that corral us.

This is the kind of action that has to be taken on the part of the Peace Forces in America and the progressive forces in America. And until they begin to do that they will not begin at all to stop imperialism; they will not begin at all to stop domestic imperialism right here at home. YOU MUST MOVE AGAINST DOMESTIC IMPERIALISM, GROWING RAMPANT FASCISM—RIGHT HERE IN AMERICA BEFORE YOU CAN END THE WAR IN VIETNAM OR ALL FORMS OF AGGRESSIVE WARS LIKE THAT AGAINST OTHER PEOPLES ABROAD. The very fact that Black, Brown, Red and other peoples in America and poor people, even poor White people, are corralled in wretched ghettos, especially those people of color and Black people whose communities are occupied in the fashion they are and murdered. No, we can't continue to allow ourselves to be duped with the notion that we're doing something good until we learn to smash imperialism right here at home. Because to smash imperialism right here at home is to smash imperialism abroad. Smashing imperialism means taking action, demanding that those prisoners of war be allowed to come home. When you say "Bring the GI's home", bring the GI's home. And we can bring the prisoners of war home by demanding that the U.S. government release political prisoners here in America. Beginning with Huey and me, right now in America we will set a precedence of opposing fascism, abroad and at home. If that is what the Vietnamese people want, to release the political prisoners and people here in America, then I say that the progressive forces have to take some action in that direction; and they will be relating directly to smashing imperialism at home and recognizing that this has to be done.

People move. Black brothers and sisters, American people, it's time that we moved against fascism at home because to smash fascism at home is to smash fascism forever abroad.

—*The Black Panther*, January 3, 1970

# 5.

# ELDRIDGE CLEAVER SPEAKS FROM EXILE

On November 24, 1968, three days before the sentence that would have returned him to prison was to go into effect, Eldridge Cleaver, Minister of Information for the Black Panther Party, former candidate for the Presidency of the United States on the Peace and Freedom ticket, and author of the best-selling *Soul on Ice*, disappeared. Today he lives in exile in Algiers. But he continues to speak out on fundamental issues confronting the people of his native land through articles, interviews, and messages. Here are his views on a number of important questions.

## Message to Sister Erica Huggins of the Black Panther Party

### Excerpt from Tape of Eldridge Breaking His Silence from Somewhere in the Third World

I'd like to send a very special word to sister Erica Huggins, the wife of our slain, murdered Deputy Minister of Information, John Huggins, who was murdered along with our Deputy Minister of Defense, Brother Alprentice "Bunchy" Carter. He's Bunchy to me.

And now, the pigs have compounded this by taking this woman, this black woman, this sister, after inflicting this horrible pain upon her by murdering the father of her newborn child. Taking her away from her child and placing her behind bars [in Connecticut] on some trumped-up charges.

I know Erica, and I know that she's a very strong sister. But I know that she is now being subjected to a form of torture that is horrible. I know that she is strong and that she will endure and sister Erica, be strong sister.

We must not rest until this sister is liberated, and if she is not out at this moment, then she should be out just as rapidly as it is possible for us to get her out. And an example to all of us, let it be a lesson and an example to all of the sisters, particularly to all of the brothers, that we must understand that our women are suffering strongly and enthusiastically as we are participating in the struggle. And I'm aware that it has been a problem in all organizations in Babylon to structure our struggle in such a way that our sisters, our women are liberated and made equal in our struggle and in regard to sister Erica, I know that the Minister of Defense, Huey P. Newton has spoken out many times that the male chauvinism that is rampant in Babylon in general, is also rampant in our own ranks.

The incarceration and the suffering of Sister Erica should be a stinging rebuke to all manifestations of male chauvinism within our ranks. That we must purge our ranks and our hearts, and our minds, and our understanding of any chauvinism, chauvinistic behavior of disrespectful behavior toward women. That we must too recognize that a woman can be just as revolutionary as a man and that she has equal stature, that, along with men, and that we cannot prejudice her in any manner, that we cannot relegate her to an inferior position. That we have to recognize our women as our equals and that revolutionary standards of principles demand that we go to great lengths to see to it that disciplinary action is taken on all levels against those who manifest male chauvinism behavior.

Because the liberation of women is one of the most important issues facing the world today. Great efforts have been made in various parts of the world to do something about this, but I know from my own experience that the smouldering and the burning of the flame demand for liberation of women in Babylon is the issue that is going to explode, and if we're not careful it's going to destroy our ranks, destroy our organization, because women want to be liberated just as all oppressed people want to be liberated.

So if we want to go around and call ourselves a vanguard organization, then we've got to be the vanguard in all our behaviour, and to be the vanguard also in the area of women's liberation and set an example in that area, and all of us to start being respectful and not condescending and patronizing, but to really understand and look upon this question, recognize, that women are our other half, they're not our weaker half, they're not our stronger half, but they are our other half and that we sell ourselves out, we sell our children out, and we sell our women out when we treat them in any other manner.

We have to be very careful about that, and Sister Erica Huggins is a shining example of a revolutionary woman who's been meted out the same kind of injustice from the pig power structure that a revolutionary man receives. So they didn't put her in a powder puffed cell. They did not make life easy for her. But the pigs recognized a revolutionary woman to be just as much a threat as a revolutionary man.

And so we recognize that we also have a duty to stop inflicting injustices of misuse of women. We have to be very careful about that, and we all know the problem. But I'm saying that it's mandatory, the Minster of Defense Huey P. Newton has said that it is mandatory that all manifestations of male chauvinism be excluded from our ranks and that sisters have a duty and the right to do whatever they want to do in order to see to it that they are not relegated to an inferior position, and that they're not treated as though they are not equal members of the Party and equal in all regards. And that they're not subjected to male practices.

And Sister Erica Huggins is a good example of a revolutionary woman who has sacrificed everything, including her husband. So Sister Erica—Right On.

ALL POWER TO THE PEOPLE

—*The Black Panther,* July 5, 1969

# The Black Man's Stake in Vietnam

The most critical tests facing Johnson are the war in Vietnam and the Negro revolution at home. The fact that the brains in the Pentagon see fit to send 16 per cent black troops to Vietnam is one indication that there is a structural relationship between these two arenas of conflict. And the initial outrageous refusal of the Georgia Legislature to seat representative elect Julian Bond, because he denounced the aggressive U.S. role in Vietnam, shows too, the very intimate relationship between the way human beings are being treated in Vietnam and the treatment they are receiving here in the United States.

We live today in a system that is in the last stages of the protracted process of breaking up on a worldwide basis. The rulers perceive the greatest threat to be the national liberation movements around the world, particularly in Asia, Africa, and Latin America. In order for them to wage wars of suppression against these national liberation movements abroad, they must have peace and stability and unanimity of purpose at home. But at home there is a Trojan Horse, a Black Trojan Horse that has become aware of itself and is now struggling to get on its feet. It too, demands liberation.

What is the purpose of the attention that the rulers are now focusing on the Trojan Horse? Is it out of a newfound love for the horse, or is it because the rulers need the horse to be quiet, to be still, and not cause the rulers, already with their backs to the wall, any trouble or embarrassment while they force the war in Vietnam? Indeed, the rulers have need of the horse's power on the fields of battle. What the black man in America must keep constantly in mind is that the doctrine of white supremacy, which is a part of the ideology of the world system the power structure is trying to preserve, lets the black man in for the greatest portion of the suffering and hate which white supremacy has dished out to the non-white people of the world for hundreds of years. The white-supremacy-oriented white man feels less compunction about massacring "niggers" than he does about massacring any other race of people on the earth. This historically indisputable fact, taken with the present persistent efforts of the United States to woo the Soviet Union into an alliance against China, spells DANGER to all the peoples of the world who have been victims of white supremacy. If this sweethearting proves successful, if the United States is finally able to make a match with

Russia, or if the U.S. can continue to frighten the Soviet Union into reneging on its commitments to international socialist solidarity (about which the Soviets are always trumpeting, while still allowing the imperialist aggressors to daily bomb the Democratic Republic of North Vietnam), and if the U.S. is able to unleash its anxious fury and armed might against the raging non-white giant of China, which is the real target of U.S. strategy the world over—if the U.S. is successful in these areas, then it will be the black man's turn again to face the lyncher and burner of the world: and face him alone.

Black Americans are too easily deceived by a few smiles and friendly gestures, by the passing of a few liberal-sounding laws which are left on the books to rot unenforced, and by the mushy speech-making of a President who is a past master of talking out of the thousand sides of his mouth. Such poetry does not guarantee the safe future of the black people in America. The black people must have a guarantee, they must be certain, they must be sure beyond all doubt that the reign of terror is ended and not just suspended, and that the future of their people is secure. And the only way they can ensure this is to gain organizational unity and communication with their brothers and allies around the world, on an international basis. They must have this power. There is no other way. Anything else is a sellout of the future of their people. The world of today was fashioned yesterday. What is involved here, what is being decided right now, is the shape of power in the world tomorrow.

The American racial problem can no longer be spoken of or solved in isolation. The relationship between the genocide in Vietnam and the smiles of the white man toward black Americans is a direct relationship. Once the white man solves his problem in the East he will then turn his fury again on the black people of America, his longtime punching bag. The black people have been tricked again and again, sold out at every turn by misleaders. After the Civil War, America went through a period similar to the one we are now in. The Negro problem received a full hearing. Everybody knew that the black man had been denied justice. No one doubted that it was time for changes and that the black man should be made a first class citizen. But Reconstruction ended. Blacks who had been elevated to high positions were brusquely kicked out into the streets and herded along with the masses of blacks into the ghettos and black belts. The lyncher and the burner received virtual license to murder blacks at will. White Americans found a new level on which to cool the blacks out. And with the help of such tools as Booker T. Washington, the doctrine of segregation was clamped firmly onto the backs of the blacks. It has taken a hundred years to struggle up from that level of cool-out to the miserable position that black Americans find themselves in. Time is passing. The historical opportunity which world events now present to black Americans is running out with every tick of the clock.

This is the last act of the show. We are living in a time when the people of the world are making their final bid for full and complete freedom. Never before in history has this condition prevailed. Always before there have been more or less articulate and aware pockets of people, portions of classes, etc., but today's is an era of mass awareness, when the smallest man on the street is in rebellion against the system which has denied him life and which he has come to understand robs him of his dignity and self-respect. Yet he is being told that it will take time to get programs started, to pass legislation, to educate white people into accepting the physically impossible, to move as fast as the black man would like to move. Black men are deadly serious when they say FREEDOM NOW. Even if the white man wanted to eradicate all traces of evil overnight, he would not be able to do it because the economic and political system will not permit it. All talk about going too fast is treasonous to the black man's future.

What the white man must be brought to understand is that the black man in America today is fully aware of his position, and he does not intend to be tricked again into another hundred-year forfeit of freedom. Not for a single moment or for any price will the black men now rising up in America settle for anything less than their full proportionate share and participation in the sovereignty of America. The black man has already come to a realization that to be free it is necessary for him to throw his life—everything—on the line, because the oppressors refuse to understand that it is now impossible for them to come up with another trick to squelch the black revolution. The black man can't afford to take a chance. He can't afford to put things off. He must stop the whole NOW and get his business straight, because if he does not do it now, if he fails to grasp securely the reins of this historic opportunity, there may be no tomorrow for him.

The black man's interest lies in seeing a free and independent Vietnam, a strong Vietnam which is not the puppet of international white supremacy. If the nations of Asia, Latin America, and Africa are strong and free, the black man in America will be safe and secure and free to live in dignity and self-respect. It is a cold fact that while the nations of Africa, Asia, and Latin America were shackled in colonial bondage, the black American was held tightly in the vise of oppression and not permitted to utter a sound of protest of any effect. But when these nations started bidding for their freedom, it was then that black Americans were able to seize the chance; it was then that the white man yielded what little he did—out of sheer necessity. The only lasting salvation for the black American is to do all he can to see to it that the African, Asian, and Latin American nations are free and independent.

In this regard, black Americans have a big role to play. They are a Black Trojan Horse within white America and they number in excess of 23,000,000 strong. That is a lot of strength. But it is a lot of weakness if it is disorganized, and the overriding need is for unity and organization. Unity is on all black lips. Today we stand on the verge of sweeping change in this wretched landscape of a thousand little fragmented and ineffectual groups and organizations unable to work together for the common cause. The need for one organization that will give one voice to the black man's common interest is felt in every bone and fiber of black America.

Yesterday, after firmly repudiating racism and breaking his ties with the Black Muslim organization, the late Malcolm X launched a campaign to transform the American black man's struggle from the narrow plea for "civil rights" to the universal demand for human rights, with the ultimate aim of bringing the United States government to task before the United Nations. This, and the idea of the Organization of Afro-American Unity, was Malcolm's dying legacy to his people. It did not fall on barren ground. Already, black American leaders have met with the ambassadors of Black Africa at a luncheon at UN headquarters. The meaning of this momentous event is lost on no one. The fact that it was the issue of Julian Bond, his denunciation of U.S. aggression in Vietnam, and the action of racist elements in the Georgia legislature which brought clearer recognition by black men that their interests are also threatened by the U.S. war of suppression in Vietnam. This dovetailing of causes and issues is destined to bring to fruition the other dream which Malcolm's assassination prevented him from realizing, the Organization of Afro-American Unity, or perhaps a similar organization under a different name. Black Americans now realize that they must organize for the power to change the foreign and domestic policies of the U.S. government. They must let their voice be heard on these issues. They must let the world know where they stand.

It is no accident that the U.S. government is sending all those black troops to Vietnam. Some people think that Vietnam is to kill off the cream of black youth. But it has another important result. By turning her black troops into the butchers of the Vietnamese people, America is spreading hate against the black race throughout Asia. Even black Africans find it hard not to hate black Americans for being so stupid as to allow themselves, to be used to slaughter another people who are fighting to be free. Black Americans are considered to be the world's biggest fools to go to another country to fight for something they don't have for themselves.

It bothers white racists that people around the world love black Americans but find it impossible to give a similar warm affection to white Americans. The white racist knows that he is the Ugly American and he wants the black American to be Ugly, too, in the eyes of the world: misery loves company! When the people around the world cry "Yankee, Go Home!" they mean the white man, not the black man who is a recently freed slave. The white man is deliberately trying to make the people of the world turn against black Americans, because he knows that the day is coming when black Americans will need the help and support of their brothers, friends and natural allies around the world. If through stupidity or by following hand-picked leaders who are the servile agents of the power structure, black Americans allow this strategy to succeed against them, then when the time comes and they need this help and support from around the world, it will not be there. All of the international love, respect, and goodwill that black Americans now have around the world will have dried up. They themselves will have buried it in the mud of the rice paddies of Vietnam.

—*The Black Panther*, March 23, 1969

## An Open Letter to Stokely Carmichael

Stokely Carmichael, Conakry, Guinea:

Your letter of resignation as the Prime Minister of the Black Panther Party [6] came, I think, about one year too late. As a matter of fact, since the day of your appointment to that position—February 17, 1968—events have proven that you were not cut out for the job in the first place. Even then it was clear that your position on coalition with revolutionary white organizations was in conflict with that of the Black Panther Party. But we thought that, in time, even you would be able to shake the SNCC paranoia about white control and get on with the business of building the type of revolutionary machinery that we need in the United States in order to unite all the revolutionary forces in the country to overthrow the system of Capitalism, Imperialism and Racism.

I know these terms are kicked around like lifeless bodies and that it is easy to allow the grisly realities behind them to become obscured by too frequent repetition. But when you see the squalor in which people live as a result of the policies of the exploiters, when you see the effects of exploitation on the emaciated bodies of little children, when you see the hunger and desperation, then these terms come alive in a new way. Since you've made this trip yourself and seen it all with your own eyes, you should know that suffering is color-blind, that the victims of Imperialism, Racism, Colonialism and Neo-colonialism come in all colors, and that they need a unity based on revolutionary principles rather than skin color.

The other charges which you make in your letter—about our new-found ideology, our dogmatism, our arm-twisting, etc.—seem to me to be of secondary importance, because, with the exception, perhaps, of the honorable Elijah Muhammad, you are the most dogmatic cat on the scene today, and I've never known you to be opposed to twisting arms or, for that matter, necks. In many ways your letter struck me as being an echo and rehash of the charges brought against the party by the bootlickers before the McClellan Committee. And since you chose this moment to denounce the party, we—and I am sure many other people outside the party—must look upon your letter in this light. The only point in your letter that I think is really you is the one about coalition with whites, because it has been this point on which our differences have turned from the very beginning.

You have never been able to distinguish the history of the Black Panther Party from the history of the organization of which you were once the chairman—the Student Non-Violent Coordinating Committee. It is understandable that you can have such fears of black organizations being controlled, or partly controlled, by whites, because most of your years in SNCC were spent under precisely those conditions. But the Black Panther Party has never been in that situation. Because we have never had to wrest control of our organization out of the hands of whites, we have not been shackled with the type of paranoid fear that was developed by you cats in SNCC. Therefore we are able to sit down with whites and hammer out solutions to our common problems without trembling in our boots about whether or not we might get taken over in the process. It has always seemed to me that you belittle the intelligence of your black brothers and sisters when you constantly warn them that they had better beware of white folks. After all, you are not the only black person out of Babylon who has been victimized by white racism. But you sound as though you are scared of white people, as though you are still running away from slave-catchers who will lay hands on your body and dump you in a bag.

As a matter of fact, it has been precisely your nebulous enunciation of Black Power that has provided the power structure with its new weapon against our people. The Black Panther Party tried to give you a chance to rescue Black Power from the pigs who have seized upon it and turned it into the rationale for Black Capitalism.

With James Farmer in the Nixon Administration to preside over the implementation of Black Capitalism under the slogan of Black Power, what value does that slogan now have to our people's struggle for liberation? Is denouncing the Black Panther Party the best you can do to combat this evil? I would think that your responsibility goes a little further than that. Even though you were right when you said that LBJ would never stand up and call for Black Power, Nixon has done so and he's bankrolling it with millions of dollars. So now your old Black Power buddies are cashing in on your slogan. In effect, your cry for Black Power has become the grease to ease the black bourgeoisie into the power structure.

By giving you the position of Prime Minister of the Black Panther Party, we were trying to rescue you from the black bourgeoisie that had latched on to your coattails and was riding you like a mule. Now they have stolen your football and run away for a touchdown: six points for Richard Milhous Nixon.

In February 1968, at the Free Huey Birthday Rally in Oakland, California, where you made your first public speech after returning to the United States from your triumphant tour of the revolutionary countries of the Third World, you took the occasion to denounce the coalition that the Black Panther Party had made with the white Peace and Freedom Party. What you called for instead was a Black United Front that would unite all the forces in the black community from left to right, close ranks against the whites, and all go skipping off to freedom. Within the ranks of your Black United Front you wanted to include the Cultural Nationalists, the Black Capitalists, and the Professional Uncle Toms, even though it was precisely these three groups who were working to murder your shit even before it broke wind. (Remember what Ron Karenga did to your meeting in Los Angeles?)

You had great dreams in those days, Stokely, and your visions, on the top side, were heroic. On the bottom side, when it came to the details of reality, your vision was blind. You were unable to distinguish your friends from your enemies because all you could see was the color of the cat's skin. It was this blindness that led you to the defense of Adam Clayton Powell, that Jackal from Harlem, when he came under attack by his brother jackals in Congress. And it was this blindness that led you to the defense of that black cop in Washington, D.C., who was being fucked over by the whites above him in the Police Department for whom he carried his gun as he patrolled the black community. In short, your habit of looking at the world through black-colored glasses would lead you, on the domestic level, to close ranks with such enemies of black people as James Farmer, Whitney Young, Roy Wilkins and Ron Karenga; and on the international level you would end up in the same bag with Papa

Doc Duvalier, Joseph Mobutu, and Haile Selassie. Yes, we opposed that shit then and we oppose it now even more strongly, especially since the Nixon Administration has stolen your program from you and, I think, included you out.

And now you are going to liberate Africa! Where are you going to start, Ghana? The Congo? Biafra? Angola? Mozambique? South Africa? If you are not aware of it, I think that you should know that the brothers in Africa who are involved in armed struggle against the Colonialists would like nothing better than for you to pack up your suitcase full of African souvenirs and split back to Babylon. They have never forgiven the tat-mouthing you did in Dar-es-Salaam when you presumed to tell them how to conduct their business. It seems to me that you are now trapped between the extremes of your own rhetoric. On the one hand, you have cut yourself off from the struggle in Babylon, and on the other hand, you are not about to become the Redeemer of Mother Africa.

The enemies of black people have learned something from history even if you haven't, and they are discovering new ways to divide us faster than we are discovering new ways to unite. One thing they know, and we know, that seems to escape you, is that there is not going to be any revolution or black liberation in the United States as long as revolutionary blacks, whites, Mexicans, Puerto Ricans, Indians, Chinese and Eskimos are unwilling or unable to unite into some functional machinery that can cope with the situation. Your talk and fears about premature coalition are absurd, because no coalition against oppression by forces possessing revolutionary integrity can ever be premature. If anything, it is too late, because the forces of counterrevolution are sweeping the world, and this is happening precisely because in the past people have been united on a basis that perpetuates disunity among races and ignores basic revolutionary principles and analyses.

You are peeved because the Black Panther Party informs itself with the revolutionary principles of Marxism-Leninism, but if you look around the world you will see that the only countries which have liberated themselves and managed to withstand the tide of the counterrevolution are precisely those countries that have strong Marxist-Leninist parties. All those countries that have fought for their liberation solely on the basis of nationalism have fallen victims to capitalism and neo-colonialism, and in many cases now find themselves under tyrannies equally as oppressive as the former colonial regimes.

That you know nothing about the revolutionary process is clear; that you know even less about the United States and its people is clearer; and that you know still less about humanity than you do about the rest is even clearer. You speak about an "undying love for black people." An undying love for black people that denies the humanity of other people is doomed. It was an undying love of white people for each other which led them to deny the humanity of colored people and which has stripped white people of humanity itself. It would seem to me that an undying love for our people would, at the very least, lead you to a strategy that would aid our struggle for liberation instead of leading you into a coalition of purpose with the McClellan Committee in its attempt to destroy the Black Panther Party.

Well, so long, Stokely, and take care. And beware of some white folks and of some black folks, because I assure you that some of both of them have teeth that will bite. Remember what Brother Malcolm said in his Autobiography: "We had the best organization that the black man has ever had in the United States—and niggers ruined it!" POWER TO THE PEOPLE.

ELDRIDGE CLEAVER, Minister of Information, Black Panther Party. July, 1969.

—Ramparts, September, 1969

## Eldridge Cleaver Discusses Revolution: An Interview from Exile

The exiled Minister of Information of the Black Panther Party, Eldridge Cleaver, surfaced last summer at the Pan-African Festival in Algiers. This interview was done at that time ·by Stefen Aust, a West German journalist.—Liberation News Service

QUESTION: What was the situation in America at the time of Stokely Carmichael's split from the Black Panther Party, and how did it contribute to the split?

ELDRIDGE: The whole approach to the problem the government is taking, black capitalism, they're using the slogan of black power to conceal that. This forced Stokely to continue articulating what he started in such a way as to make it clear he's not involved in black capitalism. But by quitting the scene and not defending his position, the whole thing has been coopted by people who are in CORE, the whole organization has gone into black capitalism. The former head of CORE, James Farmer, has become the top man in the Nixon administration to implement that, the man who succeeded Farmer as the head of CORE, Floyd McKissick, he has gotten

himself an organization, a business firm which he calls Floyd Mc-
Kissick Inc., and a lot of funds are funneled through him.

We regard this as the advent of the neo-colonialist phase of our
peculiar situation in the United States because it corresponds to the
moment the colonial power decides to grant a measure of independence to the colony and replace the colonial regime with a regime
of puppets. And this is what they're doing now in the United States
by pulling certain levels of the black bourgeoisie into the power
structure and developing for them a vested interest in the capitalist system. So these really defiant positions, the people who pre-
tended to be revolutionary, are accepting funds.

The government will give anybody money. They offered money
to the Black Panther Party; they offer it to everybody, and they don't
care what your line is, they just want to get you involved in their
programs, then they begin to put the squeezes on you to get you
dependent.

A lot of people are accepting this money and they're using the
slogan Black Power by equating black capitalism with power. And
this is one of the very bad things that has happened as a result of
what Stokely was talking about. We offered him the position of
Prime Minister of the Party to give him a base which he no longer
has as a result of his problems with SNCC and the decomposition
of SNCC itself. But he abandoned the field. Now he's talking about
the struggles in Africa. He wants to liberate Ghana; it just doesn't
stand up.

The key thing to me, he made a statement that I think is very
key. He said, "You guys are on top now, but just watch, I'll be back
up there." So that whole type of thinking is an ego trip and constantly making these invidious comparisons. We were talking to him
when we first came here because we thought he would realize the
mistake he had made and apologize to the Party, and we would then
accept him back into the Party because we had long been uptight
about where he was functioning. He said he did not know the Mc-
Clellan Committee was engaged in investigations of the Party at the
time he issued his resignation and charges. But the charges he lodged
against the Party seemed to echo the charges of these stooges who
were mumbling before the McClellan Committee. When this was
brought to his attention he said he didn't know the McClellan
Committee was involved in an investigation. And in light of not
knowing this, he said he was willing to make a statement to clarify
the situation and to make it clear that he did not have anything to
do with the McClellan Committee's attack, so it boiled down to a
question of how to do that, and he was procrastinating, and then he
made that final statement, something snapped in me, and I was no
longer willing to go along with it.

I had been the one who was trying to salvage the situation and give him a chance to apologize to the Party, and everyone else was perfectly willing to let him go and not go to the expense. So when he took the position he took, we called him up and just told him we were not going to try to arrange that other thing that we were talking about, and that we would accept his resignation as he wrote it and deal with it as he put it forth. And that's the last we've heard of him.

QUESTION: His two most important issues in this letter were first, calling the Party dogmatic, and second, condemning the alliances with white radical movements.

ELDRIDGE: I think these two are very related because when he refers to dogmatism, what he is actually referring to is the fact that we are a Marxist-Leninist Party, and implicit in Marxist-Leninism is proletarian internationalism, and solidarity with all people who are struggling and this, of course, includes white people. So that since his main object is non-alliance with whites, and turning one's back on whites and having no policy towards them at all, just to ignore them, he has to come down heavy on both those points in order to maintain his position. And we consider this position to be racist.

We recognize that we cannot function in this way, particularly these days when nationally and internationally they're using negritude as a way to create divisions amongst people, and the domestic counterpart of this international approach is the use of black capitalism, black consciousness. We call it cultural nationalism in the United States, and it's been made very clear how they finance certain cultural nationalist organizations. They have already exposed themselves as being tools of the power structure by their activities. So that another definition is required to make distinctions between friends and enemies when they are coming in all colors. And we feel that the only safe guides to action are the revolutionary principles of Marxism-Leninism, that they are relevant at this point for that reason and we choose to work on that basis and let the rest of that go because black people have already gained their consciousness, they have a sense of their identity, which was lost in the United States. At the time that this was happening, it was very progressive, it was a very good thing that was coming about. But after people had assimilated that and were reminded of who they were and everything, to maintain that position and not to go any further becomes reactionary.

This is what has happened to Stokely and a lot of other people, a lot of other people get hung up culturally in that sense, but Stokely has gotten hung up politically in that sense. There's a false distinction people make between culture and politics, and then after making this false distinction, he confuses culture with politics again. So that it's like an error compounded with an error, and we can't deal with that.

QUESTION: Being critical of cultural nationalism, how do you see the role of this African cultural festival?

ELDRIDGE: Well I think it brought together all of the experienced ideological lines, it forced certain things into the open, and it really serves to drive home to a lot of people that this negritude and cultural nationalism are stumbling blocks to the people's liberation struggles rather than assistances. I think that a lot of the conversations I have had here have been repeated over and over again, people who are involved in the process of struggle for liberation at this moment, seem to be more keenly aware of the negative aspects of this as opposed to those who have already gotten independence and have some very reactionary regimes in power, because they're using this. The people who are struggling are open to all assistance they can get, and they don't want to foreclose any avenue by some simple-minded ideological positions.

But those who are already in power and have gotten their liberation on this false basis, they're content to keep it going. One very interesting thing that I've heard people talking about is that following World War II when all the colonies were fighting for their liberation on the basis of nationalism rather than building a strong revolutionary party. This has proven to be a mistake historically. It was the easy way out because it is easier to mobilize people on the basis of nationalism than it is to create a strong Marxist-Leninist organization. The counter-revolutions that have set in and have put many of these nationalist regimes out of power and saddled the people with these oppressive regimes, again demonstrate the point that the only governments that have really been able to survive this sweep have been those governments who have gotten their liberation and created, or even had before, or created during the struggle or after the struggle, a strong Marxist-Leninist Party. And I think this is borne out by the experience of China, Cuba and the Eastern European Socialist countries, including the Soviet Union. That no matter what you say about some of the revisionist policies that are rampant in that area, still I will always choose those Socialist regimes over capitalist regimes. There is something there that is able to withstand the attempt by the imperialists and capitalists to roll back the tide. They found this easy to do in countries that are held together only by very narrow nationalism.

QUESTION: Do you think the role of nationalism in the movement for liberation is no longer important?

ELDRIDGE: I think it will have a continuing importance and there is a proper way to deal with nationalism. I don't think there is necessarily a distinction between, or should I say a conflict between, nationalism and proletarian internationalism, because it's been shown many times that if you can't love those around you, which is a form of nationalism, relate to those within your own entity, then you can't relate to those beyond you, and by the same token if you can relate to those beyond you, and not be able to relate to those near you, then there's still a problem. I'm talking about this full blown nationalist approach to the problem that completely obscures class contradictions and class problems and unites people over class lines and fitting the whole nation out for problems later on. Because on that basis, the bourgeoisie, which is always better educated at this stage, is able to move into the apparatus of the government because people with skills are required, and when they move in they also get the power, and because things are organized on a nationalist base, there's nothing there to counteract them usurping the power, organizing coups and turning the tide back. I think people are moving away from that, particularly young people, young students who are in these countries, most of them are very conscious and most of them are turning to Marxism-Leninism.

QUESTION: The main issue in the split of the American SDS was the relation to the black movement. What do you think of the split, what do you think is the task of the white mother country radicals in this special situation now?

ELDRIDGE: I think the people who were disrupting SDS were the people who had this faulty analysis of the situation, they were still functioning on the basis of an analysis of what we call the Old Left. They are not recognizing the ethnic struggles that are going on in the United States which often obscure the past struggle. The people in SDS who we work with have related to the analysis we have made and they see that it is functional because in the United States you have Mexican-Americans, Puerto-Ricans, Indians, Eskimos, Chinese-Americans, black Americans, white Americans and many other ethnic groups. These ethnic groups have been divided from each other and they are in such a posture at this time that there's no point in trying to make the mistakes that have been made in the past by trying to pull them all into one homogeneous organization without taking all these peculiarities into consideration. We say that's putting the cart before the horse. What we have to do is take the people as they are right now, pull them together into organizational machinery, and then create other machinery that they can be pulled into once they get that consciousness. This is done through a process of coalition, and it does function, and it's functioning right now, and developing, and we're able to deal with much more of the problems then we were when we were trying to pull poor people into one group and continue depleting a lot of our energies by a lot of in-fighting over that. These people who are in PL and who are very dogmatic, and who did not want to recognize what was happening in the other communities and start to impose their own ideological perspective upon the people, did get rebuffed, I consider them splitting from SDS as a fitting rebuff, to the situation they were trying to perpetuate.

QUESTION: After spending so much time in the Third World, have you changed your views on American policy, can you say anything about experiences you have had since you left the United States?

ELDRIDGE: I've been more confirmed in the position and attitude that the Black Panther Party had. I recognize now that some of the things we were doing and trying to do are even more important than we realized they were, particularly in the directions we struck out in, in trying to get around the obstacles that were created by Stokely Carmichael and SNCC, but which we feel were historically necessary—with black power. We took a different course in the United States, and we did it out of necessity. After coming into contact with other people who are revolutionaries but are not black, you see how important it is in order to work with them. I've been appalled to a greater extent than I ever dreamed that I could have been by the visible results of colonialism and imperialism. We in the United States who are oppressed, in comparison to what I've seen around the world, it seems as though we are oppressed between slices of silk, because there's nothing comparable to the poverty I've seen around the world, there's nothing comparable in the United States, even in the most oppressed areas.

I recognize that the United States government is the number one enemy of mankind and very much involved in perpetuating all these things which I have seen, through their international organizations such as NATO, SEATO and through the United Nations. They are able to perpetuate the stagnation of people and to corrupt their attempts to industrialize their countries. This, I think, has had a great influence on me, also a lot of pure revolutionary fervor that I have encountered amongst people has served to stimulate more dedication within myself.

QUESTION: Don't you think it's very important that the liberation fronts in the Third World work very closely with the Black Panther Party?

ELDRIDGE: Not only with the Black Panther Party, but with all revolutionary forces within the United States. Certainly, I think it has been demonstrated here at this festival in Algiers, which has been held under the auspices of the OAU (Organization of African Unity) but also of the whole government of Algeria, the fact that they had the courage to invite us, the fact that they had the courage to invite myself, considering the situation that existed, I think this has gone a long way toward strengthening solidarity.

It had a very strong impact on the United States, I'm sure, and I think that the important thing about this is that in the past there have been individuals, black People from the United States who have come over to make certain contacts and made certain promises that they were unable to fulfill, and for the first time a strong nationwide organization is making contact with these people, and because our relations do not depend on any one person for its perpetuation, that this will have to strengthen these links and create channels that can be perpetuated in the future. These are some of the very positive aspects that I see in this.

QUESTION: Are there any concrete plans for cooperation, such as sending delegations to other countries?

ELDRIDGE: Naturally we want to cooperate and aid each other in any way that we possibly can. A lot of this of course cannot be talked about, we can say that the people have expressed great gladness at the development in the United States, the fact that revolutionary vanguards are being created. It gives them great hope to know that even in Babylon, a revolution can be struggled for. And it helps them in their struggle because they say that if those guys can do it over there, then what's wrong with us here!? We all know that we are dealing with the same enemy. Just to know that there is someone in the same fight with you always strengthens your dedication.

QUESTION: Do you think the United States had changed since you left?

ELDRIDGE: I think the repression has increased markedly, and this means that the effectiveness of the Party's attack on the power structure was becoming intolerable to the power structure itself. One of the important things that developed after I left was the Breakfast for Children Program that the Party adopted. This was a way for the Party to strengthen its links with the community and to get thousands and thousands of people across the country involved in the program, exposed to the Party. And these people got very angry when the government started attacking the Breakfast for Children Program. There has been much more acceptance of the Party.

It's very interesting that many of the things that we were advocating, that we had been spearheading while I was there, took on more urgency and more acceptability after I left, because people had to relate to that. It's just like—from talking to the brothers in the delegation that came here from the United States, just to hear them talk, there was a long time when the Black Panther Party was shot through with cultural nationalism, and we're trying to get out of that bag. The brothers who are here now are brothers who have been in the Party almost from its beginning and I had a chance to watch them develop, see in them resistance to the direction we were trying to take, in terms of relations with white revolutionaries, so that there has been a complete change in that.

I heard one brother refer to the people of Scandinavia as our

Scandinavian brothers and sisters, and this particular cat at one time when we were trying to mobilize people from the community to go out to the courthouse and join in a demonstration at the court for Huey Newton when he went to trial, he refused to get into the sound truck because the sound truck was being driven by a white guy.

It was necessary for this guy to drive the sound truck because he had the license and the permit and it just had to be that way. But he refused to get into the sound truck, and now he is the one who made the statement I referred to. That indicates to me that things have changed and that a lot of things that we were trying to do while I was there have become accepted. That's just one, there are other things, but that's one of the most difficult.

There is a lot of development. The Party is stronger and much larger. I think that the great mushrooming and developing of the Party ideologically is one of the most important things that has happened. We always did relate to Marxism-Leninism, but there was a great difficulty in maintaining Party discipline. It wasn't functional, it wasn't really clear how you could apply democratic centralism in that situation, with the cats we had to deal with.

One thing that's important, a lot of people don't understand why a lot of people were purged from the Party. During the time when Huey Newton was going to trial, we dropped a lot of our programs because of the necessity of mobilizing as many people as possible. We virtually closed the membership, we did not make any public announcement, and we started just pulling people in. We knew who the Panthers were, but in order to maximize the number of people we pulled in, we did not argue with people if they put on a black leather jacket or black berets, or said that they were Panthers. They just walked in and said they support Huey Newton and they wanted to join our organization. We didn't have time to conduct our political education classes on this, which is a very important process in our recruitment, that the brothers maintain. After the trial of Huey Newton was over and the verdict was in, it was a question of going back to our other activities that we had been involved in. At that time, a lot of people who came into the organization in that campaign, to free Huey, they proved to be very undisciplined, and non-functional, and they created a lot of problems for the Party and they were not amenable to political education classes. So we just came down hard.

I wasn't there at the time, I was aware of it, I knew what was happening and why it was happening, and a lot of these people were defined as not being members of the Party. And those who wanted to become members of the Party were required to go through political education classes. So that a lot of people who were purged have been admitted back into the Party, but a lot of them were purged for a cause and it will be a long time—if ever—before they will be readmitted.

QUESTION: What do you plan for yourself for the future: What kind of political work do you want to do?

ELDRIDGE: I think there's a lot I can do making contacts for the Party on the international situation, I have a book that I want to finish, but really, I must return to the United States, that's what I want to do. That's really what I'm working on, getting that ready.

QUESTION: Now that the NLF has almost won the Vietnam war and entered this new stage of fighting imperialism, does this change anything?

ELDRIDGE: I think it will be very positive, if you think back you will remember that the whole approach of U.S. imperialism at the time was that the liberation forces in Vietnam had to be defeated, or else other people will get the idea that they can fight for their freedom too. And I think that this has proven that a tenacious fight in the end will be victorious. This is now happening. The United States will, I think, force people to fight just as hard for their liberation; on the whole I think this will strengthen the determination of people to fight on to victory.

QUESTION: Do you think that the persecution of the Black Panther Party now in the United States demands that you create a new kind of tactic to deal with that?

ELDRIDGE: Those things they've been doing have been frame-ups, and a lot of people think we are not serious when we say that, but what they do and what they have been doing is sending in a few provacateurs who will indulge people in conversations about blowing up bridges, or blowing up supermarkets. And on the basis of a few frivolous words that have been passed, they blow it up into a full scale conspiracy and arrest all these people and put ransom on them as opposed to bail, drain our finances; they know what they're doing and this is the technique they use in the United States to keep the Party on the defensive.

I made the decision that I was not going to submit to this type of chicanery and go to jail when it's very clear that they are manipulating the situation. And I think this is something we are all going to have to get into, because we cannot come up with $200,000 bail. When you think of 21 people in New York, 16 people in Chicago, it adds up to a king's ransom, and we don't have that kind of money, we have no process for getting that kind of money, so I think the people who are dedicated to functioning in a revolutionary manner will start adopting the attitude that they will not be arrested. And they ought to be ready at all times to defend themselves, so that when the man comes down on them and tries to arrest them, these cats are going to start dealing with it right on the spot, because that's more desirable than laying up in a penitentiary rotting away.

QUESTION: And is the United Front Against Fascism part of this tactic to create solidarity?

ELDRIDGE: It's a very important move in that regard, but there's another front that I think needs to be created, and this is something that I have been working on and which I intend to continue working on, and it's something we've been calling the North American Liberation Front. I think it's very timely, because many people see the situation that we are confronted with as one in which politics have been transformed into war, and there's no point in kidding ourselves anymore; what we have to do is fight. We have the terrain there to fight. Many people think that armed struggle carried out in the mountains in Cuba or in Vietnam is one thing, and that it could not happen in the United States. But the United States has more mountains than all of these other areas, it has the advantage of mountainous areas, and a highly organized situation, and it has rural areas. It's so large that the government forces would be forced to spread out very thinly, at the same time that dissatisfaction in the ranks of the United States Army is at an all-time peak. The stockades and military prisons are overflowing with people who have deserted and don't want to fight in Vietnam. And I think that the contradictions that have arisen within the ranks of the United States Army will continue to increase, more so when they are finally turned against the American people.

—*The Black Panther*, October 11, 1969

# The Fascists Have Already Decided in Advance to Murder Chairman Bobby Seale in the Electric Chair: A Manifesto

CONCERNING: The pre-planned political murder of Bobby Seale, Chairman of the Black Panther Party, in the electric chair in the state of Connecticut.

The Primary Task of the American Revolution, at this point in our history, is to defeat the Number One maneuver of the fascist power structure, which is to make an example of Bobby Seale by putting him to death in the Electric Chair in the state of Connecticut.

The fascists have already decided in advance to murder Chairman

Bobby Seale in their all-out effort to destroy the leadership of the Black Panther Party and to intimidate our membership in particular and all other progressive people and organizations. This should be crystal clear even to a blind man. The vicious political persecution of Chairman Bobby Seale ranges in time over a four year period—from the very beginning of the Black Panther Party—and, geographically, it follows a twisted trail of trumped-up charges from Oakland, Sacramento, Berkeley, San Francisco, Chicago, and now to Connecticut. The plot against Bobby Seale in particular is so outrageously obvious that even these shameless pigs should not have the gall to try to pull it off.

But the fact that they are going full speed ahead with their disgraceful conspiracy should make it clear to the American people, once and for all, that a desperate hour is upon us and we have no time to lose if we are to salvage the situation. Because one thing must be made absolutely clear to America: no matter what the White people of America are prepared to accept, Black people do not accept this ultimate attempt to bind and gag Bobby Seale with death because of the fearless leadership that he has given to our people.

Black people will never accept this premeditated decision of the fascist power structure to murder Chairman Bobby Seale in the Electric Chair. So that the question is now posed, pure and simple: Is America going to have a Class War or a Race War? The fascists have already declared war upon the people. Will the people as a whole rise up to meet this challenge with a righteous People's War against these fascist pigs, or will Black people have to go it alone, thus transforming a dream of interracial solidarity into the nightmare of a Race War?

Our brothers are being murdered in their sleep by the shock troopers of the power structure; our offices are being subjected to all-out military attack; our lawyers are being sentenced to prison along with us; and the fascist Nixon Administration has unleashed the political police of the F.B.I. and thrown away all pretenses of justice and equality under the law. Lip-service to the Constitution of the United States of America has been replaced by outright fascist terror and naked repression. Hundreds of our Party members have been jacked-up on highly political charges. Scores of our party members languish in jails and prisons, subjected to scandalously high bails that are tantamount to RANSOM. Throughout the length and breadth of this depraved land, the situation is the same. It is nothing but an attempt to sabotage the 400 year struggle of our people for freedom and liberation.

Our Minister of Defense, Huey P. Newton, teaches us that in order to have security from the unceasing aggressions of the enemy, we must always be in a position to inflict a political consequence upon the aggressor for each act of aggression. This attempt to murder Chairman Bobby Seale coldbloodedly in the Electric Chair is an open provocation and the ultimate aggression against Black people. It is a calculated step taken by fascist pigs in the unfolding of their vicious blueprint of genocide against Black people. We, Black people, if we are forced to go it alone, must be prepared to unleash the ultimate political consequence upon this racist nation. The ultimate political consequence which Black people have in their power to unleash is RACE WAR. Indeed, we have been and at this very moment are the victims of a systematic racist repression. The Black Panther Party, as everyone knows, has taken a leading role in trying to avoid precisely this disastrous RACE WAR which the fascist oppressors have been working day and night to bring about. But we cannot and will not continue this policy to the point of racial suicide. We will not sacrifice Chairman Bobby Seale on the altar of interracial harmony if White people continue to sit back and allow this ghastly plot to go forward. So if the so-called freedom loving White people of America do not stand up now, while there are still a few moments of time left, and put an end to the persecution of Chairman Bobby Seale, then Black people will have to go it alone and step forward alone. This will mean the end of our dreams for the Class War which America needs and the beginning of the Race War which America cannot endure. This is the political consequence which America faces because of this unspeakably evil attempt to murder Chairman Bobby Seale in the Electric Chair.

Eldridge Cleaver
Minister of Information
Black Panther Party

—Manifesto issued April, 1970, by the Black Panther Party

# 6.

# DAVID HILLIARD SPEAKS

David Hilliard, Chief of Staff of the Black Panther Party, is one of the early members of the Party and has conducted widespread political education for the organization. Here are several of his speeches and an interview. The latter arose out of a remark made by Hilliard during a speech on November 15, 1969, at San Francisco for which he was indicted by a Federal Grand Jury.

# The Ideology of the Black Panther Party

The ideology of the Black Panther Party is the historical experiences of Black people in America translated through Marxism-Leninism. When we review the past history of Black people in this country, we realize that after 400 years we are victims of the oppressive machinery that gags, binds and chains Black men who speak out in defense of their alleged constitutional rights.

Many people act as if they were surprised at what's happening to the Chairman of the Black Panther Party, Bobby Seale, but I think a careful examination of who our persecutors are will clear the minds of the masses of people that could not see through the so-called judicial smokescreen of justice. These people that tortured and gagged and chained Bobby are the descendants of pirates. Genocidal murderers of the Red Man; users of the atomic bomb upon the Japanese people. The enslavers and exploiters of Blacks in this country right up until this very day.

The Black Panther Party since its inception has always used the weapon of example to educate the masses. When the Minister of Defense, Huey P. Newton, sent a delegation of armed Panthers to the California state Capitol this was a process of educating the people by example that Blacks did not have their rights guaranteed by the constitution to bear arms in defense of their lives against racist mobs of fascists in or out of uniform. So that Huey P. Newton made the statement "an unarmed people are either enslaved or subjected to slavery at any given time." So given Bobby's situation it is crystal clear what he meant.

I think we should get back to the legality of the U.S. constitution in respect to Black people. The rhetoric of the constitution was never in the first paragraph meant for people of African descent. After violating Bobby's 1st amendment rights, his 8th amendment rights on through the 6–13–14 amendments it seems to me the whole damn thing is invalid in regards to Blacks in particular.

As long as we are hung up in theory alone, without ever testing for ourselves the reality of the laws of the courts of this system, we must expect more Bobby Seales, more cruel and inhumane treatment. We must remember this country is run by a slave oligarchy and brigandish criminals who have no respect for its people, be they Black or White; its primary interest is capitalism. So when we talk about the ideology of the Black Panther Party we are talking about the experiences of Blacks in racist, fascist America.

It is sometimes hard to understand how people react to the term fascist. They think the fascists left when the Hitlerites were defeated. I relate to what Eldridge says, "that the American flag and the American eagle are the true symbols of fascism." The American historian has a way of justifying this system by using Germany as the most vicious enemy against mankind, this is perhaps true for the people of Jewish descent. But when we really check this shit out, starting with the genocide of the Indians, the 50,000,000 Black people slaughtered by the oppressors when taken against their will at the point of guns, over 400 years ago, right here in America. Then reminding ourselves of the genocidal and imperialist war against the Vietnamese people, the burning of Blacks on the sacred cross of Christianity. Then it becomes easier to relate to the chieftains of fascism, imperialism, racism; and Bobby Seale's demand for his right to self defense.

How criminal and guilty these people must be to go to the last rung on the ladder of injustice, in the gross violaton of the Chairman of the Black Panther Party's human rights; at a time when the entire oppressed peoples of the world are raising up in arms against them. So for the American people we outline your first political education class. The criminal hall of pig justice, the courts where Black men are railroaded from California to Chicago, because these pigs that judge other men and women; particularly Black men and women, are the guilty ones.

The laws that they try to make us respect are oppressive laws, slave laws, laws that protect them and persecute us. I think that above and beyond the old evil, crooked judge and gag, Bobby left a scar on the minds of all those who relate to words without asking questions.

So we say Right On Chairman Bobby, for you have without making a sound exposed the ugly, fascist racist, farce of American Patriotism starring Judge J. J. Hoffman the people's enemy number 1?

Remind that old racist motherfucker Hoffman, to tell the pigs at Chicago O'Hare airport to put back up the sign that says, "what you are, speak so loud I hardly hear anything you are saying."

Chief of Staff,
David Hilliard

—*The Black Panther*, November 8, 1969

# Black Student Unions

### Speech delivered at San Francisco State College

The first thing that struck my mind was the composition of the leaflets. I couldn't even get past the first line, I didn't know what the word tenure meant. So I had to go in my little briefcase and try and figure out what the problem was on the campus. So after learning the definition of tenure, I got a little enlightened on what the problem is that the teachers are having here on the campus.

I think the one thing we have to hold clear in our minds is that the campus only occupies the teachers and the students 7 or 8 hours a day; and after that they're back into the community. So that it's impossible to talk about waging any type of struggle, if the community is not a part of that struggle. So if we have problems, we have to bring the community into the campus. We have to stop isolating ourselves from the community. Because the very people on the campus live in the community. And they come from the community; so therefore, the universities are also a part of the community. So we have to relate to Eldridge's article, "Education and Revolution." He outlined it very clear how we have to move, what we have to do. He's made it clear that the Board of Regents, the Board of Trustees, the Administrators whoever the people are in power, that they are designated as enemies. Because these people are members of military regimes, they're politicians, they're very powerful people outside of the community.

When I look around on San Francisco State College campus for the revolutionaries last year that so gallantly, so bravely, and courageously stood up for what they demanded in their Black studies program; it's not the same. It seems that they've taken a defeatist attitude. Well, I'm saying that perhaps out of the teachers we can make some revolutionaries on this campus. And we can put Hayakawa where he belongs,[7] and we can show the tactical squad that we're not terrorized by their violence. We're powerful because we out number them. And that there's nothing that they can do to stop our emancipation, there's nothing they can do to stop you from regaining your humanity. That's what our struggle is about, it's about revolution. It's not just about teachers holding their jobs. It's about teachers educating, and telling the truth on a very oppressive and corrupt system.

The leader of the Korean people Kim Il Sung, has said that, "reactionary ideas of the imperialist, are the main tools used to produce ideological degeneration in people and make them politically deformed." So that it's the duty of the teachers to teach revolution:

it's the duty of the teachers to join the revolution. Because they're not teachers if they're not teaching something relevant to the community. And we don't make any distinction between members of the A.F.T.,[8] White people and the Black students on our campuses. We don't make any distinctions between the White students on our campuses and the B.S.U. As a matter of fact, we want to expand the B.S.U., so that we can usurp all the revolutionary individuals, all the organizations; and put together a more formidable force, so that we can withstand the repression that's being meted out against us. That's the only way that we're going to make the American revolution.

The Black Panther Party is not going to support any B.S.U. policy that asks for an autonomous Black studies program that excludes other individuals. Because we recognize that our repression is being meted out by a very vicious government. A government that doesn't make any distinctions between revolutionaries. And as Eldridge has said, the only reason that the Black Panther Party is suffering the brunt of repression with such a magnitude is because our resistance requires that kind of repression, and that the same repression will be meted out to you, if you take the same position.

So we're not going to be duped into aligning ourselves with cowards, with renegades from the revolution. We're here to make the revolution, we're aware that we're revolutionaries; and we want you to be revolutionaries. And that you must be revolutionaries if you want peace in this country. You must be revolutionaries if you want to maintain the so-called democracy that you so often speak about, if you want to have freedom of speech. Because the only people that enjoy freedom of speech seems to be deaf mutes, those that have nothing to say, those who are afraid to say anything.

So recognizing that, the teachers have to get into the community; they have to wage campaigns. They have to organize, and they have to bring those people from the community on the campuses; whether the pigs like that or not. Because the pigs don't own these institutions. These institutions are here for the people, and it's the people that are going to put these pigs in their rightful places. They need to be institutionalized, they need to be in prison, they need to be done away with. And that's the kind of language that you have to get used to using. You have to get used to speaking in that idiom, because that's the language of revolutionaries.

You have to keep a very watchful eye on the people that stand up and use super revolutionary slogans; but you can always catch them in various devious places. Watch these people. Judge these people by their actions and not by their words. Because the whole revolution has been infiltrated; it's been infiltrated culturally, and it's been infiltrated ideologically. So we have to be able to make distinctions between people who are really dedicated to our cause and people who are just opportunistically getting on the band wagon because it's a popular trend. These are the things you have to think about. We're either going to be revolutionaries or we're going to be the children of fascists.

We know how to judge our friends from our enemies. We're not confused. We're not so confused that we cannot point out on the one hand the left capitulationist, and on the right the modern revisionist, they're very easily distinguishable. These are the people that advocate revolution from the high tower top and when the repression comes down you can't find them. We know who these people are so I don't have to call their names.

But I think that it would be proper to put an organization together on this campus that represents White people, that represents the oppressed Latin American people, that represents the Black People, that represents the Red man, that represents all the oppressed people in this country. Until we do that, then the oppressor will be victorious. The oppressor will gain all the victories, and we'll just be stagnant, arguing and debating about jobs. There's not going to be any jobs, there's not going to be any employment, there's not going to be any peace until there's peace for everybody. We're going to have to work in a concerned effort to get that, (applause). We have to work with the people, we have to work with students, students with teachers. And when we set up committees to voice our grievances, let the students have the power. Let the students make the decisions, and not fall victims to a committee of tin pot bourgeois thinking individuals. Our power lies in the masses. Our power lies in the oppressed people that's out there, that's making conditions comfortable enough for the teachers to be able to have these universities, so that they can espouse revolutionary ideas.

So when we have our Central Committees, let our Central Committees be an organ governed by the will of not only the Black students on this campus, but for the Latin Americans, and all other oppressed peoples, and all other progressive people on this campus. Let's have an organization that we call the Afro-American, Asian, Latin Alliance. Motherfuck the B.S.U., because the B.S.U. is too narrow. We recognize nationalism, because we know that our struggle is one of national salvation. But this doesn't hinder our struggle, to make alliances with other people that's moving in a common direction, but rather it strengthens our struggle. Because it gives us more energy, it gives us a more powerful force to move and to withstand the repression that's being meted out against us. And when we have racists on our campuses, that advocate those kind of splits, then let's isolate those people by setting up a tricontinental organization on the campuses. Let's designate these people as being enemies, because they're ultra-nationalists, because they're racists. And they cannot say that they're revolutionaries, because if they were revolutionaries they would recognize the need for putting together an organization that represented all ethnic categories of people. And they would recognize that the ruling class is only one composite of oppression. That oppression is manifested in those that control the level of power in this country.

So those are the things that we have to talk about when we have meetings. Those are the kind of decisions that the members of the A.F.T. have to talk about. The A.F.T. are intelligent people, so perhaps sometimes the organizations on the campuses that are not very politically mature, not just book worshipers; I mean people that have engaged in struggle, people that have suffered the brunt of the oppressor. Sometimes these people are hung up too much in their own national identity, to recognize that we're here to create a revolution that benefits all of the people, and not just some of the people. So it is our duty to wage arduous struggle against these people. There can never be any antagonistic contradictions between revolutionaries. We don't make any distinction between other fraternal organizations and other fraternal parties. Those are ideological differences, and we can solve those differences if we want to. But if we choose to take a racist stand, and allow the administrators, Hayakawa, the predecessor of Sato, to allow this man, this imperialist, this fascist, to maintain control of all the people on this campus; then I say that you deserve that. Because we can put Hayakawa into flight anytime we get ready. We can run Hayakawa not only off this campus, but we can run him back to imperialistic Japan. Because the man ain't got no motherfucking power. He's a bootlicker, for a Mafioso named Alioto[9] and we recognize that, and we should make him know that (applause).

That's what we have to do. We have to talk about organizing on our campuses, not aside from our community, but our campuses should reflect the community. Because the things that take place on the campus, are the very same things that you're faced with in the community; and that's racism. So we have to get rid of that. Because these imperialists, these fascists they use racism as a bridge to delay our emancipation; to cause acts of racism, to cause the disruptions between the young White progressives and the Black revolutionaries. But it's our duty to set the record straight, and it's our duty to weed out all the opportunists and all the revisionists and take a revolutionary stand.

ALL POWER TO THE PEOPLE
David Hilliard
Chief of Staff
Black Panther Party

—*The Black Panther*, December 27, 1969

# If You Want Peace You Got to Fight for It

**Speech delivered at San Francisco Moratorium Demonstration, November 15, 1969**

There's too many American flags out here, and our Minister of Information, Eldridge Cleaver, says that the American flag and the American eagle are the true symbols of fascism. ALL POWER TO THE PEOPLE. Black power to Black people, Brown power to Brown people, Red power to Red people, and Yellow power to Ho Chi Minh, and Comrade Kim Il Sung the courageous leader of the 40,000,000 Korean people.

The Black Panther Party takes the position that we want all Black men exempt from military service and that we believe that Black people should not be forced to fight in the military to defend a racist government that does not protect us. We will not fight and kill other people of color in the world, who like Black people are vicitims of US imperialism on an international level, and fascism domestically. So recognizing that, recognizing fascism, recognizing the occupation of all the pigs in the Black community, then it becomes evident that there's a war at home, there's a war of genocide being waged against Black people right here in America.

So then, we would like to ask the American people do they want peace in Vietnam. Well, do you? (audience) "Yes." Do you want peace in the Black communities? (audience) "Yes." Well you goddamned sure can't get it with no guitars, you sure can't get it demonstrating. The only way that you're going to get peace in Vietnam is to withdraw the oppressive forces from the Black communities right here in Babylon. So that we have a suggestion for that, we have a proposal, we have a message for that. We have a petition that we're circulating on a national level to control the pigs in the Black community; and we know that those pigs are not going to move of their own volition. We know that those pigs are not going to stop murdering Black people in the Black community. We also recognize that White people are oppressed in the White community so that our petition is applicable in their community.

But we have to make some very clear distinctions in terms of minor danger and major danger. We say that the major danger is right here in America because the Black community is occupied territory and the pigs of the power structure are killing Black people with the same lack of compunction, the same outrage and hatred that they killed the courageous people of Vietnam. So that we're not going to let you get around that. We're not going to let you talk about waging a struggle in support of people 10,000 miles from here, when you have problems right here in fascist America. We recognize that a whole lot of people get uptight and they think that the Black Panther Party is just making up shit, that they're distorting history when we say that this country is fascist. But I think just a little reexamination of your history will show to you that the American people, that the history of this country promulgates and it sets a precedence for any fascism that has ever taken place on the stage of world history.

Adolf Hitler was a fascist. The man was an animal. The man was a monster. He was a jingoist, a warmongerer. But Adolf Hitler did not create fascism. Adolf Hitler did not create the Black Legion.[10] Black people were enslaved and killed in the millions before Hitler even came on the scene. The Red man was exterminated in this country and Hitler don't take responsibility for that. So that this country has a blood stained history. This country is a country that was built on war, it was built on the ruins it was built on the sweat and blood of its Black people. So that the history of the Black Panther Party, the ideology of the Black Panther Party is nothing more than the historical experiences of Black people in this country translated by way of Marxism-Leninism. Because we recognize that Marxism-Leninism is not a philosophy for Russians, it is not a philosophy for Chinese but it's a philosophy for any people that's moving against an oppressive power structure such as the capitalistic fascist system of the American society. And we have adopted that. And that we're putting it into practice because it is proven beyond a doubt that it's truly in the service of the proletariat.

We would just like to ask the American people, we would like to ask all the mothers in the audience, all the wives who have husbands that are prisoners of war, that have been lost in action, do you want your sons home? Do you want your sons home? (audience) "Yes." Well we have a proposal for that. Our Minister of Information, Eldridge Cleaver is in Algeria. He spent two months in Korea, at the Pyongyang Journalist Conference, and there he spoke with members of the National Liberation Front of Vietnam. So that we propose to the mothers whose sons are political prisoners of war or wives whose husbands are lost in action. That they submit to the Black Panther Party their name, rank and serial number and we will turn this over to the Minister of Information of the Black Panther Party, and we will begin to negotiate for freedom for Huey P. Newton and Bobby Seale, because they're political prisoners of US fascism. That's the way that we want to help people. So that if you can relate to that then we can relate to the American people. If you can't relate to

freedom for our Chairman Bobby Seale and our Minister of Defense
Huey P. Newton then we say that we can't relate to the American
people.

We say down with the American fascist society. Later for Richard
Milhous Nixon,. the motherfucker. Later for all the pigs of the
power structure. Later for all the people out here that don't want to
hear me curse because that's all that I know how to do. That's all
that I'm going to do. I'm not going to ever stop cursing, not only
are we going to curse, we're going to put into practice some of the
shit that we talk about. Because Richard Nixon is an evil man. This
is the motherfucker that unleashed the counter-insurgent teams upon
the BPP. This is the man that's responsible for all the attacks on
the Black Panther Party nationally. This is the man that sends
his vicious murderous dogs out into the Black community and in-
vade upon our Black Panther Party Breakfast Programs. Destroy
food that we have for hungry kids and expect us to accept shit like
that idly. Fuck that motherfucking man. We will kill Richard
Nixon. We will kill any motherfucker that stands in the way of our
freedom. We ain't here for no goddamned peace, because we know
that we can't have no peace because this country was built on war.
And if you want peace you got to fight for it.

ALL POWER TO THE PEOPLE

—*The Black Panther*, November 19, 1969

## Interview with CBS News, December 28, 1969

REPORTERS:
George Herman, CBS News
Bernard Nossiter, Washington Post
Ike Pappas, CBS News

MR. HERMAN: Mr. Hilliard, the clashes between the Black Panther
leaders and the police are now the subject of at least three investi-
gations, one by the Justice Department, one by a group of Black
Congressmen, and one by a group headed by former Supreme
Court Justice Arthur Goldberg and former Attorney General Ramsey
Clark. What do you hope for from any or all of these investigations?

MR. HILLIARD: We hope that these investigations will serve as a
convincing indictment against the oppressive United States govern-

ment and its killer police. The Black Panther Party has all along said that the police were the main forces of oppression in our communities and also we have made a trip to New York City to the UN last year to apply for NGO status. So it has become very clear that the government is working in cohorts with the local agencies, the police, in a brutal attempt to try to liquidate the Black Panther Party. So out of that investigation we hope to bring the truth to the American people so that we can have peace in our communities.

MR. HERMAN: Mr. Hilliard, all three of these investigations are being conducted by people either in or very close to the establishment, the Justice Department, former officials of the federal government, present members of Congress. Do you really think that one of these investigations will find what you claim, oppression by the government against the Black Panthers?

MR. HILLIARD: I think that already the Black Congressmen, headed by Congressman Diggs, have shown concern for their own national salvation. Of course, we do not have faith in the Justice Department, because the Justice Department is the symbol of injustice as far as its Black subjects are concerned. We refer to Goldberg as a fox that watches over the chickens. So we do not expect any equality. We do not expect justice from the other individuals. But we do have faith in our own people and the very fact that they have come forth to try to bring out the criminal indictments against the police and the other agencies of the United States government shows, if nothing else, that there is solidarity with the Black people. So we see that as being victorious.

MR. NOSSITER: Mr. Hilliard, you speak of criminal activities of police. But don't the Panthers stock and collect guns themselves? Isn't this an invitation to the police to take action?

MR. HILLIARD: First of all, the Panthers do not stock guns. We are very aware of the gun laws. We advocate each individual having a shotgun in their homes, as spelled out under the Constitution of the United States. It is not our purpose to assemble large caches of weapons. If we have weapons, we would distribute the weapons in the community for self-defense, but we do not have armories. And, even if we did, we would expect the same treatment under the law that is given to members of the Ku Klux Klan, people like the Thorensons or the Birchites.

MR. PAPPAS: Mr. Hilliard, the Justice Department denies what you say, that there is an organized attempt to destroy the Black Panthers. But, if what you say is true, how successful has it been, has this campaign been against you?

MR. HILLIARD: I don't think that we can say it was successful. What it has done is it brought to the attention of the American people the atrociousness of the American government in terms of its subjects, people moving for their freedom. The very fact that they attack us so openly shows that they are very brutal people, that they are a barbarous, criminal element within society. But, as far as their successfulness is concerned, they are not successful. They can never exterminate the Black Panther Party because the Black Panther Party is not just a party for itself but, rather, it is a party for the people, and its ideas—

Mr. Pappas: Well, most of your leadership has been either jailed or is in exile, or some of them are dead. There is a leadership gap, obviously, in your organization. It seems to me that if there is a campaign against you, it has been successful to a certain point.

Mr. Hilliard: Most people would like to think that, especially the enemy, but we're satisfied that they can never exterminate the Black Panther Party. In order to do that, they would have to commit genocide because what we are working for is already spelled out within the constitution of the United States. We are asking for the basic necessities for human life so, therefore, it would be impossible for them to exterminate or really have a successful extermination campaign against our Party. Our Party is manifested in the people.

Mr. Herman: Mr. Hilliard, you say that what you are after is manifested in the constitution and yet you personally have said that you advocate the very direct forceful overthrow of the government. You are under indictment, as I understand it, for advocating the assassination of President Nixon. That doesn't sound to me like it is all within the constitution.

Mr. Hilliard: What is within the constitution is our right to free speech.

Mr. Herman: Yes.

Mr. Hilliard: And as far as my threatening the president, this is a violation of my First Amendment right. I did not threaten the life of the president. In the context of a speech that I made, I stated very emphatically that we would kill anyone that stands in the way of our freedom and, of course, the newsmen and the news media is another instrument by which the government dupes and hypnotizes the people. So the very fact that the newsmen themselves are ideological lackeys for the system, they have mouthwashed the criminal elements in the society and they have made the victims look like the criminals and the criminal look like the victim. I never said we would assassinate the president.

Mr. Herman: Do you feel that Richard Nixon is standing in the way of your freedom?

Mr. Hilliard: I think that anybody that picks up guns against the oppressed people or anybody that endorses programs that maintain the oppressive structure as it is, is in the way of our freedom.

Mr. Herman: Is that Richard Nixon?

Mr. Hilliard: Richard Nixon is the chief spokesman of the American people and, if the man is not responsible for the people in government, like the FBI agencies or the local police, then he should stand up and let the American people know that he does not endorse the kind of campaigns that have been waged against the Black Panther Party.

Mr. Nossiter: Let us get this point clear. Are you saying that you were incorrectly quoted when you were quoted as saying "we should kill president Nixon?"

Mr. Hilliard: I am saying that my whole speech was taken out of context, and this is nothing new. I think that the policy that the United States has adopted is the same policy put forth by Adolf Hitler, the big lie policy. And the big lie policy is to take things out of context.

Mr. Nossiter: Well, whether this statement was taken out of context or not, was it a statement that you made, Mr. Hilliard?

Mr. Hilliard: It was a statement that I made in the framework of a lot of other words.

Mr. Nossiter: Right.

Mr. Hilliard: So that the rhetoric as stated was joined with some other words, but I did not specifically say that we want to assassinate the president of the United States. We are not that stupid.

Mr. Pappas: I don't want to belabor this point, but I was in San Francisco. I was at the Moratorium Day ceremonies and I heard you make the speech and, within the context of what you said, I believe it went "We will kill Richard Nixon. We will kill anyone, any blankety-blank who stands in the way of our freedom." And it is a very simple question: Do you think Richard Nixon is standing in the way of your freedom? Number two, would you kill him?

Mr. Hilliard: I would say this: I would say that Richard Nixon is the chief spokesman for the American people. He is the highest official in this land. If Richard Nixon stands in opposition to freedom guaranteed to us under the alleged constitution, then the man is designated as enemy. But I did not and I will not here designate—I will not take the responsibility of saying assassinate anybody.

Mr. Nossiter: Well, what you are suggesting, Mr. Hilliard, is that this was a metaphor, a figure of speech out in San Francisco.

Mr. Hilliard: I am saying that it was political rhetoric. We can call it metaphor. It is the language of the ghetto. This is the way we relate. Even the profanity, the profanity is within the idiom of the oppressed people. So in the context of that speech I said that and I am not going to take that back.

Mr. Nossiter: Okay. Then let me ask you this: Is your revolutionary—are your revolutionary slogans, are these too metaphors? Is this also rhetoric or do Panthers literally believe that a violent over-throw of the government must take place in this country?

MR. HILLIARD: Let's just say this: Let's say that we could have our freedom without a shot being fired, but we know that the imperial-ists, that the fascists on a very local level would not withdraw from the arena without violence. They have proven themselves very violent and thus far they haven't done anything to insure us our freedom. We do not ask for violence. We were in the forefront of peaceful demonstrations for peace abroad, while right here at home we are being victims of attacks day and night by the criminal agencies manifested in the police departments. So we do not advocate vio-lence. Our slogan is that we want an abolition to war, but we do understand that in order to get rid of the gun it will be necessary to take up the gun.

MR. NOSSITER: You say that you don't favor violence, and I gather that what you are suggesting is that you only use in your view your weapons for defensive purposes. Is that correct?

MR. HILLIARD: That's right. We have—

MR. NOSSITER: All right. If this is so, then why does your party newspaper—and I see you have a copy of one in front of you—use as a repeated slogan, "kill the pigs"? Doesn't this suggest to an unwary reader, who isn't aware when you are being literal and when you are using metaphor, that indeed it is their duty to go out and kill police?

MR. HILLIARD: There is nothing in this paper that says kill the pigs. We only advocate killing those that kill us. And if we designate our enemy as pigs, then I think that it would be justified to kill. You see, what you people do is you turn the terminology around. What you try to do is you try to make us all violent and you people all civilized and peaceful, but what we understand is that it is all right to use violence if you are using violence for a change, a change for the better. So we make a distinction between the reactionary violence manifested in this system, the main oppressor of all men and in violence used in behalf of the oppressed people to throw off the shackles of colonialism and oppression. So that violence on our part would be justified.

MR. HERMAN: But, without trying to put my own interpreta-tion on it, let me ask you your interpretation of this quote, which I find in a newspaper attributed to you. I don't know whether it is correct or not, but let me read it to you and you can say. "We advo-cate the very direct overthrow of the government by way of force and violence by picking up guns and moving against it, because we recognize it as being oppressive and, in recognizing that, we know that the only solution to it is armed struggle."

MR. HILLIARD: Let's say this, let's quote from your very same

Constitution, where you say that: ". . . when a long train of abuses and usurpations, pursuing invariably the same object, evinces a design to reduce them under absolute despotism, it is their right, it is their duty, to throw off such government, and to provide new guards for their future security." Now this is from the Declaration of Independence.

MR. HERMAN: Are you saying that time has now come?

MR. HILLIARD: And if it is good for the American people, then we say it is good for the oppressed people of the world.

MR. HERMAN: Are you saying that the time has come when the masses of people have been pushed to the wall, when they cannot any longer redress their grievances through the legal political machinery of this country.

MR. HILLIARD: We are not the decision-makers, the masses are. If the masses think it is time to overthrow this system, then there is nothing you or the President or anyone else can do.

We have about thirty chapters throughout the United States.

MR. HERMAN: That would be what, 5,000 or 10,000 people?

MR. HILLIARD: It may be. It may be more than that.

MR. HERMAN: Do you have the feeling that this small group 5,000 or 10,000, really represent the masses of the Black people?

MR. HILLIARD: I am saying that the ideas spelled out in our ten-point program and platform represent the basic desires and needs of the people.

MR. HERMAN: How do you know?

MR. HILLIARD: Because these are ideas taken from the masses. These are not just a bunch of abstract ideas that fell from the sky and ended up on our paper. This is a survey, what we asked for, things that were promised to us over 400 years ago.

MR. HERMAN: But aren't some of these things that you have down on the paper in your demands and so forth, aren't some of them paraphrases of Mao Tse-tung and Che Guevara, rather than the Black masses?

MR. HILLIARD: There is nothing here that paraphrases per se Mao Tse-tung or Che Guevara, but the ideas, the desires asked for, the aspirations in our program are the same that all of the oppressed people in the world ask for, and that is freedom of self-determination. The ultimacy is national salvation.

MR. NOSSITER: Mr. Hilliard, is your back really to the wall? Here you are on national television. Here are all kinds of moderate Black groups that have come to take up your cause, at least on the legal side. Doesn't this indicate that perhaps the society is much more responsive and much more open to legitimate demands than your rhetoric sometimes suggests?

MR. HILLIARD: I don't think that television is the big payoff. We could ask for a lot of other things. More so than television, I would rather be in our communities feeding hungry children, setting up, trying to erect institutions that would educate the people, the children in our communities so that they would not have to wage war in your name, or his, or this man's.

MR. PAPPAS: Mr. Hilliard, there are twenty million Black people in this country and, if you say you have maybe five thousand or even ten thousand members, that still is not twenty million. How are you going to get them, the rest of the Black people, over to your side? We understand that you are having difficulty getting people to join with you in your philosophy.

MR. HILLIARD: Well, first of all, I never quoted you any figure. I told you that we had about thirty chapters. But our program is the method for our organizing people. We are organizing them around our ten-point program, a program that spells out the basic desires and needs of all people. And the very fact that the Black Panther Party is a party that relates to internationalism as the key to eradicating racism in this country shows that we are much stronger than even you imagine.

—*The Black Panther*, January 10, 1970

# 7.

# FRED HAMPTON SPEAKS

On April 27, 1969, Fred Hampton, chairman of the Illinois Black Panther Party, delivered the following speech. On December 4, 1969, Hampton was dead in bed, murdered in a police raid on an apartment at 2337 W. Monroe Street in Chicago. (Mark Clark, Panther member from Peoria, Illinois, was also killed; four other Panthers were critically wounded, and three were arrested unharmed. One policeman was slightly wounded.) State's Attorney Edward V. Hanrahan held a press conference later that day, displaying what he said was the arms cache recovered from the apartment and saying that the police had fired only because they had been attacked by the Black Panthers. But it soon became clear that the police had massed a heavy concentration of machine-gun and shotgun fire at one living-room wall and into two bedrooms, and that there was little if any sign of return fire. In short, the murder of Fred Hampton was part of a pattern of constant arrests, repeated raids on Black Panther headquarters and assassination of the movement's leadership in order to destroy the Black Panther Party. A Federal Grand Jury investigating the murders reached the conclusion that the police charge that they had fired in self-defense was false, but no police officials were indicted.

Hampton's speech describes, as he put it, "what the Black Panther Party is about."

# You Can Murder a Liberator, but You Can't Murder Liberation

ALL POWER TO THE PEOPLE.
What we are basically going to be talking about today is what the pig is doing to the Panthers all around the country. We are going to have to talk about what we are going to have to do about the repression that they are putting on the Black Panther Party. We are not worried about getting off it—let's try to deal with it.

We got to talk first of all about the main man. The main man in the Black Panther Party, the main man in the struggle today—in the United States, in Chicago, in Cuba and anywhere else—the main man in the liberation struggle is our Minister of Defense, and yours too, Huey P. Newton. He's the main man because the head of the imperialist octopus lies right in this country and whoever is dealing with the head of the octopus in this country is the main man. He's in jail now. We must tell the world that Huey P. Newton was tried by the pigs and they found him guilty. He was tried by the people, who found him not guilty, and we say let him go, let him free, because we find him not guilty. This is our relentless demand. We will not let up one day, we will not give up the struggle to liberate our Minister of Defense, Huey P. Newton and we will continue to exert pressure on the power structure and constantly bombard them with the people's demand that Huey P. Newton be set free.

It was Huey P. Newton who taught us how the people learn. You learn by participation. When Huey P. Newton started out what did he do? He got a gun and he got Bobby and Bobby got a gun. They had a problem in the community because people was being run over—kids were being run over—at a certain intersection.[11] What did the people do? The people went down to the government to redress their grievances and the government told them to go to hell: "We are not going to put no stoplights down there UNTIL WE SEE FIT." What did Huey P. Newton do? Did he go out and tell the people about the laws and write letters and try to propagandize 'em all the time? NO! Some of that's good, but the masses of the people don't read—that's what I heard Huey say—they learn through observation and participation. Did he just say this? NO! So what did he do? He got him a shotgun, he got Bobby and he got him a hammer and went down to the corner. He gave Bobby the shotgun and told him if any pig motherfuckers come by blow his mother fuckin brains out. What did he do? He went to the corner and nailed up a stop sign. No more accidents, no more trouble. And then he went back—another situation like that. What'd the people do? They looked at it, they observed; they didn't get a chance to participate in it. Next time what'd they do? Same kind of problem came up. The PEOPLE got THEIR shotguns, got THEIR nine milimeters, got THEIR hammers. How'd they learn? They learned by observation and participation. They learned one thing. When there is a fire you gather round the fire. Huey got a shotgun and everybody gathered round him and Bobby. They saw what was going on and they had a chance to participate in it. As the vanguard leader he taught the people about the power structure; he led the people down the correct road of revolution. What are we doing?

### Breakfast for Children

Our Breakfast for Children program is feeding a lot of children and the people understand our Breakfast for Children program. We sayin' something like this—we saying that theory's cool, but theory with no practice ain't shit. You got to have both of them—the two go together. We have a theory about feeding kids free. What'd we do? We put it into practice. That's how people learn. A lot of people don't know how serious the thing is. They think the children we feed ain't really hungry. I don't know five year old kids that can act well, but I know that if they not hungry we sure got some actors. We got five year old actors that could take the academy award. Last week they had a whole week dedicated to the hungry in Chicago. Talking 'bout the starvation rate here that went up 15%. Over here where everybody should be eating. Why? Because of capitalism.

What are we doing? The Breakfast for Children program. We are running it in a socialistic manner. People came and took our program, saw it in a socialistic fashion not even knowing it was socialism. People are gonna take our program and tell us to go on to a higher level. They gonna take that program and work it in a socialistic manner. What'd the pig say? He say, "Nigger—you like communism?" "No sir, I'm scared of it." "You like socialism?" "No Sir, I'm scared of it." "You like the breakfast for children program?" "Yes sir, I'd die for it". Pig said, "Nigger, that program is a socialistic program." "I don't give a fuck if it's Communism. You put your hands on that program motherfucker and I'll blow your motherfucking brains out." And he knew it. We been educating him, not by reading matter, but through observation and participation. By letting him come in and work our program. Not theory and theory alone, but theory and practice. The two go together. We not only thought about the Marxist-Leninist theory—we put it into practice. This is what the Black Panther Party is about.

### Subversives

Some people talk a lot about communism, but the people can't understand and progress to the stage of communism right away or because of abstract arguments. They say you got to crawl before you can walk. And the Black Panther Party, as the vanguard party, thought that the Breakfast for Children Program was the best technique of crawling that any vanguard party could follow. And we got a whole lot of folks that's going to be walking. And then a whole lot of folks that's gonna be running. And when you got that, what you got? You got a whole lot of PIGS that's gonna be running. That's what our program's about.

The Black Panther Party is about the complete revolution. We not gonna go out there and half do a thing. And you can let the pigs know it. They come here and hide—they so uncomfortable they sitting on a taperecorder, they got their gun in their hair—they got to hide all this shit and they come here and do all this weird action. All they got to do is come up to 2350 West Madison any day of the week and anybody up there'll let them know, let the motherfucker know: Yes, we subversive. Yes, we subversive with the bullshit we are confronted with today. Just as subversive as anybody can be subversive. And we think them motherfuckers is the criminals. They the ones always hiding. We the ones up in front. We're out in the open, these motherfuckers should start wearing uniforms. They want to know if the Panthers are goin' underground—these motherfuckers IS underground. You can't find 'em. People calls the pigs but nobody knows where they at. They're out chasing us. They hiding—can't nobody even see 'em.

When people got a problem they come to the Black Panther Party for help and that's good. Because, like Mao says, we are supposed to be ridden by the people and Huey says we're going to be ridden down the path of social revolution and that's for the people. The people ought to know that the Black Panther Party is one thousand percent for the People. They write a lot of articles, you know, niggers'll run up to you in a minute—when I say niggers I mean white niggers and black niggers alike—niggers'll run up to you and talk that shit about, Man, I read in the Tribune today. Well you say, Man, fuck it right there. If you didn't read it in the BLACK PANTHER paper, in the MOVEMENT—then you ain't read shit.

### Mickey White

We in the Black Panther Party have another brother I want to take some time to rap about. This brother is constantly on our mind. This brother's name is Michael White—Mickey White. This brother is beautiful. He's being held now in jail for one hundred thousand dollars bail. Some of you who listen to the radio might have heard about brothers in the state chapter, our field secretary of Defense Captain, brother Nathaniel Junior and Brother Merrill Harvey being laid up on some phoney gun charge. We don't say the Panthers don't want guns, but we already got guns and we don't have to go and try and steal or connive to buy any guns from anybody. What they are trying to do is to squash out the Black Panther Party— they're trying to squash out the leadership. Trying to squash out Bobby Rush, the Deputy Minister of Defense. Trying to squash out Chaka and Che, the Deputy Minister of Education.

Mickey White was in that bullshit with Nathaniel Junior and Merrill Harvey. Last week when they went to court even the judge in court said, you all gonna get a fair trial whether you deserve it or not. These are the types of actions we are confronted with. Mickey White is in solitary confinement and doesn't get to come out of his cell for anything at any time. And he might be in that cell for the rest of his life. His bond is $100,000. That's $10,000 cash.

Mickey White is a proven revolutionary. He's not nobody we THINK is going to be a revolutionary. He's not nobody we trying to make a revolutionary. He's a proven revolutionary. All of you have to understand that Mickey White is a Panther in ideology, he's a Panther in word and he's a Panther in deed. He's a Panther that understands it's a class struggle—not a race question. You have to understand the pressures the Black Panther Party goes through saying this. You can see the pressures the Black Panther Party goes through by making a coalition with whites.

When the Black Panther Party stood up and said we not going to fight racism with racism US said "NO, we can't do that because it's a race question and if you make it a class question then the revolution might come sooner. We in US ain't prepared for no revolution because we think that power grows from the sleeve of a Dashiki." They are armed with rhetoric and rhetoric alone. And we found that when you're armed with rhetoric and rhetoric alone a lot of times you get yourself hurt. Eldridge Cleaver told them, even though you say you fight fire with fire best, we think you fight fire with water. You can do either one, but we choose to fight with water. He said, we're not going to fight racism with racism, we're going to fight racism with solidarity. Even though you think you ought to fight capitalism with black capitalism, we're going to fight capitalism with socialism.

We got a whole lot of people being busted and you don't even know about all these people. There's one here you definitely have to know about and that's our Deputy Minister of Defense—Bobby Rush. Our Deputy Minister Bobby Rush was busted on some bullshit with a gun thing. He's got three gun charges. He's been convicted of one with a six month lead. He's out on appeal now. I know a lot of you people say, well goddamn, you got a Mickey White defense fund, an Eldridge Cleaver defense fund, a Merrill Harvey defense fund, a Nathaniel Junior defense fund, a Huey Newton defense fund, a Fred Hampton, Jule, Che, and Chaka defense fund—and I just can't keep up with all these defense funds. But since we are the vanguard party we try to do things right, so we got one defense fund so you don't get mixed up on what name to send it to. We'll decide who it goes to. You can just send it to Political Defense Fund, 2350 West Madison. If you want to send something to Breakfast for Children, you can send it to 2350 West Madison also, and you can earmark that money to go to the Breakfast for Children program.

We got Mickey on our mind tonight—and everybody knows we got Huey P. Newton on our mind tonight. We got every political prisoner in jail on our mind tonight. Eldridge Cleaver—all of these people either dead, or in exile or in jail. A lot of people understanding this will lose real faith in the vanguard by not understanding what we're talking about.

A lot of these people will go up to you in a minute and say, "Why all these people being taken, why haven't they shot it out with some pigs." Well, what do we say? If you kill a few, you get a little satisfaction. But when you can kill them ALL you get complete satisfaction. That's why we haven't moved. We have to organize the people. We have to educate the people. We have to arm the people. We have to teach them about revolutionary political power. And when they understand all that we won't be killing no few and getting no little satisfaction, we'll be killing 'em all and getting complete satisfaction.

**Go with the People**

So what should we do if we're the vanguard? What is it right to do? Is it right for the leadership of that struggle to go faster than the followers of that struggle can go? NO! We're not going to be dealing in commandism, we're not going to be dealing in no tailism. We say that just as fast as the people can possibly go, that's just as fast as we can take it.

While we take it we must be sure that we are not missing the people in the valley. In the valley we know that we can learn to understand the life of the people. We know that with all the bullshit out there, you can come to consider yourself on the mountain top. I may even consider myself one day on the mountaintop. I may have already. But I know that in the valley there are people like Benny and there are people like me, people like Mickey White and people like Huey P. Newton and Bobby Seale. And that below the valley are people like Bobby Hutton, people like Eldridge Cleaver. We know that going into the valley is a dangerous thing. We know that when you go out to the valley you got to make a commitment.

A lot of people think the revolution is bullshit, but it's not. A lot of us think that when you get in the revolution you can talk your way out of things, but that's not true. Ask Bobby Hutton, ask Huey Newton, ask Eldridge Cleaver, Mickey White and Dennis Mora. Ask these people whether it's a game. If you get yourself involved in a revolutionary struggle then you've got to be serious. You got to know what you're doing. You got to already have practiced some type of theory. That's the reason we ask people to follow the leadership of the vanguard party. Because we all theorizing and we all practicing. We make mistakes, but we're always correcting them and we're always getting better.

We used to run around yellin 'bout Panther Power—the Panthers run it. We admit we made mistakes. Our ten point program is in the midst of being changed right now, because we used the word "white" when we should have used the word "capitalist". We're the first to admit our mistakes. We no longer say Panther Power because we don't believe the Panthers should have all the power. We are not for the dictatorship of the Panthers. We are not for the dictatorship of Black people. We are for the dictatorship of the people.

The difference between the people and the vanguard is very important. You got to understand that the people follow the vanguard. You got to understand that the Black Panther Party IS the vanguard. If you are about going to the people you got to understand that the vanguard leads the people. After the social revolution, the vanguard party, through our educational programs—and that program is overwhelming—the people are educated to the point that they can run things themselves. That's what you call educating the people, organizing the people, arming the people and bringing them revolutionary political power. That means people's power. That means the people's revolution. And if you're not about being involved in a people's revolution then you got to do something. You got to support the people's revolution.

**Complete Satisfaction**

The Black Panther Party is the vanguard party. You better get on the Black Panther Party. If you can't get on, goddamit you better get behind. If you can't get behind goddamit, you better get behind somebody else so you'll at least be able to follow indirectly, motherfucker. We ain't asking you to go out and ask no pig to leave us alone. We know that the pigs fuck with us cause they know we're doing something.

Cause a lot of dudes walk around and write articles about it. I know some revolutionary groups say these niggers are runnin around saying these things—the PL [12] motherfuckers talking that bullshit, couldn't even find things to criticize. They was so far in the ground. What was they doing? Organizing groundhogs, educating groundhogs, arming groundhogs and teaching groundhogs revolutionary political power.

I say that we're the first group to come above ground where the people can follow you and see you. And if you make a mistake it's better than not even being at all. When I made that mistake I made it for the people, and I correct it for the people. You don't hear there was a raid on PL's office last night. You ain't never heard that. When you hear of PL busted in New York, PL's leader in jail with no bars, PL leader run out of the country, PL leader shot 18 times while he was running with his back turned and hands tied up, PL leader gets breakfast for children for 1800 people a week. You ever hear it? Ya never heard it. I want to hear it. If you do hear it, it'll be because of the Black Panther lead. I'm not putting all these things out and saying PL doesn't know 'em. But I'm saying that when people write something like this, a lot of people don't understand it. And I wanted to take the time to explain it.

There are some things that PL says that are valid. Don't misunderstand me. We don't get mad because in some way or another PL is trying to better the Black Panther Party by trying to criticize it. But I just want to let you know, ain't nothing all right and ain't nothing all wrong. We're not all right—though we trying to get that way. We make mistakes but we understand that we gonna make some more mistakes. And we gonna try and correct these mistakes and we gonna try and keep on moving.

So what do we say? Don't get the pigs offa us cause we can stand em. We jail Mickey White, we should let em murder Bobby Hutton, we should let em run Eldridge Cleaver out of the country. Why? Because you can jail a revolutionary, but you can't jail the revolution. You can run a freedom fighter around the country but you can't run freedom fighting around the country. You can murder a liberator, but you can't murder liberation.

Kill a few and get a little satisfaction. Kill some more and you get some more satisfaction. Kill 'em all and you get complete satisfaction. We say All Power to the People—Black Power to Black People and Brown Power to Brown People, Red Power to Red People and Yellow Power to Yellow People. We say White Power to White People EVEN. And we say Panther Power to the vanguard Party and we say don't kill a few and don't kill some more. As a matter of fact we rather you didn't move until you see we ready to move, and when you see we ready to move you know we not dealing with a few, we not dealing with some more. You know that when we get ready to move we dealing from complete—that's what we're after—total, everything, everybody—complete satisfaction.

POWER TO THE PEOPLE

—*The Movement*, January, 1970

# 8.

## BLACK PANTHER WOMEN SPEAK

In February, 1970, Kathleen Cleaver, Communication Secretary of the Black Panther Party, living in exile in Algiers with her husband, Eldridge, was asked by a reporter from the Women's Page of the Washington *Post* what was a woman's role in the revolution. "No one ever asks what a man's place in the Revolution is," she replied in part. Very early in the history of the Black Panther Party, Huey Newton, Bobby Seale and others moved to eliminate male chauvinism in the Party. From the early period, too, black women were important in the work of the Party. Nor was their activity confined to the typewriter and mimeograph machine. Panther women spoke at rallies and meetings and were interviewed in the underground press. Here are articles and speeches by five women active in the Black Panther Party, and a speech by the mother of a woman member of the Party.

# Liberation and Political Assassination

by Kathleen Cleaver

With the assassination of Dr. Martin Luther King in Memphis, Tennessee on April 4 and the attempted assassination of Eldridge Cleaver in Oakland on April 6, the Federal Government launched its national, systematic, and timetable plan to liquidate the leadership of the black liberation struggle. The systematic attempt to liquidate the leadership of the Black Panther Party starting with the bullet fired into Huey P. Newton in October is but the most advanced stage of a national conspiracy in the mother country against black people in the colony because the leadership of the Black Panther Party was the most advanced in this country. The relationship of Dr. King's assassination to the attempted assassination of Eldridge Cleaver within two days of each other must be understood clearly in order to see the political direction the present leadership of the Federal Government has taken.

### LBJ Resigns

On April 1, the most profound political shock since the assassination of John F. Kennedy issued from the White House and shot across the world like lightning: President Johnson would not run for re-election. The entire political apparatus in the mother country went into a new phase. The white left was thrown into disarray, afraid that Robert Kennedy's presidential campaign would usurp their following; announcements of phony peace negotiations with Vietnam threatened to destroy the issue they were organized around. The white liberals were led to believe they had an opening and could win with McCarthy; however, liberalism in leadership was ended with the assassination of President Kennedy. While both the white left and the white liberals were being distracted by a tactical maneuver by LBJ, the white fascists were emboldened by the increasing display of police power and the disintegration of middle-class liberalism. For the announcement of President Johnson, the murderous dictator perpetrating the most barbarous war in human history against the people of Vietnam, who has never given any indication of a desire to relinquish power or to stop the war in Vietnam regardless of the opposition of the white middle class, clearly means that the elections have been negated as a decision making process. Political decisions can no longer be implemented with a ballot, but with a bullet.

**MLK Killed**

On April 4, a bullet went through Martin Luther King's neck. Before the chaos and bewilderment generated by President Johnson's shock tactic statement settled, another even more profound political shock electrified the world and exploded in the black colony. The political apparatus of the colony went into a new phase, thrusting the revolutionaries, radicals, and militants into the front. potential national leadership simultaneously. In this vacuum, much On April 6, bullets directed for Bobby Seale murdered Little Bobby Hutton and wounded Eldridge Cleaver who was immediately taken to the state penitentiary for life imprisonment. Immobilizing Eldridge Cleaver and destroying his ability to communicate with the political groups he was leading generated a profound state of chaos into the political apparatus of the Bay Area, of Alameda County in particular, where the most advanced political apparatus had been built around the issue of freeing Huey P. Newton.

The national move to decapitate the leadership of the black liberation struggle initiated with the assassination of Martin Luther King had its most powerful impact here in Oakland with the shooting and imprisonment of Eldridge Cleaver. For six months he had worked to build a defense campaign for Huey P. Newton, Minister of Defense of the Black Panther Party, indicted for murder and attempted murder and awaiting trial on May 6. The powerful political forces he was harnessing into a political apparatus organized around the issue of Huey P. Newton had national and international significance. The attempted assassination and imprisonment of Eldridge Cleaver was directed against the mobilization and coordination of the forces. April 6, the day Eldridge was shot, was exactly one month prior to Huey Newton's trial on May 6. The entire focus of all of his political organizing and direction, the full strength of the movement he had structured and initiated, was directed towards guaranteeing Huey Newton's freedom, and was building up a tremendous momentum towards the opening of Huey Newton's trial.

**Pattern of Oakland Pigs**

The attempted assassination of Huey P. Newton in October initiated the move to liquidate the leadership of the Black Panther Party and thereby destroy its organization of the black community. This attempt was totally unsuccessful as the leadership of the Party was actively picked up by Eldridge Cleaver and Bobby Seale when he was released from jail in December. In January, as a warning, the San Francisco gestapo kicked down the door of Eldridge Cleaver's home at 3:30 am and invaded his house with guns drawn without either a search warrant or an arrest warrant. In February, following a

massive show of community support for Huey P. Newton at the Free
Huey Rally at the Oakland auditorium, the Berkeley gestapo surrounded Bobby Seale's home with shotguns and kicked in his door
at 3:30 am, arresting him and his wife on charges of conspiracy to
commit murder without either a search warrant or an arrest warrant,
and arresting friends of his in the Black Panther Party outside his
home. On April 3, the Oakland gestapo raided the St. Augustine's
Church in West Oakland where Bobby Seale would lead the black
community meetings held by the Black Panther Party. Twenty gestapo armed with shotguns invaded the church but left when they discovered Bobby Seale was not there. During the month of March
they had framed up absurd charges attempting to send Bobby to
jail in Berkeley municipal court, Oakland municipal court, and in
Alameda County superior court. On April 6, Bobby Hutton
was murdered, Eldridge Cleaver wounded and arrested, David Hilliard
and several other captains and members of the Black Panther Party
arrested following a massive attack on the party by the Oakland
pigs. And, finally, on April 25, the Chief of the Oakland pigs held a
press conference denouncing the Black Panther Party as a threat to
the peace and the Peace and Freedom Party as creating anarchy.

**Pattern of Fed. Govt.**

The Federal Government has moved with the speed of lightning
against the leadership of the black liberation struggle on a national
scale through all the police departments of the cities across the
nation in a calculated and systematic plan following the assassination
of King. The planned liquidation of the leadership of the Black
Panther Party in the Bay Area is a microcosm of what has been done
across this country. Following the rebellions initiated by King's assassination across the black colony, in which the police were por-
trayed as restrained onlookers by the white press, mass arrests,
jailings, beatings, and elimination of militant spokesmen and political
organizers in the colony were initiated without any coverage by the
press. The elimination of King as a national leader, the elimination
of scores of political organizers and spokesmen in Boston, Buffalo,
New York, Chicago, Detroit, Washington, D.C., Oakland and scores
of other cities, and the attempted assassination and imprisonment of
Eldridge Cleaver and the disruption of the political campaign to
liberate Huey P. Newton, followed up with the arrest of Reies
Tijerina in New Mexico last week is all one coordinated move to
destroy the leadership of the black liberation struggle and its allies.
     The most powerful tool developed politically for Huey's defense
was the coalition between the Black Panther Party, the Peace and
Freedom Party, the Mexican American Community, and the student peace movement represented by the Stop the Draft Week
organizing committee. The coalition between the most dynamic and

potentially explosive political forces in the mother country and in the colony generated tremendous power to the demands of its participants: FREE HUEY. The attack on Eldridge Cleaver was an attack on the political apparatus he had engineered to support Huey Newton, an attack on the political ideas he had projected and set into motion. The demand for Free Huey had obtained a revolutionary momentum in Alameda County, and plans were in motion to move nationally with this mechanism and this demand. The bullets fired at Eldridge Cleaver were intended to stop this move.

The assassination of Dr. King was a move on a national scale similar to the attempted assassination of Eldridge Cleaver on a local scale; both attacks were against the politics of coalition. Dr. King had also moved to combine powerful forces for change into a single movement against poverty and racism. He had initiated organizing projects in Appalachia among poor whites, had moved to establish an alliance with the leadership of the Mexican American community, and had deepened his struggle from civil rights to peace to an attack on poverty, combining it all into one fight for justice. Reies Tijerina was the Southwest Coordinator of the Poor People's March Dr. King was organizing and his recent arrest on April 27 on trumped up charges for which he was already out on bail only further reveals the national conspiracy to stop the Poor People's March and the coalition activities of colonized peoples.

The attempted assassination of Eldridge Cleaver also indicates a sinister move to deprive the black community of leadership at both ends of the colonial spectrum, from liberal to revolutionary, to wipe out existing national leadership and potential national leadership simultaneously. In this vacuum much damage can be done to the black nation in this crucial stage of building national organization. The dual moves initiated by the Black Panther Party coordinated by Eldridge Cleaver of merger with SNCC and coalition with the Peace and Freedom Party, of moving to unite with other organizations in the colony working for the same purposes as the Party and to align with other organizations in the mother country working for similar ends portended a move for national leadership. Regardless of the destruction of our leadership cadre and its imprisonment and elimination, the Black Panther Party will move and is moving to assume national leadership in the black liberation struggle because it meets the needs of the black nation. The entire thrust of this attack by the national government of the mother country is to destroy the political leadership of the colony in order to force our people into a confrontation with superior military power at an early stage and to wipe us out with firepower. Removing the militant, radical, and revolutionary leadership of the black community will allow its deceivers and decoys to then come into the colony to co-opt, control, then kill the blacks who remain unorganized and unpolitical.

**Jail or Murder**

The level on which the national government of the mother country is forced to deal with the political developments in the colony, on the level of assassination and imprisonment, no longer on the level of phony negotiations and pacification, indicates that our struggle has developed an even more powerful threat to the established patterns of exploitation and racism.

The assassination of President Kennedy followed by the assassination of Malcolm X, the assassination of Martin Luther King followed by the attempted assassination of Eldridge Cleaver indicates a definite pattern, a conspiracy of police forces from the local to the international level. In all of these assassinations there has been coordination with the CIA and the local police forces, and an inability to locate the real assassin. The role of the police forces has become one of such high national prominence, one responsible for executing top-level national policy. With the national decision making activity of the mother country being carried out by the local police forces, the national defense of the black colony lies in the Black Panther Party, its Ten Point Program, and its focus on the activities of the police.

**Bullet Silences**

The right-wing fascist element of this mother country madness has one outstanding political drawback: it cannot produce any charismatic or brilliant orators to advance its cause. These above mentioned four victims of police assassination plots had one thing in common with each other: they were all brilliant orators. The bullet has been called in to silence the oratory of the political leaders from the white liberal to black revolutionary arenas as well as destroy their political work. The price of speaking the truth, or even beautiful and inspiring lies, has become murder. These are political decisions made and implemented with the bullet.

**LBJ Throughout**

During all these assassination plots, LBJ has been President and benefactor. LBJ is a President notorious to unbelievable proportions for his outright corruption and high-level gangsterism. The pattern of assassination falls at his doorstep, on the front door of the White House. True, political power grows out of the barrel of a gun. The only question is whose politics: Huey P. Newton's or LBJ's? Power to the pigs or power to the people? Martin Luther King and Eldridge Cleaver both stood for power to the people. One was a minister of the church, the other a minister of the Black Panther Party. The Black Panther Party will prevail.

—*The Black Panther*, May 18, 1968

# On Cultural Nationalism

by Linda Harrison
East Oakland Office

Cultural nationalism is recognized by many who think in a revolutionary manner as a distinct and natural stage through which one proceeds in order to become a revolutionary. Such is not always the case, and many people remain at the level of a cultural nationalist all of their lives. In the United States, cultural nationalism can be summed up in James Brown's words—"I'm Black and I'm Proud."

Cultural nationalism manifests itself in many ways but all of these manifestations are essentially grounded in one fact; a universal denial and ignoring of the present political, social, and economic realities and a concentration on the past as a frame of reference.

This phenomenon is not unique to this stage of the revolution in which we find ourselves; neither is it unique to the United States Black "citizens" struggle for freedom. Frantz Fanon in THE WRETCHED OF THE EARTH said of this phenomenon that "There is no taking of the offensive—and no redefining of relationships. There is simply a concentration on a hard core of culture which is becoming more and more shrivelled up—inert and empty."

Those who believe in the "I'm Black and Proud" theory—believe that there is dignity inherent in wearing naturals; that a buba makes a slave a man; and that a common language; Swahili; makes all of us brothers. These people usually want a culture rooted in African culture; a culture which ignores the colonization and brutalization that were part and parcel; for example; of the formation and emergence of the Swahili language. In other words cultural nationalism ignores the political and concrete, and concentrates on a myth and fantasy.

A man who lives under slavery and any of its extensions rarely regains his dignity by rejecting the clothiers of his enslaver; he rarely regains his dignity except by a confrontation on equal grounds with his enslaver. All men can die, and this is the only thing that equalizes them. Under many systems those with money die less often. Any confrontation which gives men, no matter what their social or economic position, an equal chance to die under equal conditions is uplifting for those who consider themselves at the bottom and degrading and toppling for those who are at the top.

To see himself on an equal plane with his enslaver is to realize
that the ones who enslave and oppress do not have the divine right
to do so. There is nothing to be proud of in colonization and slavery
and only out of the initiative of the oppressed can come something
meaningful and amending to his existence.

Quoting Fanon "The desire to attach oneself to tradition or
bring abandoned traditions to life again does not only mean going
against the current of history but also opposing one's own people—"
Cultural Nationalists in their finery support many of the evils which
have put them in the position of servitude. In the absence of constructive and corrective platforms and actions, the support and
profit from "Being Black" they become profit seekers selling ear-
rings at 400% mark up and buba's from dime store yardage at Saks
5th Avenue prices. Sort of a hustler trying to become respectable.
Exploiting those with weaker minds and weaker pocketbooks.

And because cultural nationalism has no political doctrine as a
rule—the limits of being black and proud are proximate. Where is
there to go after a woman has got a natural—to the natural shop
of course!!—and pay $5.50 for a hairdo, $2.00 for oil spray; $2.00
for comb out conditioner, $3.50 for a line and comb-out, and then
to the dress shop for a traditional wrap priced at $25.00 to $50.00.
On the way to and from this shopping and spending they are still
observing the oppression and exploitation of their people—in different clothes.

Because cultural nationalism offers no challenge or offense against
the prevailing order; the influx of "Black and Proud" actors, movie
stars, social workers, teachers, probation officers and politicians is
tremendous. Bourgeoisie and upper class standing is no handicap to
the "Black" and vice versa. The power structure, after the mandatory
struggle, condones and even worships this new found pride which
it uses to sell every product under the sun. It worships and condones anything that is harmless and presents no challenge to the
existing order. Even its top representatives welcome it and turn it
into "Black Capitalism" and related phenomenon. Everyone is black
and the bourgeosie continue to hate their less fortunate black brothers and sisters; and the oppressed continue to want. The "Black"
social worker continues to work for the degrading welfare system,
and the "Black" probation and parole officers continue to violate their probationers and parolees.

We have no nation without a fight against those who oppress us.
We have no culture but a culture born out of our resistance to
oppression. "No colonial system draws its justification from the
fact that the territories (and people) it dominates are culturally
nonexistent. You will never make colonialism blush for shame by
spreading out little known cultural treasures under its eyes." The

peoples of Africa had cultures. It is only racism and economic necessities and whims that enslaved these countries and people. Apes have cultures—they are put into zoos. Economics transcends cultures in the capitalistic context. That is to say that capitalism will always use as its basis for expansion a real or imagined economic necessity. It will of course justify with racist conclusions and explanations of the progress that they bring to the "Natives" and "Savages," and no culture in the world, except a revolutionary culture will stop or halt or destroy that advance. Colonialism, slavery, neocolonialism, and other extensions of capitalism thrive over a thousand and one cultures.

"It is around the peoples struggles that African-Negro culture takes on substance—and not around songs, poems or folklore." A culture that does not challenge wholly and resolutely the dominant and exploitative forces—political, economical, and social forces—is a culture which is either pre-slavery, pre-colonialistic or completely made up and in either case completely useless. And cultural nationalism is most always based on racism. We hear "Hate Whitey" and "Kill the Honkey". These statements ignore the analysis—intellectual analysis such as those made by Eldridge Cleaver on the relationships between the government and the pigs—and marines etc.; and they ignore the possibility of allies. In all cases cultural nationalism—in the midst of struggle, seeks to create a racist ideology. To be a racist in America is certainly justified, but it is a handicapped position to take as a revolutionary.

"Adherence to African-Negro culture and to cultural unity of Africa is arrived at in the first place by upholding unconditionally the people's struggle for freedom. No one can truly wish for the spread of African culture if he does not give practical support to the creation of the conditions necessary to existence of that culture . . ."

How can a cultural nationalist claim to love and to be proud of a country—and a continent that has suffered for hundreds of years in colonialism and slavery, and is still suffering in all the cleverly disguised and open forms of these institutions? How can he himself deny the political realities of his own life in America by dressing up in a maternity smock (brightly colored) to participate in the culture of a people torn by revolution and revolt? How can a cultural nationalist claim adherence to the cultures of Africa, when the culture of Africa is a revolutionary culture? Solidarity with the revolutionary people all over the world has brought about a common culture to people who know nothing of each other except that they suffer under similar systems of exploitation; degradation, and racism. That their people have undergone much the same changes and that in no case will the people regain their dignity and find their freedom except through a face to face and equal confrontation through revolutionary tactics and actions. "A revolutionary culture is the only valid culture for the oppressed!!"

All quotations except the last one from THE WRETCHED OF THE EARTH by Fanon.

—*The Black Panther*, February 2, 1969

# The Struggle Is a World Struggle

by Connie Matthews

Speech delivered at the Vietnam Moratorium demonstration, San Jose State College, October 15, 1969

POWER TO THE PEOPLE. I have listened to all the speeches that have gone on before me. I have been reading the newspapers, reading the stuff that the so-called radical groups have been putting out and you are talking about the atrocities in Vietnam, you are talking about repression in the United States. I wonder whether you people really do understand what's going on. I have to ask myself this question because in 1967 there was a World Tribunal which was held in Roskilde in Denmark and there the world condemned the United States for the atrocities committed in Vietnam and found her guilty of war crimes and the United States said—Later for the World, because we rule the World. It was announced on the news that there would be demonstrations tomorrow against the war and Nixon said this morning that it makes no difference to his strategy in Vietnam.

Now, I am not trying to negate or to diminish the efforts that you are making in holding these demonstrations. What I am trying to say to you is that the time has come when we have to move in another direction. We have to understand that by peaceful demonstrations, by trying to negotiate, that we are not going to get anywhere. We have to understand that the struggle at this moment is a world struggle, it's a world proletarian struggle; two things—the oppressed versus the oppressor. You have to understand that we must stop talking in terms of countries, we have to talk about internationalism because the United States has now gone to the moon, they will go to Mars, they will go to Venus next, so that it is not just a question anymore of the planet earth. And you want to take a trip around the world and visit some of the countries I

# IMPERIALIST PLANS...

have visited to see what American imperialism has done. Eldridge
Cleaver, our Minister of Information, in his last article from exile,
which is in the last issue of our newspaper (there are some copies
here) has stated that the oppression in the United States, and the
way that people live in ghettos here is as if you have been placed
in silk sheets compared to what American imperialism has done in
the other countries of the world.[13]

Now whenever the Vietnamese fight, and they are fighting, and
they have won the war, they are fighting for you here. You have to
understand this and I use Chairman Bobby Seale's statement—We
are in the belly of the whale here [14]—but you have to do your
thing because you are helping to enslave those millions of people
in Asia, Africa and Latin America, because you are covertly con-
doning what the administration is doing. Because power must belong
to the people. You are responsible for that administration being in
power and just demonstrating and marching and saying—We don't
dig this—won't do any good to anyone.

Now, you know the Black Panther Party started off and we said
that we understood that this thing was a class struggle. We understood that there are Black people who are pigs and we understood
that there are White people who are pigs. What we are trying to
say is that we want a United Front of all ethnic oppressed groups,
regardless of race, color, creed or what have you, because the ultimate
aim is to overthrow this establishment. Sartre said that Europe the
dying mother of capitalism gave birth to a monster, imperialism,
and this is the United States of America. You have to understand
that what the Black Panther Party is doing is for you and for the
rest of the world. Now you have to rally behind the Black Panther
Party and to support the Black Panther Party. It's o.k. when a bunch
of niggers get out on the streets and say we hate all White people.
Nixon endorses this, Nixon endorses Black capitalism, because he
knows that what he is going to do is to get a few so-called elite
Black people and create yet another division and this is why I am
glad I am talking to a group of students and the thing that I notice
is that there are over 400 Black students here at San Jose State
and that none of these students thought that the war in Vietnam
has anything to do with them or else they would be in this goddamned room. And they should understand that those Vietnamese
are fighting and dying for them. Now, to get back to the point,
Nixon believes that by brainwashing you students, because you are
the ones who are going out tomorrow to continue what Nixon has
brainwashed you into believing everything is o.k. You have got
to get hip to this thing, because you are the ones who are going
to be the leaders and the establishment tomorrow, you are going
to be the bank managers, members of the administration and all the

rest of it and you have got to get hip to the fact that you cannot allow this thing to continue. You have got to get hip to the fact that what the Black Panther Party wants is to take the wealth from out of the hands of the few, and it is only controlled by about 250 people who run the world. This seems absurd, but there are only about 250 to 300 big capitalists in this country. They are the ones who put who they want in power, they are the ones who control and rule the world and say what should be done in this country and for that matter the world. Now the future rests with you people who are here today.

You can see what has been going on in Chicago and I can tell you that the so-called mother country radicals have been a disappointment. I was in Court there and they don't take this thing seriously. They do not understand that the trial in Chicago, the outcome, will set the precedence in the United States as to whether the people have any freedom or not. They seem to think this is all a big joke, with Abbie Hoffman doing somersaults in Court and all that kind of bulls--t. Now, I am saying you have had what is known as group freedom and you are trying to find individual freedom. We are all one people, this is all one country, in fact in the whole world we are all one people, so until everyone has known what group freedom is you are not going to be able to exist in your hippie and yippie societies with individual freedom. And I am saying that over the last six months Nixon has launched a massive repression against the Black Panther Party that is unheard of. When I have spoken in other countries, like France, Germany or even England, people find it hard to believe that Americans, people like you can sit here and watch this sort of thing happening and you do nothing about it. Chairman Bobby Seale, at the beginning of his trial in Chicago was sick, and he wasn't allowed to have a doctor, he has no lawyer, he has no rights he is unable to defend himself, because Charles Garry, his lawyer, is lying on his back in the hospital right here in California, and because he is a Black man it doesn't matter. He shouldn't have anyone to defend him. I am now saying to you here, that I do not think you are trying hard enough, I don't think you understand fully what's going on. I think you need to get out of your bag and your safe complacency in these colleges. I think you need to go and work in those communities, but before you go into the communities and propagate the wrong ideology, arm yourselves with the right ideology, understand what the struggle is about. It is the oppressed against the oppressor. You middle-class people, because I do not believe that any of you here are capitalists, there are only about 300, you are definitely in a vacuum and you are going to have to take sides at some stage or other and make sure that you take the right side, because if you don't you are not going to have any place to go, because the people must win.

The Vietnamese are a good example of the people being victorious. Because with all of America's technology and her greatness she has been unable to defeat the Vietnamese. Every man, woman and child has resisted. You want to see what is going on in Vietnam. All the men have had to go to the front and you should see how those women and children safeguard their villages. It is probably very difficult for you in the middle of all this to see it clearly, but this is why you have the greatest responsibility. The people who understand what is wrong, because it has to come from within as well as from outside.

We have a petition for community control of police, and those of you who are not familiar with it, get yourself familiar with it, because this is one of the ways in which we are trying to get the power back into the hands of the people. Here on your colleges you have these demonstrations and you go about saying that you don't want this and you don't want that, and you want this and you want that, and then you sit down and you say you have won. You haven't won anything because you must realize that the people who control the colleges are the same people who were put there because they have power in the communities. So your job is in the communities. The two things are tied up together. Don't try to put them in compartments. I think the time has come for all you young people here in the United States to take a look at yourselves. Look inside first. Try and grasp what the Black Panther Party is trying to do, try and understand how many lives we have lost, because we are trying to educate you. We are the Vanguard because of 400 years, of sweat, blood toil and tears. But we are not going to start the revolution, it's when you people are educated fully that this thing is going to have to happen, and I am trying to say that if you sit by in this complacency you know what will happen?—This so-called United States of America was built up at the expense of genocide of 50 million Indians and you people have romanticized it and called it "Cowboys and Indians." Think about that s--t. Six million Jews were murdered and people sat by and didn't believe it was happening. You sit by now and understand that this is happening right here, and that the power is in your hands, because you are the people so this country belongs to you, so you are the ones who are going to have to stop it and you are going to have to stop it not just by concentrating on one aspect but all facets of what's going on. What I am trying to say is, educate yourselves, in turn educate your people, the people in the communities. Whenever you go out you talk about it. You talk about the whole thing, the reason why they divided us up into ethnic groups, into races, because as Fanon has said—capitalism and racism—one is cause and the other effect. They did not bring Black people over from Africa as slaves because we were Black. They brought Black people over so capitalism could thrive. When capitalism reached its highest form—imperialism—they had to define methods to keep the divisions.

The United States is advancing so rapidly technologically, that most of you will become redundant, you will have no jobs and in fact nothing. The dollar at present is worth only about 75 cents, and all you people here who live on credit cards, watch it. They have you hoodwinked. If you have been watching the stock market and the world monetary fund system, they have told you that the German market is floating. There are no changes. While the German mark is floating the dollar has decreased and watch—over the next six months or so what will happen. You are the ones who are going to feel it most. Not the poor oppressed people, because they have nothing anyway. But you in the middle, who think you have something, who have those bills and those $20,000 houses, you are the ones who are going to find out that the mortgage or interest or whatever it is that you are going to have to pay back is about twice what you thought originally. Get yourself hip to all this, do some research, you are the students, get with it and educate your people because the Black Panther Party is out there in the front but we can't stay out there in the front forever. We will stay until everyone of us is killed or imprisoned by these racist pigs, but then someone will have to take over. So don't let us all die in vain.

POWER TO THE PEOPLE

—*The Black Panther*, October 25, 1969

# I Joined the Panthers

by Joan Bird

Joan Bird, twenty-one-year-old Black Panther Party member, accused of conspiracy to commit murder, among other charges, spent nearly a year and a half in prison, pending her trial as part of the Panther 21 case in New York, until she was released on July 6, 1970, on $100,000 bail. In the pre-dawn raids on the homes of Panthers named in the conspiracy cases, she was severely beaten. In October, 1969, Miss Bird sent a letter to the press telling the story of her persecution. It was printed eight months later. The following excerpt deals with the events that led up to Miss Bird's joining the Black Panther Party.

I was born in New York City 20 years ago. I grew up in the Harlem Community and attended parochial elementary school, Resurrection, and from there went on to Cathedral High School for Girls.

Growing up in the typical black ghetto community I clearly recognize the ills of poverty, embedded there among my people. We suffer day to day . . . trapped into hunger, disease and complete destitution, which is so actively present in our lives. Having loving and concerned parents I am indeed lucky, but there are many in Harlem who have none to turn to for help. Their world is blatant.

My ambition: to become a nurse. I thought I could sincerely help my people with this perspective in mind. After graduating from Cathedral in 1967, I entered Bronx Community College, majoring in nursing. During this period, I felt this was not enough. I needed and wanted to be fully aware of myself, the changing world, my people's true identity and their roles in society and the need for us to unite if we are ever going to achieve any sort of power.

I first heard and read about the Black Panther Party in the summer of 1968 right after the incident in Brooklyn Court when 200 policemen violently attacked members of the Black Panther Party. Having lived in Harlem all my life, I was aware of bad cops and police brutality, but this was more than I had ever dreamed of.

I wanted to know more about the Black Panther Party and its purpose so I went to the office on Seventh Avenue and met a few of the brothers. They related to me the necessity for all oppressed people to be politically aware of the fascism which has crippled them for centuries. I read the 10-point program and what brothers like Malcolm, Huey, Eldridge and Che were talking about began to make sense.

I became a Party member and actively participated in its various programs—free breakfast for the children, free clothing for the people, political education classes open to the public and finding out the immediate needs of the people by going into the community. I continued to go to school at night and devoted my days to working with the people. I was never tired by this schedule because doing anything to help my people gave me the energy to go on.

—*The Black Panther*, June 27, 1970

# We Will Win:
# Letter from Prison by Afeni Shakur

**Afeni Shakur is one of the Panther 21 in New York accused of conspiracy. The letter was written while she was imprisoned in the Women's House of Detention in lieu of $100,000 bail.**

We feel that you are indicting, arresting, incarcerating, trying, and probably convicting us on an erroneous image of us that you have received from the daily press and we know that this daily press is not only erroneous but also brutally racist. We feel before we go on, since it is our lives that are in jeopardy, we would appreciate it if we could shed at least some facts about our organization, its goals, as to why these charges are not only illegal, unconstitutional, but also ridiculous to say the least.

The Black Panther Party was formed three years ago in Oakland California by Huey P. Newton—but was it? Black Panther historians argue themselves over the beginning at the spirit of the Black Panther Party. Some say it had its beginnings around 400 years ago when you first decided that we were not human beings. Others attribute it to the 100 million or so that you killed on slave ships. Others to Gabriel Prosser, Denmark Vesey, Nat Turner and of course Toussaint L'Ouverture.[15] Some even say it began at the time of the fugitive slave act and the Dred Scott decision. But all agree that this spirit is there and has been for quite sometime. And all agree on the modern adaptation of it—that Frantz Fanon put it on paper, that Malcolm X put into words, and that Huey P. Newton put it into action. It is a spirit that has been stifled for centuries but cannot be and will not be stifled any longer.

We know that you are trying to break us up because we are the truth and because you can't control us. We know that you always try to destroy what you can't control. We know that you are afraid of us because we represent a truth of the universe. We are not being tried for any overt act nor for attempt to commit any overt act—we are being tried for bringing within our minds the focusing of the ideas of centuries and trying to bring this knowledge into a workable plan to liberate our people from oppression. We are being tried only because we know you and because we are not afraid of you. We know of your history of lies, deceit and slavery. We know that you now have 80% of the world in slavery. We know how you turn nation against nation, tribe against tribe, brother against brother. We know that you are blood-thirsty, pitiless and inhuman. We have seen you justify the most inhuman crimes—the worst of which was the destruction of men's hearts and minds. We know of your greed. We know that 10,000 army bases does not make this a "free world" except free for your exploitation and imperialism. How many civilizations have you destroyed?

In this country we know that we are not 2nd class citizens—we know that we are not citizens at all. We know that the 13th, 14th and 15th amendments did not liberate us—that they only legalized slavery and expanded the Dred Scott decision to include the Indians, Spanish speaking and poor whites. We know that things have not gotten any better—but only progressively worse. We know that this is the rich man's courts, laws, and justice. It is his skies, and air—we can only look at it and breathe it if he says so. We know that wealth is not the fruit of labor but the result of organized protected robbery. But you teach the poor workers to be honest. We know that the Almighty dollar which everyone is taught to revere is only guaranteed by slavery and exploitation. We know that we live in a world inhuman in its poverty. We know that we are a colony, living under community imperialism. The U.S. that we see is not one of freedom, beauty, and wisdom, but of fear, terror, and hate. This is a nation of *your* laws, run by your police, and based on protecting your economic strength. The poor are politically, economically and legally non-existent that is why in jail, 80% of the inmates are non-white and all are poor. Yet even your sociologists and criminologists admit that 80% of these are innocent.

We see that inhuman treatment but are told that we do not. We see men beaten to death in jail but are told that they died of "natural causes" but we are liars. Just as we are always presumed guilty. We heard the judge tell us that "The law didn't apply to us," but it isn't in the record—and of course we lie. We are born criminals and liars. We know we are innocent but we are liars. The people know we are innocent but they don't count. The prisoners know we are innocent but they too are liars. The guards and even the captains of the guards know we are innocent but they can't testify. They will lose their jobs. We can prove we are innocent. But we wonder does it really matter. We can prove it in detail and we will, but just in general the charges against us in this indictment are ridiculous and are contradictory to our basic beliefs. We have never been asked as a people whether we wanted to be governed by your God, your laws, your justice, your customs, your speech, dress, and ethics. We do not. We have no respect for them. We have no respect for your laws, taxes, your gratitude, sincerity, honor and dignity—you have no respect for them yourself. You don't respect us—thus we don't respect YOU.

We admit that we do not want you to "elevate" us to be workers who are only free enough to see our labors to you. We will not be your killers any longer—nor will we be "elevated" to become your accomplices. You will not reform nor improve upon this system—we feel that it cannot be reformed and we do not want it improved—we demand that it be changed. We realize that you have filled the army, the jails, and the dope seller lists with our young people—we demand their release. We realize that you cannot give us the right to anything—either we have it or we do not. That we must be independent we must stop being dependent—and now. We cannot do it by moderation—that is a contradiction and an impossibility—you do not stop a child from starving by moderation—you do not stop murder by moderation. We realize that freedom is a duty and it is our duty to get this freedom for our people and to yield to no one in obtaining it. We will be beggars no longer. You brought the nigger into existence and now, finally, we are destroying him.

We know that your economic system is a chain around our necks and we are breaking all of your chains. We will identify with the needs of our people—the oppressed. You do not want us to rule you and we do not want you to rule us. We will rule ourselves, make our own progress, our own mistakes, our own friends, and our own enemies. We will judge our own. We will mend enmities that you have created and make enemies of your friends. We will live. We will have a humanistic, disciplined mutual cooperation as our goal. The question becomes—does the state rule the people or do the people rule the state? You are the state and we say "All Power to the People" and the people will have the power. But you will try to stop us. You will oppress us until we stop you and we will stop you. History shows that wars against oppression are always successful. And there will be a war—a true revolutionary war—a bloody war. No one not you nor us nor anyone in this country can stop it from occurring now. And we will win. We admit all of this. But, and this is important, the charges you have against us we are innocent of. You see for one thing we study Malcolm X—and he said: "I believe in anything that is necessary to correct unjust conditions . . . I believe in it as long as it's intelligently directed and designed to get results. But I don't believe in getting involved in any kind of political action or other kind of action without sitting down and analyzing the possibility of success or failure." What success could we have achieved, what results could we have obtained that would correspond with our goal? You have accused us of conspiring to murder innocent people by the use of terrorism. We feel that in itself is an insult to our intelligence and our seriousness. The technique of terrorism is always the same— bombs—usually against soldiers and always against our enemies. The people who shop in those stores are not our enemies. Why would we want to hurt or kill or burn them? All of the workers and most of the shoppers, especially, around Easter are our people. As Frantz Fanon says, "The decision to kill a civilian is not an easy one and no one takes it lightly. No one takes the step of placing a bomb in a public place without a battle of conscience." Why should we do that?

What would we have gained as Black Panthers, as Black People, as Poor People as Human Beings? We are not melodramatic—we are not, at least not willingly, martyrs and we are not crazy—we are revolutionaries and as such we will do what is necessary and only what is necessary—when and only when that action will actually be furthering the interest of our struggle. All else, as in this indictment, is folly.

—*Rat*, January 7–20, 1970

# A Word for Panther Parents

**by Mrs. Jewel Barker**

**Mrs. Barker delivered this speech at the memorial rally held December 6, 1969, 201 So. Ashland in honor of Fred Hampton and Mark Clark. She is the mother of Panther Ann Campbell.**

I have but one thing that I would like to ask of the Black mothers and fathers in this country and all over the world. You have given much to your sons and daughters. You have overcome insurmountable forces of evil against you. You have paid the supreme price. You have given to the world the best. Stand behind it. Do not be ashamed. I have but one child. I gave her to the cause. She works for you, because she knows where Vietnam really is. She said to me one day, she said "Mother, they are not oppressing us in Vietnam, they are not killing the soul brothers in Vietnam, they are not shooting through doors and killing Black women in Vietnam, they're doing it here!" Yes, mothers and fathers, I would like to say to you that you have listened to the television, the radio, and you have read the newspapers, but you have not walked out of your doors to the Breakfast Centers to see what your children are trying to do. Don't listen—walk and find out for yourselves. And when you see the tremendous forces that are working against the beautiful work your children are trying to do, I think you will be very glad to stand up and be counted. Remember this: prayer is good. If Fred could be murdered while he slept, remember what can happen to you while you're on your knees.

I pledge allegiance to my parents and I hope that you will understand the necessity of standing behind your beautiful sons and daughters who are working so fervently, working for the salvation of all mankind. Don't let anybody tell you that you have failed. Don't sneak in corners and hide when your children cry "All Power to the People." Don't sneak in corners and hide when they ask you to help build a Medical Center that will accommodate all poor people. Support them in their struggle.

Father Clemens said yesterday that he was ashamed of his generation. You have no need to be ashamed. Be our judges. Be our jurors. You are our peers. Make it real for our children. And this is the only way. The only way is through the struggle of our children and generations to come. Not through the birth control pill; no, not through hungry children, not through fine minks and big Cadillacs, and not through money. And if you love Fred Hampton, he wouldn't appreciate your being here saying all these beautiful words, but you will fight for Fred, you will hold up Fred's banner.

POWER TO THE PEOPLE

—*The Black Panther*, December 13, 1969

# 9.

## COMMUNITY ACTIVITIES

"Breakfast for Children pulls people out of the system and organizes them into an alternative. Black children who go to school hungry each morning have been organized into their poverty, and the Panther program liberates them, frees them from that aspect of their poverty. This is liberation in practice. . . . If we can understand Breakfast for Children, can we not also understand Lunch for Children, and Dinner for Children, and Clothing for Children, and Education for Children, and Medical Care for Children? And if we can understand that, why can't we understand not only a People's Park, but People's Housing, and People's Transportation, and People's Industry and People's Banks? And why can't we understand a People's Government?" So wrote Eldridge Cleaver from exile in an article entitled "On Meeting the Needs of the People," published in *The Black Panther* of August 16, 1969. In this section, the reader will find examples of community activities conducted by the Black Panther Party: the Free Breakfast for School Children program, Liberation schools and other programs.

# To Feed Our Children

The Free Breakfast for School Children is about to cover the country and be initiated in every chapter and branch of the Black Panther Party. This program was created because the Black Panther Party understands that our children need a nourishing breakfast every morning so that they can learn.

These Breakfasts include every nutrient that they need for the day. For too long have our people gone hungry and without the proper health aids they need. But the Black Panther Party says that this type of thing must be halted, because we must survive this evil government and build a new one fit for the service of all the people. This program is run through donations of concerned people and the avaricious businessmen that pinch selfishly a little to the program. We say that this is not enough, especially from those that thrive off the Black Community like leeches. All of the avaricious businessmen have their factories etc. centered in our communities and even most of the people that work in these sweat shops are members of the oppressed masses.

It is a beautiful sight to see our children eat in the mornings after remembering the times when our stomachs were not full, and even the teachers in the schools say that there is a great improvement in the academic skills of the children that do get the breakfast. At one time there were children that passed out in class from hunger, or had to be sent home for something to eat. But our children shall be fed, and the Black Panther Party will not let the malady of hunger keep our children down any longer.

The Breakfast has already been initiated in several chapters, and our love for the masses makes us realize that it must continue permanently and be a national program. But we need your help, and that means money, food, and time. We want to turn the program over to the community but without your efforts and support we cannot. We have had a few mothers to come down to the breakfast in the mornings to cook and serve, but not hardly enough. This is the people's program, for the people, and we want the people to assist in it. We are holding a community meeting May 3, 7:30 pm at St. Augustine's Episcopal Church on 27th and West in Oakland, concerning the Breakfast Program. We will have a movie of the children participating in the Breakfast, your children, to show to all of the members of our community. Speakers from the Black Panther Party shall inform you on the achievements of the Breakfasts, and the ways that you can assist. Hunger is one of the means of oppression and it must be halted.

POWER TO THE PEOPLE

—*The Black Panther*, March 26, 1969

# Why the Free Breakfast?

The Free Breakfast for Children is just one of the programs being carried out by the Black Panther Party that can be attributed to Huey P. Newton. Huey P. Newton, organizer and Minister of Defense of the Black Panther Party says that the Party must go forth to meet the basic desires and needs of the people. Huey says the members of the Party are oxen to be ridden by the people.

How is the Party ridden by the people? Panthers working the breakfast program get out of bed at approximately 6:00 a.m. every school day. They set tables, clean facilities, cook and prepare the food, they direct traffic to see that the children cross the streets safely. After a day's breakfast has been completed, the Panthers attend to the constant task of procuring food from the merchants who do business in the community, to see that the program is constantly supplied with the necessary food. Why a Breakfast for Children Program? The answers to this question need be answered for only those who belong to the upper or so-called middle class. The majority of Black, Mexican-American, Orientals and poor Whites know from their American experience that it is impossible to obtain and sustain any education when one has to attend school hungry.

Huey P. Newton knew that these conditions existed and that the American school system has not seen fit to alleviate them. Validity has been added to Huey's knowledge by the fact that the Free Breakfast program has spread like wild fire across the United States wherever Black Panther Chapters and Branches exist.

The Free Breakfast for Children program is a socialistic program, designed to serve the people. All institutions in a society should be designed to serve the masses, not just a "chosen few". In America this program is revolutionary. In capitalist America any program that is absolutely free is considered bad business. The Black Panther Party is a vanguard organization and a vanguard organization educates by example. The Black Panther Party is educating the people to the fact they have a right to the best that modern technology and human knowledge can produce.

"The world belongs to all the people."

FOR TOO LONG OUR CHILDREN HAVE GONE HUNGRY

—*The Black Panther*, October 4, 1969

# Liberation Schools

What are revolutionaries? "Revolutionaries are changers." This response comes from the eager lips of the youngsters participating in the first liberation school sponsored by the Black Panther Party. The liberation school is the realization of point five of the ten point platform and program, that is, "We want education for our people that exposes the true nature of this decadent American society. We want education that teaches our true history and our role in the present-day society." We recognize that education is only relevant when it teaches the art of survival. Our role in this society is to prepare ourselves and the masses for change. The change we want is within this decadent society. It's the implementation of the 10 point platform of the Vanguard Party. It's the destruction of the ruling class that oppresses and exploits the poor. It's the destruction of the avaricious businessman (the youth in the liberation school call him the "big, fat, businessman"). It's the destruction of the lying, deceiving politicians, and most important of all, the destruction of the racist pigs that are running rampant in our communities.

Liberation schools will replace for the summer the Free Breakfast for School Children that was initiated in the beginning of this year and has since spread in chapters and branches of the party throughout the country. Liberation School is the second of the many socialistic and educational programs that will be implemented by the Black Panther Party to meet the needs of the people. The first program began Wednesday, June 25 at 9th and Hearst Streets in Berkeley, California. The program is a success with the maximum participation coming from the youth and volunteers throughout the community. The curriculum is designed to meet the needs of the youth, to guide them in their search for revolutionary truths and principles. Brunch and a well-balanced lunch is served daily. Three days of the week are spent in class. Thursday is Film day and Friday is set aside for field trips throughout the community. The 30th of June marked the opening of two additional schools in East Oakland, and Hunters Point in San Francisco, California. Additional programs are scheduled to begin in the very near future throughout the Bay Area and across the country.

The youth understand the struggle that's being waged in this society. It's evident by their eagerness to participate in the program. They understand that we're not fighting a race struggle, but in fact, a class struggle. They recognize the need for all oppressed people to unite against the forces that are making our lives unbearable. Their understanding manifests itself in their definitions, i.e. Revolution means Change; Revolutionaries are Changers; Liberation means Freedom and by their collective view of themselves as being part of a BIG FAMILY working, playing, and living together in the struggle. The beauty of socialism is seen through their daily practice while involving themselves in the program.

We call upon the people within the community to join the Vanguard Party in putting forth the correct examples for our youth through their active participation in our liberation schools across this country.

Community Political Education classes will also be starting in the evening for adults. The education of the masses is primary to the Vanguard Party. People, take part in this revolutionary program to continue the struggle for freedom in this country."

ALL POWER TO THE PEOPLE!
ALL POWER TO THE YOUTH!

—*The Black Panther*, July 5, 1969

## The Youth Make the Revolution

by Val Douglas

Children come through the doors ready to eat, learn and play. They know that when they come in, their breakfast is being prepared, because the Black Panther Party knows the importance of having breakfast in the morning. It wakes them up and gives them strength to exert their energy.

Being an assistant teacher, I have an opportunity to be amongst the children and start a conversation, and stimulate their minds to seeing clearly the state of repression that we are living in. What is so fascinating for the teachers and parents is to see how quickly their minds work, and are able to elaborate and go into detail. We know that our children are brilliant, all you have to do is show them and guide them in the right direction. Most of the children raise their hands without even being asked, to speak of the ten point platform and program, what is happening in their community, pigs, and Panthers. They are given posters and can tell you all of the names, such as; Huey, Bobby, Eldridge, and others. And when you speak of Eldridge they say, "he's free, he's eating watermelon and the pigs can't touch him."

They are eager to learn and exchange ideas, because the curriculum is based on true experiences of revolutionaries and everyday people who the children can relate to. One Mother of five told me that her children made satisfactory grades in school, but when she saw the work they were doing in the Liberation School, such as; choosing articles and writing about them or giving an oral report about an event that happened in the world, she smiled with pride; she said, "their work shows that they can relate to what is happening to them and other poor people in the world." Some of the children who can't even write, try because they understand that we are there to help each other. We have a basic topic each day:

Monday is Revolutionary History Day
Tuesday is Revolutionary Culture Day
Wednesday is Current Events Day
Thursday is Movie Day
Friday is Field Trip Day
(The topics can be changed around for the benefit of the people working in a Liberation School)

This is basic, but we have a Curriculum Coordinator who arranges a curriculum each week. We also take the children outside for exercises. They all raise their hands to lead in the exercises. You watch them strong and full of vigor. They march to songs that tell of the pigs running amuck, and Panthers fighting for the people.

We have children in the Liberation School ranging from 2–13. The older ones are becoming more and more helpful to their younger brothers and sisters. At the age of 10–13 children have seen and experienced things for themselves, where as, they understand the need for their younger brothers and sisters to fully understand why there is a need for a Liberation School. We call ourselves the Big Family along with the rest of our class brothers and sisters all over the world. We want the children to especially understand the class struggle, because people of all colors are being exploited by the same pigs all over the world. Most of the Liberation Schools are in areas where poor people of all colors live who are being exploited and oppressed, because of this it is easier for them to relate to the class struggle when they see people of different races who are just as poor as they.

Our young children are becoming more and more disciplined each day, simply because they can relate to what is being taught. One four year old, Sonya, told her fellow student who is three that he was too big to be crying, and don't you want to hear about Huey P. Newton and Bobby Seale. "She", got the three year old to stop crying. We know that the children are going to rebel against their teachers and older people, but we know that the most important thing is to get the children to work with each other, because there's not going to be a Black Panther Party around all the time to set things straight. They're going to have to depend and relate to each other. We have small fights and arguments, but when they do occur we sit down and discuss the matter and come to a conclusion, a unity of will, because we know that if we don't solve the problem then and there, the children will be holding grudges against each other.

In the past the colleges, and recently high school students have been voicing their demands and opinions. These children will teach their other brothers and sisters, and even the elementary schools will be expressing their disgust of the situation they are in. They are the ones that will carry on the struggle, and we are happy to say that in the next couple of weeks, Liberation Schools will be springing up all over the Nation, just like the Breakfast for School Children.

ALL POWER TO THE YOUTH
Liberation School, 9th & Hearst
Berkeley
—*The Black Panther*, August 2, 1969

## People's Medical Care Center

by Lincoln Webster Sheffield

In the current drive to exterminate the Black Panther Party, scant attention has been focused by the establishment press on the Panther programs aimed at serving the people. One of these programs in Chicago is the People's Medical Care Center, located in the Lawndale ghetto on the West Side. The center is named for Spurgeon "Jake" Winters, a martyred Panther killed by police last year.

The only publicity the center has received came when city authorities attempted to close it a few days after it opened in December, charging numerous building and Board of Health violations.

But the center has remained open, in spite of this harassment, and it regularly treats more than 100 patients every week.

One of the center's volunteers is Mrs. Sylvia Woods, a licensed practical nurse.

"We have ten doctors, twelve nurses, and two registered technicians who officially serve in the Free Medical Center," Mrs. Woods told me. "We also have a large number of interns who come and help regularly, from medical schools around the city."

Part of the center's work includes training community people to perform services wherever possible. "For example," said Mrs. Woods, "we are training some of the young people to do laboratory urinalysis and blood tests, and teams of people from the community are organized to canvass the neighborhood and bring the center to the people. Most of the people in Lawndale are so poor they never go to a doctor until they are practically dying. Our teams take their blood pressure, medical histories, and in general determine if there are people suffering from illness.

"If illness is discovered, whether chronic or just simple ailments, the person is urged to visit the center, where an examination, treatment, and prescription are all free."

In a typical evening of duty, Mrs. Woods may help to treat 20 or 30 people, some of whom come in after being referred by the survey teams, and many who come after hearing from friends and neighbors about the center.

"The center opens at 6 o'clock every evening," she said, describing a typical night's work. "Last night, when I got to the center, there weren't any patients in yet, so I worked with some Panthers straightening and cleaning up the reception area.

"At about 6:20, our first patients arrived. They were two children, 14 and 12 years old, who needed a routine health examination for school. When I worked for the Joslyn Clinic in Maywood, these examinations cost at least $10. But at the Panther center, they are absolutely free. If the parents happen to be on welfare, I don't know what they did before we had the center, because welfare wouldn't pay for school examinations.

"I took the histories of the two youths, and we did a complete urinalysis and blood test. Then, each was examined thoroughly by a licensed pediatrician. Neither had had DPT (diphtheria-tetanus toxoid) shots, so they were administered. Both patients were in generally good health, except that the oldest had a cold. He was given medication, and we made an appointment for him to return. There was, of course, no charge for any of this.

"Next, a 21-year-old woman came in. She was seriously ill and aborting her first pregnancy. She was examined, given some medication for pain, and taken to a hospital that has agreed to take some of our patients.

"Next, we had several more young people who came in for routine examinations, and then a mother brought in a four-month old baby who had a bad cold. The baby was examined by the pediatrician, and a throat culture was taken. This baby had been going to the well-baby clinic operated by the Board of Health, but had not yet received any of the normal shots. After the examination and discussion with the mother, an appointment was made for the baby to return for continued treatment and the shots."

Among others who came in that evening, Mrs. Woods said, was a young woman who had contracted venereal disease, several other children, and a woman suffering from a "cold" for three months.

"All these people were treated free, no questions asked about 'ability to pay' or anything. On hand to take care of all these people were a pediatrician, a general practitioner, two interns, and two nurses."

The center does not stop at treating medical problems. A member of the Black Panther Party is on hand at all times to serve as a "people's advocate." He interviews each patient.

"The people's advocate makes the center more able to deal with the entire range of people's problems," Mrs. Woods said. "After being examined, the patient and his or her parents if a minor discuss any other problems they may have with the representative of the Panthers. The people's advocate will try to find out if the patient has any difficulties at home, such as paying the rent, finding clothes for the family, food, or whether they may be having trouble studying, or in school—almost any kind of problem is relevant.

"Whenever possible, the Panthers will help with the problem, no matter what it is. For example, we discovered that many of the school children, aside from problems like going without breakfast, faced serious strain from the difficulty of finding a place to study or play, safe from the hazards of the street. So we opened up the center to them during the afternoon, before the regular hours, where they can play quietly, or study, paint or do whatever they wish."

Most diseases the center has treated, frequently discovered by the canvass teams and previously unknown to the patient, are bronchial ailments, heart disease, diabetes, apparent mental retardation, and high blood pressure.

The success of the Spurgeon "Jake" Winters People's Medical Care Center has inspired similar efforts by other organizations, particularly those in the "rainbow coalition" with the Panthers. Both the Young Lords and the Young Patriots have opened centers, although they are not yet operating on as full a schedule as the Panthers.

—*Daily World*, May 16, 1970

# Pocket Lawyer of Legal First Aid

This pocket lawyer is provided as a means of keeping black people up to date on their rights. We are always the first to be arrested and the racist police forces are constantly trying to pretend that rights are extended equally to all people. Cut this out, brothers and sisters, and carry it with you. Until we arm ourselves to righteously take care of our own, the pocket lawyer is what's happening.

1. If you are stopped and/or arrested by the police, you may remain silent; you do not have to answer any questions about alleged crimes, you should provide your name and address only if requested (although it is not absolutely clear that you must do so.) But then do so, and at all times remember the fifth amendment.

2. If a police officer is not in uniform, ask him to show his identification. He has no authority over you unless he properly identifies himself. Beware of persons posing as police officers. Always get his badge number and his name.

3. Police have no right to search your car or your home unless they have a search warrant, probable cause or your consent. They may conduct no exploratory search, that is, one for evidence of crime generally or for evidence of a crime unconnected with the one you are being questioned about. (Thus, a stop for an auto violation does not give the right to search the auto.) You are not required to consent to a search; therefore, you should not consent and should state clearly and unequivocally that you do not consent, in front of witnesses if possible. If you do not consent, the police will have the burden in court of showing probable cause. Arrest may be corrected later.

4. You may not resist arrest forcibly or by going limp, even if you are innocent. To do so is a separate crime of which you can be convicted even if you are acquitted of the original charge. Do not resist arrest under any circumstances.

5. If you are stopped and/or arrested, the police may search you by patting you on the outside of your clothing. You can be stripped of your personal possessions. Do not carry anything that includes the name of your employer or friends.

6. Do not engage in "friendly" conversation with officers on the way to or at the station Once you are arrested, there is little likelihood that anything you say will get you released.

7. As soon as you have been booked, you have the right to com-

plete at least two phone calls—one to a relative, friend or attorney, the other to a bail bondsman. If you can, call the Black Panther Party, 845–0103 (845–0104), and the Party will post bail if possible.

8. You must be allowed to hire and see an attorney immediately.

9. You do not have to give any statement to the police, nor do you have to sign any statement you might give them, and therefore you should not sign anything. Take the Fifth and Fourteenth Amendments, because you cannot be forced to testify against yourself.

10. You must be allowed to post bail in most cases, but you must be able to pay the bail bondsmen's fee. If you cannot pay the fee, you may ask the judge to release you from custody without bail or to lower your bail, but he does not have to do so.

11. The police must bring you into court or release you within 48 hours after your arrest (unless the time ends on a week-end or a holiday, and they must bring you before a judge the first day court is in session.)

12. If you do not have the money to hire an attorney, immediately ask the police to get you an attorney without charge.

13. If you have the money to hire a private attorney, but do not know of one, call the National Lawyers' Guild or the Alameda County Bar Association (or the Bar Association of your county) and ask them to furnish you with the name of an attorney who practices criminal law.

—*The Black Panther*, March 23, 1969

# In Memory of Dr. Martin Luther King

Martin Luther King is dead—the victim of a white racist bullet. The entire nation has assumed a cloak of mourning. The Commander-in-Chief of the United States Army pays official tribute to Martin Luther King and to non-violence. But although officials on all levels of government give public praise to the man and his deeds, they are all too silent in pledging themselves to the concrete actions that are needed to deal with the evils in American society that Dr. King dedicated his life to eliminating. As a response to the racism that took his life, and as a tribute to the man, we make the following demands upon those who now hold power in this country:

### Existing Police Forces Must Be Withdrawn
### from All Black Communities

It is the police who are the main perpetrators of violence against Black people. They are the official agents of a white racist society which enforces the will of that society upon the Black and other national minority communities. They are not of that community, cannot understand its problems, and do not identify with it and its needs. Their ignorance of the community leads them to deal with it through violence and gives an official stamp of approval to the idea that white racist violence is an appropriate response to the needs and demands of the Black community. Existing police forces should be replaced by a new police force responsible to the Black community and consisting of men who live in that community.

### Massive Economic Aid Should Be Provided
### to Rebuild the Black Communities

The United States spends over 40 billion dollars per year in Vietnam. At least that amount should immediately be redirected to meet the needs of America's oppressed communities. Ghetto housing must be rebuilt and turned over to the occupants. Adequate jobs and services must be provided to all ghetto residents, and these must be turned over to the cooperative control of the ghetto residents. White racism is a reactionary response to the just demands of Black people. Ultimately, white racism will not be eliminated until those demands are adequately met.

### Control of the Institutions of the Black Community
### Must Be Turned Over to That Community

Not only control over jobs and housing, but also control over the schools and courts of the Black community must be turned over to that community. Only the residents of a community have a true understanding of its needs and desires. As long as white society dominates the institutions of the ghetto, racial tensions will continue to exist. No people is free unless it can determine its own destiny.

We believe that those who mourn the death of Dr. Martin Luther King, but do nothing to eliminate the white racism and oppression that has characterized America for the past three hundred years are merely mocking him and the Black community. We will judge men not by their words, but by their deeds, not by their sentiments, but by their programs. America must stop mourning Dr. King and must begin satisfying the needs and desires of its Black community.

BLACK PANTHER PARTY
PEACE & FREEDOM MOVEMENT
LOS ANGELES COUNTY

# Petition Statement for Community Control of Police

SUMMARY OF POLICE CONTROL AMENDMENT THAT MUST BE ESTABLISHED IN THE CITIES AND COMMUNITIES OF AMERICA TO END FASCISM

This amendment to a City charter would give control of the police to community elected neighborhood councils so that those whom the police should serve will be able to set police policy and standards of conduct.

The amendment provides for community control of the police by establishing police departments for the major communities of any city; the Black community, the predominantly White area, the Mexican American Communities, etc., etc. The departments would be separate and autonomous. They can by mutual agreement use common facilities. Each Department will be administered by full time police commissions. (Not single police chiefs.) The Commissioners are selected by a Neighborhood Police Control Council composed of fifteen members from that community elected by those who live there. Each department shall have five Community Council divisions within it. (Or number of departments ratioed to population.)

The Councils shall have the power to discipline officers for breaches of Department policy or violations of law. (Against the people). They may direct their police Commissioner to make changes in department wide police policy by majority vote of the said department commissioners. The Council can recall the Commissioner appointed by it at any time it finds that he is no longer responsive to the community. The community can recall the council members when they are not responsive to it.

All police officers must live in the department they work in, and will be hired accordingly.

—*The Black Panther*, June 14, 1969

## Defend the Ghetto

IN OUR STRUGGLE FOR NATIONAL LIBERATION, we are now in the phase of community liberation, to free our black communities from the imperialistic control exercised over them
by the racist exploiting cliques within white communities, to free our people, locked
up as they are in Urban Dungeons, from the imperialism of the white suburbs.

OURS IS A STRUGGLE against Community Imperialism. Our black communities are colonized and controlled from outside, and it is this control that has to be smashed,
broken, shattered, by whatever means necessary.

THE POLITICS IN OUR COMMUNITIES are controlled from outside, the economics of our
communities are controlled from outside, and we ourselves are controlled by the racist
police who came into our communities from outside and occupy them, patrolling, terror-
izing, and brutalizing our people like a foreign army in a conquered land.

THE BLACK PANTHER PARTY IS THE REVOLUTIONARY ORGANIZATION STRUGGLING TO FREE OUR
PEOPLE FROM OPPRESSION, BY POLITICAL AND PHYSICAL MEANS. WE HAVE TO GET ORGANIZED,
AND WE HAVE TO DEFEND OURSELVES. --- JOIN THE BLACK PANTHER PARTY ---

# BLACK    PANTHER    PARTY
1808A Fulton Street, Brooklyn

## Community Discussion Groups

# COMMUNITY DISCUSSION GROUPS

### WOULD YOU LIKE TO HAVE A MEMBER OF THE B.P.P. COME TO YOUR HOME AND DISCUSS:

1. •The Ten-Point Platform and Program of The BLACK PANTHER PARTY and What it Means To Black People,

2. •The Need For COMMUNITY CONTROL OF POLICE.

3. •The Need For Black People To Become REGISTERED VOTERS So They Can Sit on Jury Panels and Give Justice To Black People.

4. •The Murders of FRED HAMPTON and MARK CLARK in Chicago.

5. •The Many Attacks on our Homes and Offices in L.A., CHICAGO, NEW YORK. etc. and The International Harrassment, Repression and Murders of The Members of The BLACK PANTHER PARTY.

HOME DISCUSSION GROUPS SHOULD NUMBER AT LEAST SIX PEOPLE. APPOINTMENTS ARE AVAILABLE BETWEEN THE HOURS OF 9 a.m & 7 p.m., SEVEN DAYS A WEEK.

CALL—
BERKELEY – 845-0103 or 0104
E. OAKLAND – 568-3334
SAN FRANCISCO – 922-0095
RICHMOND – 237-6305

ALL POWER TO THE PEOPLE
BLACK PANTHER PARTY Natl. Hq.
3106 SHATTUCK AVE. BERK.

# 10.

## BLACK PANTHERS IN COURT

The picture of Bobby Seale gagged, shackled, and bound during the Chicago conspiracy trial shocked the entire world, as did the cruel contempt sentence imposed upon him by Judge Julius Hoffman. Millions at the same time admired and respected the Chairman of the Black Panther Party for his courage in insisting upon his constitutional rights.

Bobby Seale was one of eight defendants in the Chicago conspiracy trial who were being tried under an amendment to the Civil Rights Act of 1968—the so-called Rap Brown Amendment—which makes it a crime to cross state lines with intent to incite a riot. The penalty for such intentions is five years in jail. Together with the other seven defendants, Seale was accused of having come to Chicago in August, 1968, with the intention of creating a riot and stirring up violence during the Democratic National Convention being held in that city. During the trial, Seale had frequent clashes with Judge Hoffman. He charged that he had been unfairly denied the counsel of his choice because Judge Hoffman had refused to postpone the trial so that Charles R. Garry, Seale's San Francisco lawyer, could attend the trial after his recovery from a major operation. Seale also charged that the judge, having refused the postponement, then refused to permit Seale to defend himself in Garry's absence and had illegally imposed a counsel upon him. On October 29, Seale was chained hand and foot to a metal chair and a gag of muslin was put in his mouth so that he could not continue to challenge the judge and interrupt the trial proceedings. During the next few days, the gag was strengthened. A few days later, in response to rising protests, Seale was allowed to enter the courtroom free of his gags and straps. When Seale continued to insist on his right to defend himself, Judge Hoffman declared a mistrial in his case; sentenced him to sixteen terms of three months each for contempt, and ordered him to remain in jail until his trial on April 23, 1970.

The first part of this section contains excerpts from Judge Hoffman's long statement citing evidence of what he described as proof of Bobby Seale's conduct in continually disrupting "the orderly administration of justice"—but which Seale maintained proved only his efforts to uphold his constitutional rights—and which preceded the judge's announcement of his sentence of contempt.

During the pre-trial hearings of thirteen Black Panthers in New York accused of conspiracy, New York Supreme Court Justice John M. Murtagh suspended the proceedings and insisted that the defendants give him assurances about their behavior during the trial. The thirteen sent a twenty-four-page response to Judge Murtagh (which he rejected) which rapidly became famous as a significant summary of Black History as well as for its clear assertion that it is impossible for black people to receive a fair trial in the United States. The entire document is reprinted in the second part of this section. It was written by thirteen defendants. Originally, twenty-one persons were arrested and charged. Eight have been severed from the case for various reasons, but the case is still referred to as the Panther 21.

The section ends with the moving concluding appeal to the jury by Charles R. Garry in the trial of Huey P. Newton. Garry has been the main attorney for the Black Panther Party. He has defended Newton and Seale, among others, and at the time of this writing is defending Seale in Connecticut. Mr. Garry is also the attorney for six Mexican-Americans in the trial known as Los Siete de la Raza.

# Bobby Seale vs. Judge Hoffman

JUDGE HOFFMAN:

Item No. 5. At the morning session on October 22, 1969, during argument on a motion of Attorney William Kunstler for leave to withdraw as counsel for the defendant Seale, the following occurred in open court.[16]

MR. SEALE: Can I speak on that and answer his argument?

THE COURT: No. This is not your motion, sir. Your motion has been decided.

MR. SEALE: In other words, I can't speak in behalf of myself?

THE COURT: Not at this time, sir.

MR. SEALE: Why not?

THE COURT: Because this is your lawyer's motion.

MR. SEALE: That ain't my lawyer.

THE COURT: This is not your motion. This is the motion of Mr. William Kunstler for leave to withdraw as your lawyer.

MR. SEALE: Well, this man has misconstrued a whole lot of things concerning my right to defend myself and he knows he did.

They can jack you up and get you to sit up there and say rotten, crazy stuff concerning my right to defend myself.

THE COURT: I would request the marshal to ask the young man to sit down.

MR. SEALE: Well, I want my right to defend myself and this man knew, I indicated to him he was not my counsel at the very beginning when I first got here and arrived here and was in jail.

THE COURT: That motion—since you will not listen to the Court, you may sit down.

Have him sit down, Mr. Marshal.

MR. SEALE: I still want my right to defend myself. A railroad operation, and you know it, from Nixon on down. They got you running around here violating my constitutional rights.

Item No. 6:

During the morning session on October 22nd, 1969, in the presence of the jury . . . the following occurred:

MR. SCHULTZ: Your Honor, before the next witness testifies, would it be possible if the Court would permit the Government— well, we haven't offered the picture, as a matter of fact. We have the picture of the boy with the black power symbol fist on his sweat

shirt that was identified by Officer Tobin and Carcerano as the boy—

THE COURT: Is that Government's Exhibit 14?

MR. SCHULTZ: That's the one. . . . We are going to move to offer that exhibit in evidence at this time. . . .

THE COURT: Show it to counsel.

MR. SEALE: That's not a black power sign. Somebody correct the Court on that. It's not the black power sign. It's the power to the people sign.

THE COURT: Mr. Marshal, will you stop the talking, please.

MR. SEALE: Yes, but that is still wrong, Judge Hoffman. It's not a black power sign. It's a power to the people sign, and he is deliberately distorting that and that's a racist technique.

MR. SCHULTZ: If the Court please, this man has repeatedly called me a racist—

MR. SEALE: Yes, you are. You are, Dick Schultz.

MR. SCHULTZ: And called Mr. Foran a racist—

THE COURT: Ladies and gentlemen of the jury, I will ask you to leave the Court. Mr. Marshal, remove the ladies and gentlemen of the jury:

(The following proceedings were had in open court, out of the presence and hearing of the jury:)

THE COURT: Mr. Seale and Mr. Kunstler, your lawyer, I must admonish you that such outbursts are considered by the Court to be contemptuous, contumacious, and will be dealt with appropriately in the future.

MR. KUNSTLER: Your Honor, the defendant was trying to defend himself, and I have already indicated my—

THE COURT: The defendant was not defending himself.

MR. SEALE: I was, too, defending myself. Any time anybody gives me the wrong symbol in this courtroom is deliberately—

THE COURT: He is not addressing me with authority—

MR. SEALE: —distorting, and put it on the record.

THE COURT: Instruct that man to keep quiet.

MR. SEALE: I want to defend myself and ask him if he isn't lying, and he is going to put that lying crap on the record. No, siree—I am not going to sit here and get that on the record. I am going to at least let it be known—request that you understand that this man is erroneously representing symbols directly related to the party of which I am chairman.

Item No. 8:

At the opening of the morning session on October 27, 1969, the following occurred in open court:

THE COURT: Ladies and gentlemen of the jury, good morning.

MR. SEALE: Good morning, ladies and gentlemen of the jury. As I said before, I hope you don't blame me for anything.

THE COURT: Mr. Marshal, will you tell that man to sit down.

THE MARSHAL: Take a seat, Mr. Seale.

MR. SEALE: I know—

THE COURT: Mr. Marshal, I think Mr. Seale is saying something there.

MR. SEALE: I know I am saying something. You know I am getting ready to speak out in behalf of my constitutional rights again, don't you?

THE COURT: I will ask you to sit down, sir.

THE MARSHAL: Sit down.

MR. SEALE: You also know I am speaking out for the right to defend myself again, don't you, because I have that right as a defendant, don't I?

THE COURT: I will have to ask you to sit down sir.

MR. SEALE: You know what I am going to say, don't you?

THE COURT: No, I don't.

MR. SEALE: Well, I said it before.

THE COURT: I don't know what you are going to say and you have a very competent lawyer of record here.

MR. SEALE: He is not my lawyer and you know I fired him before that jury was even picked and put together.

THE COURT: Will you ask him to sit down, Mr. Marshal?

THE MARSHAL: Sit down, Mr. Seale.

MR. SEALE: What about my constitutional right to defend myself and have my lawyer?

THE COURT: Your constitutional rights—

MR. SEALE: You are denying them. You have been denying them. Every other word you say is denied, denied, denied, denied, and you begin to oink in the faces of the masses of the people of this country. That is what you begin to represent, the corruptness of this rotten government, or four hundred years.

THE MARSHAL: Mr. Seale, will you sit down.

MR. SEALE: Why don't you knock me in the mouth? Try that.

THE MARSHAL: Sit down.

THE COURT: Ladies and gentlemen of the jury, I regret that I will have to excuse you.

MR. SEALE: [To the jury] I hope you don't blame me for anything and those false lying notes and letters that were sent that said the Black Panther Party threatened that jury, it's a lie and you know it's a lie, and the government did it to taint the jury against me.

(The following proceedings were had in open court, out of the presence and hearing of the jury:)

MR. SEALE: You got that? This racist and fascist administrative government with its superman notions and comic book politics. We're hip to the fact that Superman never saved no black people. You got that?

MR. KUNSTLER: I might say, your Honor, you know that I have tried to withdraw from this and you know that Mr. Seale—
THE COURT: I don't know what you tried to do. I know your appearance is of record, and I know I have your assurance orally of record that you represent this man.
MR. KUNSTLER: You have a withdrawal of that assurance, your Honor. You knew that on September 30th, you knew that Mr. Seale had discharged me.
THE COURT: You represent him and the record shows it.
MR. KUNSTLER: Your Honor, you can't go on those semantics. This man wants to defend himself.
THE COURT: This isn't semantics. I am not fooled by all of this business.
MR. SEALE: I still demand the right to defend myself. You are not fooled? After you have walked over people's constitutional rights?
THE MARSHAL: Sit down, Mr. Seale.
MR. SEALE: After you done walked over people's constitutional rights, the Sixth Amendment, the Fifth Amendment, and the phoniness and the corruptness of this very trial, for people to have a right to speak out, freedom of speech, freedom of assembly, and et cetera. You have did everything you could with those jive lying witnesses up there presented by these pig agents of the Government to lie and say and condone some rotten racists, fascist crap by racist cops and pigs that beat people's heads—and I demand my constitutional rights—demand—demand—
Call in the jury.
THE COURT: Will the Marshal bring in the jury, please.

Item No. 9:
During the direct examination of the witness William Frapolly on October 27, 1969, the following occurred:
MR. SEALE: I object to that because my lawyer is not here. I have been denied my right to defend myself in this courtroom. I object to this man's testimony against me because I have not been allowed my constitutional rights.
THE COURT: I repeat to you, sir, you have a lawyer. Your lawyer is Mr. Kunstler, who represented to the Court that he represents you.
MR. SEALE: He does not represent me.
THE COURT: And he has filed an appearance.
Ladies and gentlemen, I will excuse you.
(The following proceedings were had in open court, within the presence and hearing of the jury:)
MR. KUNSTLER: May I say I have withdrawn or attempted to withdraw.
MR. SEALE: The defense filed a motion before the jury ever heard any evidence, and I object to that testimony.

THE COURT: For your information, sir, I do not hear parties to a case who are not represented by lawyers. You are represented by a lawyer.

MR. SEALE: I am not represented by a lawyer. I am not represented by Charles Garry for your information.

THE MARSHAL: Sit down, Mr. Seale.

THE COURT: Now you just keep on this way and—

MR. SEALE: Keep on what? Keep on what?

THE COURT: Just sit down.

MR. SEALE: Keep on what? Keep on getting denied my constitutional rights?

THE COURT: Will you be quiet?

MR. SEALE: I object to that man's—can't I object to that man there sitting up there testifying against me and my constitutional rights denied to my lawyer being here?

Now I still object. I object because you know it is wrong. You denied me my right to defend myself. You think black people don't have a mind. Well, we got big minds, good minds, and we know how to come forth with constitutional rights, the so-called constitutional rights. I am not going to be quiet. I am talking in behalf of my constitutional rights, man, in behalf of myself, that's my constitutional right to talk in behalf of my constitutional rights.

THE COURT: Bring in the jury, Mr. Marshal.

MR. SEALE: I still object to that man testifying against me without my lawyer being here, without me having a right to defend myself.

Black people ain't supposed to have a mind? That's what you think. We got a body and a mind. I wonder, did you lose yours in the Superman syndrome comic book stories? You must have, to deny us our constitutional rights.

THE COURT: Are you getting all of this, Miss Reporter?

MR. SEALE: I hope she gets it all.

(The following proceedings were had in open court, out of the presence and hearing of the jury:)

MR. SEALE: Taint the jury against me, send them threatening letters that I never sent, and you know it's a lie, you keep them away from their homes and they blame me every time they come in this room because they are being kept away from their homes, and you did it.

THE COURT: Are you going to stop, sir?

MR. SEALE: I am going to talk in behalf of my constitutional rights.

THE COURT: You may continue, sir, with the direct examination of this witness.

And I note that your counsel has remained quiet during your dissertation.

Mr. Seale: You know what? I have no counsel here. I fired that lawyer before that jury heard anything and you know it. That jury hasn't heard all of the motions you denied behind the scenes. How you tricked that juror out of that stand there by threatening her with that jive letter that you know darned well I didn't send, which is a lie. And they blame me every time they are being kept from their loved ones and their homes. They blame me every time they come in the room. And I never sent those letters, you know it.

The Court: Please continue with the direct examination.

On October 28, 1969—this is Item No. 10—on October 28, 1969, during the afternoon session, while the witness William Frapolly was testifying on cross-examination, the following occurred in open court:

The Court: Mr. Weinglass, do you want to cross-examine this witness?

Mr. Seale: I would like to request to cross-examine the witness.

The Court: You have a lawyer here.

Mr. Seale: That man is not my lawyer. The man made statements against me. Furthermore, he violated Title 1892 of the United States. Well, you are still violating it.[17]

The Marshal: Sit down, Mr. Seale.

Mr. Seale: You violated the Code. You violated the United States laws against my rights.

The Court: Mr. Marshal, will you ask Mr. Seale to sit down in his chair?

Mr. Seale: You are violating Title 42, United States Criminal Code. You are violating it because it states that a black man cannot be discriminated against in his legal defense.

The Court: Will you sit down, Mr. Seale?

Mr. Seale: It is an old reconstruction law and you won't recognize it. So I would like to cross-examine the witness.

The Court: Will you sit down, sir?

Mr. Seale: I still want to cross-examine the witness.

The Court: You may not.

A Marshal: May I remove the jury, please?

The Court: Ladies and gentlemen of the jury, you may be excused.

After the jury was excused, the defendant Seale continued to refuse to obey the order of the Court to remain silent. Thereupon the following occurred in open court:

The Court: Let the record show that the defendant—

Mr. Seale: Let the record show you violated that and a black man cannot be discriminated against in relation to his legal defense and that is exactly what you have done. You know you have. Let the record show that.

The Court: The record shows exactly to the contrary.

MR. SEALE: The record shows that you are violating, that you violated my constitutional rights. I want to cross-examine the witness. I want to cross-examine the witness.

THE COURT: Bring in the jury, Mr. Marshal, and we will let them go for this evening.

I admonish you, sir, that you have a lot of contemptuous conduct against you.

MR. SEALE: I admonish you. You are in contempt of people's constitutional rights. You are in contempt of the constitutional rights of the mass of the people of the United States. You are the one in contempt of people's constitutional rights. I am not in contempt of nothing. You are the one who is in contempt. The people of America need to admonish you and the whole Nixon administration.

Let me cross-examine the witness. You won't even let me read— you wouldn't even let me read my statement this morning, my motion this morning, concerning the fact that I wanted a copy of the transcript for my own legal defense.

THE COURT: Bring in the jury.

Is he getting the jury?

THE CLERK: Yes, your Honor.

THE COURT: Tell him to just bring them before the box.

MR. SEALE: I want to cross-examine the witness.

MR. HAYDEN: Let the record show the judge was laughing. [Mr. Hayden is a defendant.]

MR. SEALE: Yes, he is laughing.

THE COURT: Who made that remark?

MR. FORAN: The defendant Hayden, your Honor, made the remark.

MR. SEALE: And me.

THE COURT: Let the record show that—

MR. SEALE: I still want to cross-examine the witness to defend myself.

The jury was then returned to the courtroom to be excused for the day, during which time, the defendant Seale continued to speak. Thereafter, the following occurred in open court:

THE COURT: You may sit down.

I must admonish the defendant and his counsel—

MR. SEALE: Counsel ain't got nothing to do with it. I'm my own counsel.

THE COURT: You are not doing very well for yourself.

MR. SEALE: Yes, that's because you violated my constitutional rights, Judge Hoffman. That's because you violated them overtly, deliberately, in a very racist manner. Somebody ought to point out the law to you. You don't want to investigate it to see whether the people get their constitutional rights. 68,000 black men died in the Civil War for that right. That right was made during the Reconstruction period. They fought in that war and 68,000 of them died. That law was made for me to have my constitutional rights.

THE COURT: Do you want to listen to me for a moment?

MR. SEALE: Why should I continue to listen to you unless you are going to give me my constitutional rights? Let me defend myself.

THE COURT: I am warning you, sir, that the law—

MR. SEALE: Instead of warning, why don't you warn me I have got a right to defend myself, huh?

THE COURT: I am warning you that the Court has the right to gag you. I don't want to do that. Under the law you may be gagged and chained to your chair.

MR. SEALE: Gagged? I am being railroaded already. I am being railroaded already.

THE COURT: The Court has that right and I—

MR. SEALE: The Court has no right whatsoever. The Court has no right to stop me from speaking out in behalf of my constitutional rights because it is denying me the constitutional rights to speak out in behalf of myself and my legal defense.

THE COURT: The Court will be in recess until tomorrow morning at ten o'clock.

THE MARSHAL: Everyone will please rise.

MR. SEALE: I am not rising. I am not rising until he recognizes my constitutional rights. Why should I rise for him? He is not recognizing—

THE COURT: Mr. Marshal—

MR. SEALE: I am not rising.

Item No. 12, on October 29, 1969, during the morning session when the cross-examination of the witness Frapolly was completed, the following occurred in open court:

THE COURT: Is there any redirect examination?

MR. SEALE: Before the redirect, I would like to request again— demand, that I be able to cross-examine the witness. My lawyer is not here. I think I have a right to defend myself in this courtroom.

THE COURT: Take the jury out, and they may go to lunch with the usual order.

MR. SEALE: You have George Washington and Benjamin Franklin sitting in a picture behind you, and they were slave owners.[18] That's what they were. They owned slaves. You are acting in the same manner, denying me my constitutional rights being able to cross-examine this witness.

THE COURT: Gentlemen, we will recess until two o'clock.

Accordingly, it is therefore ordered that pursuant to the authority vested in this Court by Rule 42(a) of the Federal Rules of Criminal

Procedure and by Title 18, United States Code, Section 401, the defendant Bobby Seale be punished for contempt. I will hear from you, Mr. Kunstler.

MR. KUNSTLER: Your Honor, I have already indicated that because I have been discharged I can say nothing for Mr. Seale. He wants to be his own attorney, as your Honor has read at least thirty or forty times from your own opinion, and I think that I would be derelict in my duty to my understanding of my right and liability as an attorney were I to speak for him now.

THE COURT: Mr. Seale, you have a right to speak now. I will hear you.

MR. SEALE: For myself?

THE COURT: In your own behalf, yes.

MR. SEALE: How come I couldn't speak before?

THE COURT: This is a special occasion.

MR. SEALE: Wait a minute. Now are you going to try to—you going to attempt to punish me for attempting to speak for myself before? Now after you punish me, you sit up and say something about you can speak? What kind of jive is that? I don't understand it. What kind of court is this? Is this a court? It must be a fascist operation like I see it in my mind, you know,—I don't understand you.

THE COURT: I am calling on you—

MR. SEALE: You just read a complete record of me trying to persuade you, trying to show you, demonstrating my right, demonstrating to you the need, showing you all this stuff about my right to defend myself, my right to defend myself, history, slavery, et cetera; and you going to sit there and say something about, "OK, now you can speak"?

What am I supposed to speak about? I still haven't got the right to defend myself. I would like to speak about that. I would like to—since you let me stand up and speak, can I speak about in behalf of—can I defend myself?

THE COURT: You may speak to the matters I have discussed here today, matters dealing with your contemptuous conduct. The law obligates me to call on you to speak at this time.

MR. SEALE: About what? About the fact that I want a right to defend myself? That's all I am speaking about.

THE COURT: No, about possible punishment for contempt of court.

MR. SEALE: Punishment? You've punished black people all your life. I mean, you, they even say you own a factory that produces raw materials to kill people in Viet Nam [the family of Judge Hoffman's wife is involved in the Brunswick Corporation which produces war materials, among other things], you know, so it's nothing, death is nothing, I mean, if that is what you're talking about, or putting me in jail, or prison, or hanging people, and all that stuff. I have nothing to say about that. I have something to say about the fact that I want to defend myself still. I want my rights, to be able to stand up and cross-examine the witnesses. I want that, so I don't know what you're talking about.

THE COURT: I have tried to make it clear.

MR. SEALE: All you make clear to me is that you don't want me, you refuse to let me, you will not go by my persuasion, or my arguments, my motions, my requests to be, to the extent of even having to shout loud enough to get on that record for that record so that they can hear me half the time. You don't want to listen to me. You don't want to let a man stand up, contend to you that that man is not my lawyer, show you and point out that fact, in fact, made motions and told you that I fired the man.

And to stand up here and say, "Look, I have the right to defend myself," continuously over and over, even to the point just recently on Friday you recognized that I did have only one lawyer by letting this man and Thomas Hayden to go and to talk to Charles R. Garry to see about coming out here for me, which begin to show me that I was beginning to persuade you to do something, at least allow somebody to investigate my situation. Now what are you talking about? Now all of a sudden on the record?

THE COURT: I want to make it clear. I don't want to be questioned any further. The law gives you the right to speak out now in respect to possible punishment for contempt of court, sir.

MR. SEALE: Well, the first thing, I'm not in no contempt of court. I know that. I know that I as a person and a human being have the right to stand up in a court and use his constitutional right to speak in behalf of his constitutional rights. That is very clear, I hope. That's all I have to say. I still want to cross-examine the witnesses, I make those requests. I make my motions, and I make those requests, and I will continue to make those requests, hoping that once in one way along this trial, you will recognize my rights as a human being, a black man living under the scope and influence of a racist decadent America where the Government of the United States does not recognize the black people's constitutional rights, and have never recognized them from 1867 to the Dred Scott case situation, in a period of slaves you never recognized them, and here you are, and all I can say is that you're probably acting in the same manner as Benjamin Franklin and George Washington. We are hep to that kind of business.

THE COURT: Oh, but you are mistaken about that.

MR. SEALE: Oh, yes, you're acting in the same manner as those courts acted in those periods of slavery history, and you know it. That's what you're doing.

If a black man stands up and speaks, if a black man asks for his rights, if a black man demands his rights, if a black man requests his rights, what do you do? You're talking about punishing. If a black man gets up and speaks in behalf of the world—

THE COURT: Are you addressing me, sir?

MR. SEALE: I'm talking. You can see I'm talking.

THE COURT: That's right, but if you address me, you'll have to stand.

MR. SEALE: Stand? Stand now. Now let's see, first you said that I couldn't stand. I got my suit. It's going to a higher court, possibly the highest court in America.

# To Judge Murtagh: From the Panther 21

We the defendants named by the state in the proceedings now pending before "Justice" John M. Murtagh, in Part 38 Supreme Court, County of New York, say:

That the history of this nation has most definitely developed a dual set of social, economic and political realities, as well as dynamics. One white, and the other Black (The Black experience, or ghetto reality) having as their roots one of the most insidious and ruthless systems of human exploitation known to man, the enslavement and murder of over 40 million Black people, spread over a period of less than three centuries.

### Blacks—not Human?

Long ago in this nation certain basic decisions were made about Black people, but *not* consulting them. Even before the Constitution was ever put on paper with its beautiful words and glowing rhetoric of man's equality and philosophical rights, human consideration had long given way before white economic necessity. Black people were to legally be defined and classified as non-human, below a horse—but definitely not a man.

Color became the crucial variable, and the foundation of the system of Black slavery. While chattel slavery is no longer upheld by the supreme law of the land, the habit and practice in thought and speech of looking at Black people from the chattel plain still persist. After much refinement, sophistication and development, it has remained to become embedded in the national character, making itself clear in organized society, its institutions, and the attitudes of the dominant white culture to this very day.

For us to state there are two realities (experiences) that exist in this nation, is a statement of fact.

When we speak of American traditions, let us not forget the tradition of injustice inflicted again, and again upon those whom tradition has been created to exclude, exploit, dehumanize and murder.

Let us not conveniently forget how the system of "American justice" systematically upheld the bizarre reasoning about Black people in order to retain a system of slave labor. And when this became economically unnecessary, how "the great American system of justice" helped to establish and maintain social degradation and deprivation of all who were not white, and most certainly, those who were Black. To be sure, the entire country had to share in this denial; to justify the inhuman treatment of other human beings, the American had to conceal from himself and others his oppression of Blacks, but again the white dominant society has long had absolute power, especially over Black people—so it was no difficult matter to ignore them, define them, forget them, and if they persisted, pacify or punish them.

**Racism Is Built In**

The duality of American society today need no longer be reinforced by laws, for it is now and has long been in the minds of men:

The Harlems of America, as opposed to those who decide the fate of America's Harlems. This is essentially a historical continuation today, of yesterday—the plantation mentality, system and division, in the cloak of 20th century enlightenment.

"Traditional American justice," its very application has created what it claims to remedy, for its eyes are truly covered: it does not see the Black reality, nor does it consider or know of the Black experience, least of all consider it valid.

Black poor people are always subject to, but do not take part in your corrupt grand jury system and process.

We as a people do not exist except as victims, and to this and much more, we say no more. For 351½ years we said this in various ways. But running deep in the American psyche is the fear of the ex-slave. He who for so long has been wronged, will be wronged no more, and in fact will demand, fight and die for his human rights.

**NO MORE!**

But why need we feel this way in the first place? Does not your Constitution guarantee man's freedom, his human dignity against state encroachment? Or does the innate fear of the rebellious slave in the heart of the slave-master continue to this day to negate all those guarantees in the cases of Black people? Does this cultural racist phobia make one forget, and abridge his own constitution, as this court has done to us? Do you not know what we mean when we say "NO MORE"? What has been done to us by your court, the District Attorney, is only a reflection of all that has been infused and permeates this racist society.

Black people have said and felt this for over 100 years. But those of the other reality, the dominant white culture, its institutions, had no ears to truly hear. The wax of centuries of slave master-slave relationship had stopped up their ears, your ears. For if our reality, the Black experience in America, is invalid, then so are the institutions and social structure that contributed to its creation invalid. If you then concede it is valid (which it most definitely is), then it must be of consequence in determining what is "justice" compared to us, (Black people).

White citizens have grown up with the identity of an American, and have enjoyed a completely different relationship to the institutions of this nation, with that, the unresolved conflicts of the ex-slaveholder.

Blacks are no longer the economic underpinning of the nation. But we continue to be willing, or unwilling, victims. There is a timeless quality to the unconscious which transforms yesterday into today.

### The Black Experience

On August 17, 1619, over a year prior to the landing of the pilgrims at Plymouth Rock, a Dutch privateer dropped anchor off Jamestown, Virginia. There she exchanged her cargo of twenty Black men, women and children for provisions. According to the Dutch sailors, these Black people had been baptized, they were "Christians" and therefore could not be enslaved under British laws. As a result of that law, we were legally defined as "indentured" servants.

By 1663, though, the "Christian" conscience had given way to the capitalist desire for maximum profits. By 1663 also the Carolinas, New York and Maryland in 1664, Delaware and Pennsylvania in 1682 perpetrated the most heinous and despicable act conceivable to the human mind, that of denying an entire race of people their freedom by relegating them to an eternal status of "chattel slavery," and this abominable feat was done through the courts, legally, and with the backing of guns—our first experience with "American justice."

But it did not stop there. Although later the "Declaration of Independence" proclaimed that "All men are created equal, that they are endowed by their creator with certain unalienable rights, that among these are Life, Liberty, and the Pursuit of Happiness," there was a most interesting omission. In the original draft there was a paragraph that Thomas Jefferson intended to include in the list of grievances against King George II. The paragraph read: "He has waged cruel war against human nature itself, violating its most sacred rights of life and liberty in the person of a distant people (African Black people), who never offended him; captivating and carrying them into slavery in another hemisphere, or to incur miserable death in their transportation thither."

This paragraph was omitted in the final document, and understandably. For not only would it have been a valid and factual indictment against King George, but also one against the "Founding Fathers" themselves.

When the "glorious" and "sacred" Constitution of the United States of America was drawn up in 1787, the "noble," "just" and "freedom loving" men who had fought a long and bloody war against the tyrannical and oppressive British regime headed by King George, for their freedom, wrote into their constitution laws that further sanctified, legalized and protected that most "peculiar institution" (slavery). Apparently they recognized the absurd and repugnant contradiction, but not sufficiently enough to do anything other than exclude the term "Negro" and "slave" from that document.

The Constitution contained three provisions that dealt specifically with the issue of slavery. The first, established the policy that in counting population in order to determine how many representatives a state might send to Congress all free persons and "three-fifths of all other persons" were to be counted (Article I Section 2). The second forbade the Congress from making any laws restricting the slave trade until 1808 (Article I Section 9), and the third, provided that runaway slaves who had escaped from any state had to be returned by any other state in which they might have sought refuge (Article IV Section 2).

### The World the Slave-Holders Made

The years passed and our wretched plight progressively worsened, the "laws" of bondage became even more institutionalized, inculcated in the dominant culture. In order to further protect and perpetuate their domination over us, the southern states passed many repressive laws called "slave codes." For us, there was no freedom of assembly. If more than four or five slaves came together without permission from a white person, that gathering in the depraved minds of the slave-masters was construed as a conspiracy. The towns and cities imposed a 9 p.m. curfew on us, there was no freedom of movement, a pass had to be carried by the slave whenever he was out of the presence of his master. And to enforce these ignoble laws, slave patrols, organized like militias were composed of armed and mounted whites. (This mentality persists to this day.

Woe to the Black man who is out very late in a white neighborhood; the police (white) suspect him immediately of being up to some foul deed, even into the ghetto, the white policeman brings this mentality.)

Although slavery had been abolished in certain states, the Black people who lived in those states were subjected to degrading laws which belied their so-called free status, and even worse, they were subject to kidnapping and being sold into slavery. This so-called free Black man was anything but free under the "American system of justice."

Throughout this horrid epoch, a few slaves managed to escape, then more slaves. The slaveholders demanded that the runaway slave laws be enforced. They pleaded to the United States Supreme Court, and that "august" body, the most powerful judiciary body in the land, the ultimate interpreters of the Constitution, answered their plea by passing the "fugitive slave law" in 1850.[10] Now for the run-away slave escaping to the North was not enough, for the Northern cities were overrun with slave-catchers.

### Dred Scott

In July 1847, Dred Scott, a Black resident of Missouri, brought suit in a Federal Court for his freedom. It read:

"Your petitioner, Dred Scott, a man of color, respectfully represents that sometime in the year of 1835 your petitioner was 'purchased' as a slave by one John Emerson, since deceased, who . . . conveyed your petitioner from the state of Missouri to Fort Snelling [Illinois] a fort then occupied by the troops of the United States and under the jurisdiction of the United States."

In essence Dred Scott was claiming that since he had been transported into territory (Illinois), in which slavery was forbidden by an act of Congress as well as state law, he was now a free man. This case was looked upon as a test to determine just what rights a Black man had in this country. It was the profound hope of many that a just and humane verdict would be rendered.

It took the Dred Scott case 10 years to reach the "sacred" halls of the Supreme Court, and when that "prestigious" group of men spoke in March 1857 through the voice of "Chief Justice" Roger Taney, the Court ruled that "people of African descent are not and cannot be citizens of the United States and cannot sue in any court of the United States," and the Black people have "no rights which whites are bound to respect"—a classic example of the "American way of justice."

### Reconstruction—the Pretense of Democracy

The Reconstruction Era was a time of great and unparalleled hope. It seemed as though Black people were finally to be accorded equal and humane treatment when the 13th, 14th and 15th Amendments were enacted.

But terror, violence, intimidation and murder still haunted us; the Ku Klux Klan did "their thing."

In 1875 Congress enacted the first significant civil rights law. It theoretically gave Black people the right to equal accommodations, facilities and access to public transportation and places of public amusement. But as Blacks well know and whites deny, there is a world of difference in America between theory and practice. For although the 13th, 14th and 15th Amendments and the civil rights act of 1875 "gave" Black people so-called freedom, the right of citizenship and the right to vote, the enforcement of those laws was an entirely different thing. The extent of enforcement was totally dependent upon the degree to which it was advantageous to the Republican Party and the Northern industrialist.

By 1876 it was decided that Black people had served their purpose and, therefore, even the pretense of Black equality was no longer necessary.

The Supreme Court in 1883 embodied that attitude in law by declaring that the civil rights act of 1875 was unconstitutional. In other decisions it displayed its remarkable and ingenious talent for interpreting the law according to the needs and interests of the dominant white ruling class. It nullified the 14th and 15th Amendments by declaring that they were Federal restrictions only on the powers of the states or their agents, not on the powers of individuals within those states. Thus it was still illegal for any states to violate or abridge the rights of Black people; but if on the other hand, private citizens or a group of them (such as the Ku Klux Klan), within any state actively prevented Black people from exercising their rights, then the crime came under the jurisdiction of the state in which the crime, or crimes, took place.

The court also ruled that if a state law did not appear on its surface discriminatory against Black people, then the federal courts had no right to investigate. But this was not enough. It was necessary to go even further, and they did.

In 1896 the Supreme Court in *Plessy vs. Ferguson*, 163 U.S. 537, upheld a Louisiana law requiring segregated railroad facilities. As long as equality of accommodations existed, the court held segregation did not constitute discrimination, and Black people were not deprived of equal protection of the law under the 14th Amendment. American justice!

Segregation automatically meant discrimination. Black people were forced to use in public buildings, freight elevators and toilet facilities reserved for janitors. On trains all Black people, even those with first class tickets, were forced to seat themselves in the baggage car. Employment discrimination and wage discrimination, "inferior" schools for Black children. All of these inhuman crimes were made legal by the highest court in the land. Typical American justice, for Black people.

### The 20th Century

In 1954 the Supreme Court, only after intense domestic pressure and unveiling internationally as a nation of hypocrites, this nation's ruling elite reversed the infamous *Plessy vs. Ferguson* decision, and ruled that segregated educational facilities were unconstitutional. But this ruling, like virtually every seemingly just decision for Black people, was almost immediately revealed as a sham, a mere gesture to pacify us and alleviate your embarrassment. For the public schools of the nation are still overwhelmingly segregated and unequal, the result of a century of duality.

In the north, in the south, in the east and in the west, all over the country Black people are accused of crimes, thrown in your jails, dragged through your courts and administered a sour dose of "American justice." We are in jail outside, and jail inside. Black people and now all poor people have been well educated in the American system of justice.

We know very well what is meant by your statement, "This court is responsible for maintaining proper respect for the administration of criminal justice and preventing any reflection on the image of American justice." Properly translated, it simply means that the farce must go on. The image must remain intact.

It is precisely these contradictions of maintaining justice as a reality or rhetorically asserting such procedure that must be resolved. The process of determining judicially by which the legal rights of private parties or the people are vindicated, and the guilt or innocence of accused persons is established has a history that is as variable as the color and the class of the individual prosecuted. It is not only doubtful, it is appalling, to say the least.

### Who Is in Contempt?

Accusations of contempt for the "dignity" of and respect for, the court indicates to us, the defendants, that a devious attempt by the court prevails, to obscure the truth of these proceedings. There is a note of glaring distinction between theory and practice within the "halls of justice" which is consistent with the judicial history as it pertains to Black and poor people. This is why the brief history. What fool cannot see that the "justice" of which you speak has a dual interpretation quite apart from the legal definition and is in keeping with "slave-master" traditions.

In light of historical fact, the perspective must be put into the proper context and true time continuum as to whether justice and

United States constitutional rights are effectively afforded unvaryingly to all who stand before the "American system" of justice, that exercises due process.

Just law, in reality, shall not be defamed by its dual application according to racial and social values because of wealth, position and influence. History provides the doubt of "American system" of justice when comparison of class orientation defines the degree of rights, respect and justice the individual shall receive. Political favors as existed then for judicial position has not varied even to the present.

With such political relationships existing have the courts, in practice, escaped from the abuse of authority which is a threat to the development of a free nation of people? Fascism encroaches in just such a manner. Historically the qualitative change in society still reveals a lack of humane interaction with the socially, economically and politically exploited and isolated Black and poor peoples. The preceeding chronology substantiates a blatant contempt for Black people and other non-white poor people, not recognizing their human rights and liberties as a matter of law, or morality, and a total disregard to our social reality, is an insult to us. We can see the yesterday in today and the history of our particular case runs upon the same tracks as does our people's long struggle.

**The Big Lie**

This court represents the most ruthless system in the world, caring nothing for the wholesale misery that it brings, while at the same time, your papers are full of verbiage of your "nobility," "righteousness," "justice," "fairness," and the "good" that you do.

We are very, very sick and tired of the BIG LIE. We cannot stand passive to the big lie any longer. We cannot accept it any longer.

It is time to state the truth, for Black people, for poor Puerto Rican, Mexican American, Chinese American, Indian and poor white people. The "Amerikkan system of justice" is a hideous sham and a revolting farce.

We must look at the situation objectively. As has been explicitly implied in the preceding, we realize that we are not 2nd Class citizens at all. We are a colonized people. (Read your own Commission Reports). We see that we are still considered chattel. We see how the Fugitive Slave Act has been modified in words, but is still being used, how the Dred Scott decision was never really reversed. That the 13th, 14th and 15th Amendments of the Constitution did not liberate us—that in fact, in social reality, they only legalized slavery and expanded the Dred Scott decision to include Indians, Spanish-speaking and poor white people.

We see that things have not gotten better, but only progressively

worse, and that includes tyranny. We completely oppose racism and
tyranny and will continue to do so. You wish us to act according to
a Decorum set down by an organization, the "American Bar Association," which is not only racist, but is also not against genocide. (Perhaps they realize the truth, and see that the American
ruling class is definitely liable, for its treatment of Black people?)

In court you ask us to submit to a code of laws . . . your laws,
not our laws (Black and poor people) but *your* laws—your laws
because we were never asked (Black people) if we consented to
having them as our laws, nor are these laws relevant to our ghetto
reality. They are *your* laws, and we find them racist and oppressive.
They, these laws, perpetuate our plantation continuation. Right
now, in 1970, 90% of the inmates of your prisons are non-white.
90%! And we (Black people, etc.) have never had the right to
decide if we wanted to be governed by laws which we had no part
in making. Yet, the primary concern of the men who drafted the
"Declaration of Independence" was the *consent* of the governed
by laws which they had a part in forming and which was relevant
to them. We are in your prison, but these are not our laws. They
are your laws, and in dealing with Black and poor people, you do
not even adhere to *your own laws*.

In fact, a leading criminologist, Dr. R. R. Korn of Stanford
University, has noted than 80% of the people now in prison were
put there *illegally* according to *your* own law. (Strange that the
overwhelming population is Black and non-white?)

### Hanging Judge

Mr. Murtagh—your record speaks for itself. You are known in the
ghetto as a "Hanging Judge." (How many Black and white poor
men did you convict without their even having counsel just in 1969
alone, in your clever slick way?) Frank Hogan and his aides are
well known in the Ghetto—very well known in the Ghetto—known
for what they are—racist and unethical. (We have knowledge of cases,
since our incarceration of Assistant District Attorneys, or D.A.'s men
posing as legal aides to get conviction). But in our case you and
Mr. Hogan have gotten together and have outdone yourselves in
denying us *all*, everyone of our "alleged" state, federal and human
rights. The record clearly shows this, when not clouded with the
mist of racism.

A) Let us clear up one basic misconception. You constantly refer
to this case as a "criminal" trial, while all of the time we *know*,
you *know*, Frank Hogan knows, the people know, the other prisoners
and even the guards know that this is *not* a criminal trial. Everyone
knows that this is a political trial, for if we were not members of
the Black Panther Party, a lot of things would never have been done
to us in the first place.

Why are we not allowed to be with other prisoners? Why are we not allowed to even talk to the other prisoners? Why are we isolated? (Something we might say or do that can open their eyes, perhaps?) Alleged murderers and rapists are not treated in this manner, even "convicted" murderers and rapists are not treated in the manner in which we were treated. Why do you persist in the big lie? It is one of many clear contradictions.

B) On April 2, 1969, hordes of "police" broke down our doors, or otherwise forced entry into our homes, and ran amuck. Rampaging and rummaging through our homes, they seized articles from us with wild abandon while having no search warrants. The "police" put us and our families in grave danger, nervously aiming shotguns, rifles and pistols at us and our families—even our children.

We were then kidnapped as were some of our families. We state "kidnap" because many of us were never shown any arrest warrant, even to this day. This is illegal. This is a blatant contradiction of your own Constitution. . . . We said nothing.

C) Upon the arrest of *some* of the defendants and before the appearance of any of the defendants, New York City District Attorney Frank Hogan appeared on national radio and national television (Channels 2, 4, 5, 7, 9, and 11) in a press conference, during which time he gave our information from an "indictment" against us in an inflammatory and provocative manner, deliberately designed to incite the people against us and to deny us even the semblance of a "fair trial." Mr. Hogan implied a lie—that we had been seized on the way to commit these alleged acts with bombs in our hands—rather than the truth—that we had no bombs and that most of us were taken out of our beds.

Subsequent to that press conference, "unidentified police sources" and "persons close to the investigation" stated falsely to the press that we, as members of the Black Panther Party were being aided and abetted by foreign governments considered hostile to your government (i.e. Cuba and China)—that we, as Black Panther Party members were stealing money from federal and/or state agencies and many other false wild charges, designed to heighten the public alarm against us and our Party, rather than diminish it, so as to create an atmosphere conducive to the extermination of the Black Panther Party and justify anything that might be done to us.

### Fair Trial Impossible

This unethical behavior gave, aided, and abetted further prejudicial pre-trial publicity, in direct contradiction to your law as outlined in the 14th Amendment of your Constitution of the United States. Due to this behavior alone, we are positive that we could not get a fair trial anywhere in this country. . . . We still said nothing.

D) When our attorneys learned of our arrest, they attempted to

IN A SOCIETY WHERE THE LAW UPHOLDS

EXPLOITATION, AND ORDER SUPPORTS

INJUSTICE AND FASCI... BY

NECESSITY BR... FINE

US TO OUR S...

IF WE BE CALLED CRIMINALS BECAUSE WE

SEEK THIS, THEN LET HISTORY JUDGE US —

BUT LET US NOT SUPPORT ... OUR SLAVERY,

LET US DIE IN F...HER... OF OUR...

LET US BREAK T... CHAINS

THAT...

see us, as we were being held in your District Attorney's office. They were refused permission to do so. At the "arraignment" a similar request by our counsel was again refused by Mr. Charles Marks who presided thereat. These refusals were in blatant violation of your law as outlined in the 6th and 14th Amendments of your Constitution of the United States. . . . We continued to be silent.

E) At this "arraignment" this Mr. Charles Marks who was presiding, refused to read, explain or give us a copy of this "indictment" against us. This is another violation of your law as outlined in the 6th and 14th Amendments of your Constitution of the United States. . . . yet, we remained silent.

F) Bail (ransom) was set at $100,000, which is ridiculous and tantamount to no bail at all. This is another violation of your own law as outlined in the 8th and 14th Amendments of your Constitution of the United States. We state that this bail is not only contradictory to your own law, but that it is also racist. When white "radical" groups are arrested, their bails do not usually exceed $10,000. When three Yemenites were charged with "conspiracy" to murder your President Nixon, and with the equipment to do such, their bail was $25,000; when Minutemen in New York were arrested and charged with a conspiracy to commit murder, the murder of 155 persons and were arrested with bombs and guns more than enough to do this. Bail was set at $25,000. We had no bombs. Our bail was $100,000. . . . We remained silent.

G) At this arraignment, this Mr. Charles Marks, the same "Judge" who is alleged to have signed the "Arrest Warrants," stated in words or substance that he was accepting all of the allegation in the "indictment" against us to be true. On subsequent hearings during May 1969 concerning reduction of ransom (bail) at which this same Mr. Marks still presided, he stated that we were "un-American" and that the law "did not apply to us" (sounds like history?). This does not quite show impartiality. . . . Yet, we said nothing.

H) Our counsel have been in front of at least 35 "Judges" concerning our bail, and this attitude permeates the "great American system of justice." All motions on this were denied, either without comment or because of the "seriousness" of the "charges," but *never* dealing with the Constitutional issues involved, and it is *your* Constitution. All of this seems to underlie "Judge" Marks' remarks. . . . Yet, we said nothing.

I) We have been treated like animals—in fact, like less than animals. On January 17, 1969, Miss Joan Bird was kidnapped, beaten, and tortured. She was punched and beaten, given the "Thumb Torture," hung upside down by the ankle from out of a third-story window of a "Police Precinct." On April 2–3, 1969, some of us were beaten as we were being kidnapped. From April 2, 1969, all of us were placed under constant abuse and harrassment, which included 24-hour lock-in, complete isolation, no library or recreation, lights kept on in our cells for 24 hours, physical assaults, deprivations of seeing our families, at times denied mattresses, medication, sheets, showers, pillow-cases, towels, soap, toothpaste, and toilet paper.

Our families have suffered abuse in visiting us, and mental anguish. One of us suffered the loss of a child because of this. Some of our families had to go on welfare because of our outrageous incarceration and ransom. We were denied mail, even from our attorneys—denied access to consult all together with our attorneys. We have been subjected to the most onerous and barbaric of jail conditions. The objective of all this was our psychological and physical destruction during our pre-trial detention.

As NEWSWEEK Magazine even states, ". . . the handling of the suspects between their arrest and their trial was something less than a model of American criminal justice," and "None of it was very becoming to the state . . ." (How well we know.) All this is a blatant violation of your own law as outlined in the 8th and 14th Amendments of your own Federal Constitution. . . . Yet, we *still* remained silent.

J) You—Murtagh. You came into the case in May 1969. You were informed of these conditions. You could have righted these blatant violations of your own law, the laws you have "sworn" to uphold. But you did not. You refused to do this . . . and remained silent. You tried to rush us pell-mell to trial, knowing full well that we were not, could not, be prepared. . . . We remained silent.

### The Government. Conspiracy

We filed motions that are guaranteed to "citizens" by the 14th Amendment of your Federal Constitution. You denied them all. You denied us the right as guaranteed in your laws in the 6th and 14th Amendments of your own Constitution, to conduct a voir dire of the Grand Jury in these proceedings, knowing full well that they did not comprise members of our peer group. . . . We remained silent.

You denied us a hearing with which to be confronted with the witnesses against us, as is guaranteed by your law in the 6th Amendment of your Constitution. . . . We remained silent.

You denied us a Bill of Particulars which is guaranteed by your laws in the 6th and 14th Amendments of your Constitution. . . . We remained silent.

Two "suspects" were kidnapped under the modification of the Fugitive Slave Act in November 1969. You gave them no bail. (No sense pretending anymore, it seems). . . . We remained silent.

You denied us every state and federal constitutional right, and we remained silent. You substantiated Mr. Marks' "the law does not apply" to us. . . . Yet, we remained silent.

### Lee Berry

K) Lee Berry. Lee Berry is a classical example of how you and your cohorts conduct the "American System of Justice" when dealing with Black people. On April 3, 1969, Lee Berry was a patient in the Veterans' Administration Hospital where he was receiving treatment as an epileptic, subject to Grand Mal seizures, which can be fatal. Lee Berry is not mentioned particularly in the "indictment." Yet, on April 3, 1969, your "police" dragged him out of the hospital. These "police" stood him up before your cohort, "Judge" Marks. Lee was "arraigned" without counsel. Bail $100,000. He was thrown into an isolation cell in the Tombs without even a mattress. In July 1969, he was physically attacked without provocation and without warning, while he was in a drugged stupor.

You were aware of his condition—you were quite aware. Numerous motions were in your "Great Court System." It took four months to even get him medication, and only in November when he had become so ill, so progressively worse that it was frightening. He finally got consent to be transferred to Bellevue Hospital. Because of the courts' decisions under your "American System of Justice," Lee Berry has had four serious operations within the last two months. Because of the courts' decisions under the great American System of Justice at this precise moment Lee Berry is lying in the shadow of death with a possible fatal case of pneumonia. At the very least, your Great Court system is guilty of attempted murder, and D.A. Hogan should be named as a co-defendant. Lee Berry is our Brother, and what is done to him, has been done to us all. . . . and we remained silent.

L) In November 1969, four white persons were arrested for allegedly "bombing" various sites in New York City. They were arrested allegedly with "bombs in their possession," but they were white. For three of them, bail was reduced 80% in two days, because "the presumption of innocence is basic among both the statutory and constitutional principles affecting bail" . . . if you are white. (The political climate is such today, even this hardly matters anymore if one is dissident.)

### We Could Be Silent No Longer

Two days after that decision, we were brought in front of you and given a superseding "indictment." We could be silent no longer. We had been insulted enough—more than enough. We had been treated with contempt, in an atmosphere of intimidation for too long.

We must reiterate—we are looking at the situation objectively. Object Reality.

At the pre-trial hearings we are confronted with a "Judge" who has admitted, in fact, had been indicted and arrested for ignoring "police" graft and corruption . . . a "Judge" who by his record shows an unblemished career of "police" favoritism and All-American racism. In your previous dealings with Black people, you have shown yourself to be totally unjust, bloodthirsty, pitiless, and inhuman. We are confronted with a District Attorney machine which has shown itself to be vigilant and unswerving in its racist policies. 90% of the inmates convicted are non-white and poor. This machine has shown itself to be unethical in its techniques and practices—even in front of our eyes—tactics which include going up and whispering to the witnesses on the stand, signalling and coaching them. We know as LOOK Magazine stated in June 1969 "how the police corrupt the truth . . . Prosecutors and Judges become their accomplices:" To cite a small example: A man, a Black man . . . was beaten to death in the Tombs in front of forty witnesses in May 1969 and the police swore that he died of a "heart attack." Yes, we *know* to what the police will swear to. All Black people, poor people, know to what the police will swear. With all this, together with the hostility inculcated in the dominant white culture towards anything Black, is shown by you and your cohorts very well indeed. Under these conditions, and considering our stand against American racism, this is not only a challenge to us and Black people, but the whole people. To relate in terms you can understand, even Racist Woodrow Wilson stated concerning fascism: ". . . This is a challenge to all mankind; there is one choice we cannot make, we are incapable of making, we will not choose the path of submission . . . we will be, we must be as harsh as the Truth and as uncompromising as Justice—true Justice is on our side". . . . To that we say, Right On!

### Court Out of Order

You have implied contempt charges. We cannot conceive of how this could be possible. How can we be in contempt of a court that is in contempt of its own laws? How can you be responsible for "maintaining respect and dispersing justice," when you have dispensed with justice, and you do not maintain respect for your own Constitution? How can you expect us to respect your laws, when you do not respect them yourself? Then you have the audacity to demand respect, when you, your whole Great System of Justice is out of order and does not respect us, or our rights.

You have talked about our counsel inciting us. Nothing could be further from the truth. The injustices we have been accorded over the past year incite us, the injustice in these hearings incite us, racism incites us, fascism incites us, in short—when we reflect back over history, its continuation up until today, you and your courts incite us.

But we will not leave it there for you and others, to distort, as some are inclined to do. There will be left no room for your courts and media to distort and misinterpret our actions. We wish for a speedy and FAIR trial, a just trial. But—we must have our "alleged" Constitutional rights. This court is in contempt of our Constitutional rights and have been for almost a year. We must have our rights first. The wrongs inflicted must be redressed. Bygones are *not* bygones. Later for that. 351½ years are enough. We must clean the slate. We do not believe in your Appeal Courts (we've had experience with 300 years of appeals generally, and 35 judges specifically). So we must begin with a mutual understanding anew. When we have our constitutional guarantees redressed, we will give the court the respect it claims to deserve—precisely the respect it deserves.

**Contempt of the People**
In light of all that has been said, in view of the collusion of the federal, state, and city courts, the New York City Department of Correction, the city police, and District Attorney's office, we feel that we, as members of the Black Panther Party, cannot receive a fair and impartial trial without certain pre-conditions conforming to our alleged constitutional rights. So we state the following: we feel that the courts should follow their own federal Constitution, and when they have failed to do so, and continue to ignore their mistakes, but persist dogmatically to add insult to injury, those courts are in contempt of the people. One need not be black to relate to that, but it is often those who never experience such actions on the part of the courts, who believe they, the courts, can never be wrong.

So, in keeping with that, and the social reality in which that principle must relate, we further state:

1) That we have a constitutional right to reasonable bail, and a few would, if they were white, be released in their own custody. We demand that, and the courts' consistent denial of that right, in effect is in contempt of its own Constitution.

2) We demand a jury of our peers, or people from our own community, as defined by the Constitution.

3) We say that because the Grand Jury system in New York City systematically excludes poor Black people, it cannot be representative of a cross-section of the community from which we come. So in effect, it is unconstitutional, and nothing more than a method

of wielding class power and racial suppression and repression. We demand to have a constitutional and legal indictment, or be released, for we are being held illegally, by malicious and racist unethical laws.

4) We demand that the unethical practice of the police and D.A.'s office, in its production of evidence, lying, and misrepresentation be strictly limited by the introduction of an impartial jury of our peers of all pre-trial hearings, to judge all motions and evidence submitted, subsequent to a new constitutional indictment.

Therefore, since you have effectively denied by your ruling of Wednesday, February 25, 1970, our right to a trial, and since this ruling will affect the future of Black and white political prisoners, we have directed our Attorneys to do everything in their power, to upset this vicious, barbaric, insidious and racist ruling, which runs head-on in contrast with the promise of the 13th and 14th Amendments of your U.S. Constitution.

Let this be entered into all records pertaining to our case.

ALL POWER TO THE PEOPLE!
Lumumba Abdul Shakur
Richard Moore (Analye Dharuba)
Curtis Powell
Michael Tabor (Cetewayo)
Robert Collier
Walter Johnson (Baba Odinga)
Afeni Shakur
John J. Casson (Ali Bey Hassan)
Alex McKiever (Catarra)
Clark Squire
Joan Bird
Lee Roper
William King (Kinshasa)

—*Rat*, March 7–21, 1970

# Closing Remarks to the Jury by Charles R. Garry in People of California v. Huey P. Newton

If the Court pleases, Ladies and Gentlemen of the Jury, Mr. Jensen (prosecuting attorney), and Defense Staff, and the rest of the members of the audience:

This is supposed to be the argument by counsel. I don't intend to argue to you. I intend to think out loud with you.

As Mr. Jensen was presenting his views and telling you what a difficult task you had before you because of the type of evidence (at least that was my reaction to what he had to say), it reminded me of *Alice in Wonderland*. Some of you probably remember *Alice in Wonderland*. The King said, "The evidence first, and then the sentence." The Queen said, "No. The sentence first and then the evidence." Alice said, "That's nonsense," and yelled, and everybody got alarmed at what she said. "The idea of a sentence first and the evidence second!"

It reminded me of that. I am too often reminded of *Alice in Wonderland* and *Gulliver's Travels*.

As I have sat in this courtroom for days like you have, at first picking the jury, asking you questions that probably infuriated you—I hope that your infuriations stopped as the evidence unfolded—I hope that it got you to thinking about the things that are going on in my beloved America and your beloved America. I hope that you remember the things that we asked you in this voir dire.

Mr. Newton and I feel as though we have a pact with you and that pact is that you be able to decipher this evidence, evaluate this evidence, without any prejudgments, and without any exterior feelings of what's going on in our cradle of freedom, so-called.

I hope you can divorce from your minds the [Democratic and Republican] conventions that you saw, the two conventions, the spectacle that was made in them of democracy. The candidates today are talking about safety in the streets, against violence and all this, which is nothing but a camouflage for curtailing civil rights and civil liberties.

Some of you, maybe one or two of you, remember the early depression. I do. I am a by-product of a great depression that we had. I am a student of FDR. I knew no other president. We know that FDR stopped the so-called crime in the street by bringing means where people could be self-reliant and at least be able to fill their tummies without begging or selling apples on the street corners. I'm going to go into this a little fuller. I thought that perhaps I ought to get into the evidentiary aspect of this case so that you will have an opportunity when we adjourn here tonight to be thinking about some of the things that we are talking about. . . .

I am going to talk briefly about Huey Newton as a person, as a man.

You have seen exposed his entire past. Frankly I wish my own past was as clean as his was. Did you see in any one of the things the difficulties that he had ever gotten into, where he had stolen so much as a loaf of bread, a pencil? Did you see anything about

his past, his juvenile record was even brought in, which is supposed to be sacred, and the only juvenile difficulty he got into was
when he was sixteen years of age when he was transferred to another
school, in Berkeley where they were all strangers and seven people
beat him up the day before. And this youngster sought some way
of defending himself. Everyone of you would have done the same
thing.

This is the background, this is the hate that Mr. Jensen said
that man had engendered within himself. Huey Newton was on
probation from 1964 and he thought until the 27th day of October,
1967, and during that entire time his probation was never revoked
for anything that happened because the probation department recognized the struggle that black people have to go through, and some
of the encounters with the police, and the conduct of the police,
weren't sufficient to revoke his probation.

One time Huey said that the probation officer called him in and
he said you have the right to have a weapon that is exposed, a
shotgun or a rifle and that admonition he carried through. You
heard the probation officer Melvin Torly testify and say "I may
have told him that his probation expired on the 27th instead of
the 28th, I may have made that mistake and I may have told him
that."

Is it any wonder a man who is walking around with the law book
and was attending law school shortly prior to this event so that
he could be an officer of the court, so that he can make his contribution as a lawyer to the profession, to the people who need
him; is it any wonder that when his probation was finished, he
thought, on the 27th, that he would be celebrating?

Huey Newton doesn't ask very much for himself. Huey Newton,
in my opinion, is a selfless man. I am sure that that came out in
his testimony. A man who is not interested in himself as a person;
he is a devoted man; he is a rare man. Mr. Jensen tried to make
this man a liar. He says he talks about love and he preaches
violence or words to that effect. He may not have said it in those
words. I am reminded of the Book of Matthew, Chapter 10, Verse
34: "Think not that I come to send peace on earth. I came not to
send peace but the sword."

I am sure that most of you have never heard that version of
Christ. This was talking to the twelve disciples shortly before his
arrest. He was telling them that he was going to be arrested. You
have heard Christ say time and time again, "Turn your swords into
plowshares." [Then] He was talking to the multitude. [But when]
he was talking to the twelve disciples on the day of his arrest,
[when] he was subsequently crucified by the people in power at that
time, he told them to sell and buy their swords. This is again found

in Luke 22:36: "Then he said unto them, 'But now, he that hath a purse, let him take it, and likewise his script: and he that hath no sword, let him sell his garment and buy one.' "

What is Huey Newton saying, what is Christ saying? Christ wasn't saying get out the sword and destroy people. He was saying that the twelve disciples in order to be able to carry out their mandate and their responsibilities would also at a time have to resort to the sword for self-defense.

Huey Newton is saying to the black community and the black ghetto there has got to be times when you will have to defend yourself by political means and any other means for your life, for your survival.

You know we fought a great war against Fascism which had as its cradle the destruction of the freedom of the human being. We fought a great war because one nation practiced genocide on six million Jews. You saw evidence of that.

We know through history that there is and there have been massacres of people. The Armenians have gone through several massacres. Other nations have gone through genocide in more ways than one, but history tells me that the black people of the world have had genocide in excess of fifty million of them. Fifty million black people throughout this world since history has been able to document, have been destroyed, eliminated. The black community today, the black ghetto, is fighting for the right of survivalship. The white community is sitting smug and saying, "Let's have more police, let's have more guns, let's arm ourselves against the blacks." They are saying that time and time again.

That is not the answer. If you think that is the answer we are all destroyed. If you think that Mayor Daley has the answer we are all destroyed. If you think that this nation with all of its power and all of its strength can eliminate violence on the street with more violence they have got another thought coming.

My client and his party are not for destruction; they want to build. They want a better America for black people. They want the police out of their neighborhoods. They wanted them out of their streets. Everyone of you here possibly know one policeman in your neighborhood. I know several people in police departments. I think they are wonderful people. I live in Daly City, I have a beautiful relationship with them. Those police live in my neighborhood within three or four blocks. I know where one of them lives. I can call on him if I need him, but in the black ghetto no police officer lives in that ghetto. Why don't they live in that ghetto? Because a man that is making eight or nine or ten thousand dollars isn't going to live in the kind of hovel that the ghetto has.

Has anybody thought of uplifting that ghetto so that it doesn't

exist in the manner that it has? These are the things that Huey
Newton and the Black Panthers and other people seek; they are
not the only ones. Professor Black initiated and gave it to you,
'TCB', taking care of business, and taking care of the wants and
desires and needs of a community that has been forgotten, a community that we don't even understand. We don't even have their
language. Mr. Jensen doesn't understand their language. It took me
a long time to understand their language. I spent ten months òn
this case and I have been in this case since November 1st. I had
to start learning. I thought I knew something about Negro America
because some of my intimate friends are Negro professionals who
have been accepted partially in our great white society. I thought
I knew them and we exchanged visits back and forth and we were
buddies. It wasn't a week or two weeks after I got into this case
and I came to the conclusion that I knew absolutely nothing about
black America.

I was ignorant—as ignorant as any white could be and I am a
person that thought I was informed. I have had to educate myself.
I have had to read everything that I could get hold of. I read one
book by a man by the name of Frantz Fanon called "Wretched of
the Earth," a book called "Listen, White Man, Listen." I have
gone down the list, the Kerner Report came out and most of you
when I voir dired you hadn't even heard of it. Some of you had
heard about it in a lip-service sort of a way.

The Kerner Report lays down the hypothesis and the problems
of black America today. White American, listen, white American,
listen. The answer is not to put Huey Newton in the gas chamber,
it is not the answer to put Huey Newton and his organization
into jail. The answer is not that. The answer is not more police.
The answer is wipe out the ghetto, the conditions of the ghetto
so that black brothers and sisters can live with dignity, so that they
can walk down the street with dignity.

I cut out a piece that I worked out and I would like to call
to your attention.

Take a look at the extent to which the slaughter of Negroes has
been killed in our language, in our vocabulary. White denotes charity,
simplicity and candor, innocent truth, and hope, while black is sin,
synonymous with sinful, inhuman, fiendish, devilish, infernal, monstrous, atrocious, horrible, nefarious, treacherous, venal.

A white lie is one made with the best of intentions while a
black one is deliberate, harmful and inexcusable. We wish to eliminate a person from favorable consideration, we blackball or black-
list him. We are able to whitewash anything except a black mark,
not even magic can overcome the preface black. We consider the
black guys as a badge of shame while at the same time we reward

the normal badge of combat with the Purple Heart, but the white flag takes a back seat to the Black Death, and everyone is familiar with the connotation of black man, black heart, black deed, black outlook, black sheep and Black Maria.

These are the things that white America, white racist America has been doing. Four years ago just a simple thing of passing a law so that the owner of a property could not discriminate against any person because of race, color or creed. Sixty-six percent of the white Californians voted against such a law. I think that we white people ought to start bowing our heads and start thinking, start thinking on Huey Newton, a Black Panther. Malcolm X, Dr. Du Bois, a great historian of the world—I had to read ten or twelve of his books so that I could understand. I could understand the language when Huey Newton is talking. When Huey Newton is presenting himself I can feel a vibration of his thoughts so that I could at least try to transmit to you, practical white jurors. . . .

This case is a diabolical attempt to put an innocent man into jail or into the gas chamber and my government should not be a party to that kind of a scheme. I want to remind you again of Alice in Wonderland. When I sit down I am finished. I wish I could say that it has been a pleasure trying this case. I can't. It is like saying I enjoyed a broken neck, or a broken heart. With my 30 years in the practice of law, turbulent practice of the law in many areas, I find that the need for this type of a trial makes me sick inside. It makes me sick inside that America that I have grown to love, to be a part of, today is the kind of an America that I don't understand and I hate.

I hate the violence that is created because of the lack of common language, understanding. I see the northern and western part of the United States creating ghettos where ghettos did not exist before, segregate and divide people, great and beautiful friends being hamstrung to the stake.

—Charles R. Garry, *Minimizing Racism in Jury Trials*, Berkeley, California, 1970, pp. 199–204

# 11.
## ALLIANCES AND COALITIONS

Early in its history the Black Panther Party, disregarding the criticism of the Cultural Nationalists in the black community, moved to achieve an alliance and coalition with all people and organizations who were prepared to move against the power structure. In 1968 the Party established a coalition with the Peace and Freedom Party in California in the campaign to free Huey Newton and in the election of that year. The Party also established alliances with a number of groups which were influenced by the Black Panthers and modeled their program and activities in their own communities on the Black Panther Party. Among them were the Young Lords, a Puerto Rican gang which had become a political movement; the Brown Berets, a group of young Chicanos (Mexican-Americans); the Young Patriots, a group of young whites who aimed to organize poor whites; and the Red Guards, a group of Chinese-Americans who organized to battle oppression in the Chinese-American communities under the slogan of "Yellow Power." The Black Panther Party also worked closely with Black Student Unions which were influenced by the ideology and program of the Black Panthers, and cooperated with black workers who were establishing black caucuses in a number of labor unions to combat racism in the labor movement and end the second-class status of many black members of trade unions.

In this section are a number of examples of the coalition activities of the Black Panther Party, as well as the programs and activities of some of the organizations and groups influenced by the Black Panthers.

On June 18, 1970, at a press conference at the Overseas Press Club, Ossie Davis, spokesman for the Committee to Petition the United Nations, announced a plan to submit another petition to the UN to end U.S. genocide against black, yellow, red and brown Americans. A minimum of one million signatures will be sought for the petition. Members of the committee which drafted the petition included Huey Newton; Black Congresswoman Shirley Chisholm; the black scholar Dr. Nathan Wright; Roger Littlehorn of the Indians of All Tribes, the group which is occupying Alcatraz Island off San Francisco; Dick Gregory, one of the co-chairmen of the committee; and Carl Blakley of the Saulteaux tribe. The first signatures on the petition were by Huey P. Newton and Bobby Seale, and the petition with their signatures is the final document in this section.

219

# The Black Panther Party Stands for Revolutionary Solidarity

The Black Panther party stands for revolutionary solidarity with all people fighting against the forces of imperialism, capitalism, racism and fascism. Our solidarity is extended to those people who are fighting these evils at home and abroad. Because we understand that our struggle for our liberation is part of a worldwide struggle being waged by the poor and oppressed against imperialism and the world's chief imperialist, the United States of America, we—the Black Panther party—understand that the most effective way that we can aid our Vietnamese brothers and sisters is to destroy imperialism from the inside, attack it where it breeds. As for the Vietnamese people, for the peoples of Asia, Africa and Latin America as well.

The aims of the Black Panther party are manifest in our 10-point platform and program. We demand the right to self-determination for all third-world peoples and we call for a United Nations-supervised plebiscite to be held throughout the black colony in which only the black colonial subjects will be allowed to participate for the purpose of determining the will of black people as to their national destiny. Our program is not much different from any liberation front's program in the third world. Because we are victims of U.S. imperialism (community imperialism) just as the people of the third world are, we see our struggle as one and the same.

History has shown that while the nations of Asia, Africa and Latin America were shackled in colonial bondage, black people in the U.S. were bound by the chains of racism and forced with its special brand of murder and terror. We see our revolutionary position vis-a-vis this evil as directly derived from the actions of liberationists like Nat Turner and Toussaint L'Ouverture. We must emulate the actions of these black heroes, combine them with the socialist perspective the party's 10-point program gives us.

⁕In the words of the party's chairman, Bobby Seale, we will not fight capitalism with black capitalism; we will not fight imperialism with black imperialism; we will not fight racism with black racism.⁕ Rather we will take our stand against these evils with a solidarity derived from a proletarian internationalism born of socialist idealism.

—Statement especially written for special supplement on The Black Panthers, *The Guardian*, February, 1970, by the national office of the Black Panther Party

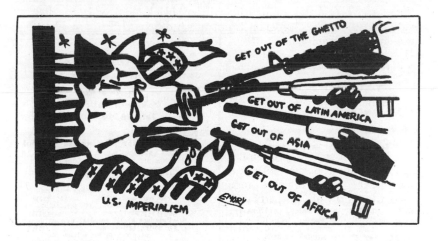

# We Must Develop a United Front Against Fascism [21]

Peoplel  Organizationsl  Groupsl  Yippiesl  Political

Partiesl  Workersl  Studentsl  Peasant-Farmersl

You the Lumpenl  Poor Peoplel  Black People,

Mexican-Americans, Puerto Ricans, Chinese, etc,

## We Must Develop A

# United Front
# Against Fascism

---

**FOR:**

Registration Blanks

Publicity Materials
Leaflets
Posters
Stickers

Travel Information for Groups

**CONTACT:**

BLACK PANTHER PARTY
2026 Seventh Avenue     3106 Shattuck Avenue
New York, N. Y.              Berkeley, California
Phone: 864-8951            Phone: 845-0104

NATIONAL COMMITTEE TO COMBAT FASCISM
c/o 58 West 25th Street
New York, New York
Phone: 675-2520 or 242-9225

**Revolutionary Conference**
**UNITED FRONT AGAINST FASCISM**
**in America**
**Oakland, California**
**July 18, 19, 20, 21.**

**Fascism:**
**The Power of Finance Capital**
This conference is called and organized
by the Black Panther Party, the International Liberation School and other
community organizations and groups.

Some objectives to develop a United
Front Against Fascism
- Community control of police on
national scale.
- Freedom of all political prisoners
and political freedom.
- Political program for all the poor,
black, oppressed workers and people
of America.
- Military off campus.
- Self defense.

# On Establishing a United Front
# with Communists

What objections can the opponents of the united front have and how do they voice their objections?

Some say: "To the Communists the slogan of the united front is merely a maneuver." But if it is a maneuver, we reply, why don't you expose the "Communist maneuver" by your honest participation in a united front? We declare frankly: "We want unity of action by the working class, so that the proletariat may grow strong in its struggle against the bourgeoisie, in order that while defending today its current interests against attacking capital, against fascism, the proletariat may be in a position tomorrow to create the preliminary conditions for its final emancipation."

"The Communists attack us," say others. But listen, we have repeatedly declared: We shall not attack anyone, neither persons nor organizations nor parties that stand for the united front of the working class against the class enemy. But at the same time it is our duty, in the interests of the proletariat and its cause, to criticize those persons, those organizations, those parties which impede unity of action by the workers.

"We cannot form a united front with the Communists, since they have a different program," says a third group. But you yourselves say that your program differs from the program of the bourgeois parties, and yet this did not and does not prevent you from entering into coalitions with these parties.

"The bourgeois-democratic parties are better allies against fascism than the Communists," say the opponents of the united front and the advocates of coalition with the bourgeoisie. But what does Germany's experience teach? Did not the Social-Democrats form a block with those "better" allies? And what were the results?

"If we establish a united front with the Communists, the petty bourgeoisie will take fright at the 'Red danger' and will desert to the fascists," we hear it said quite frequently. But does the united front represent a threat to the peasants, the petty traders, the artisans, the toiling intellectuals, No, the united front is a threat to the big bourgeoisie, the financial magnates, the Junkers and other exploiters, whose regime brings complete ruin to all these strata.

"Social-Democracy is for democracy, the Communists are for dictatorship; therefore we cannot form a united front with the Communists," say some of the Social-Democratic leaders. But are we offering you now a united front for the purpose of proclaiming the dictatorship of the proletariat? We make no such proposal for the time being.

"Let the Communists recognize democracy, let them come out in its defense, then we shall be ready for a united front." To this we reply: "We are adherents of Soviet democracy, the democracy of the toilers, the most consistent democracy in the world. But in the capitalist countries we defend and shall continue to defend every inch of bourgeois-democratic liberties which are being attacked by fascism and bourgeois reaction, because the interests of the class struggle of the proletariat so dictate."

"But the tiny Communist Parties do not contribute anything by participating in the united front brought about by the Labor Party," say, for instance, the Labor leaders of Great Britain. Recall how the Austrian Social-Democratic leaders said the same things with reference to the small Austrian Communist Party. And what have events shown? It was not the Austrian Social-Democratic Party headed by Otto Bauer and Karl Renner that proved right but the tiny Austrian Communist Party which at the right moment signaled the fascist danger in Austria and called upon the workers to struggle. For the whole experience of the labor movement has shown that the Communists with all their relative insignificance in numbers are the motive power of the militant activity of the proletariat. Besides this, it must not be forgotten that the Communist Parties of Austria or Great Britain are not only the tens of thousands of workers who are supporters of the Party, but are parts of the world Communist movement, are sections of the Communist International, the leading party of which is the party of a proletariat which has already achieved victory and rules over one-sixth part of the globe.

"But the united front did not prevent fascism from being victorious in the Saar," is another objection advanced by the opponents of the united front. Strange is the logic of these gentlemen! First they leave no stone unturned to ensure the victory of fascism and then they rejoice with malicious glee because the united front which they entered into only at the last moment did not lead to the victory of the workers.

"If we were to form a united front with the Communists, we should have to withdraw from the coalition, and reactionary and fascist parties would enter the government," say the Social-Democratic leaders holding cabinet posts in various countries. Very well. Was not the German Social-Democratic Party in a coalition government? It was. Was not the Austrian Social-Democratic Party in office? It was. Were not the Spanish Socialists in the same government as the bourgeoisie? They were, too. Did the participation of the Social-Democratic Parties in the bourgeois coalition governments in these countries prevent fascism from attacking the proletariat? It did not. Consequently it is as clear as daylight that participation of Social-Democratic ministers in bourgeois government is not a barrier to fascism.

*"The Communists act like dictators, they want to prescribe and dictate everything to us."* No. We prescribe nothing and dictate nothing. We only make proposals concerning which we are convinced that if realized they will meet the interests of the toiling people. This is not only the right but the duty of all those acting in the name of the workers. You are afraid of the "dictatorship" of the Communists? Let us jointly discuss them and choose, together with all the workers, those proposals which are most useful to the cause of the working class.

Thus all these arguments against the united front will not bear the slightest criticism. They are rather the flimsy excuses of the reactionary leaders of Social Democracy, who prefer their united front with the bourgeoisie to the united front of the proletariat.

No. These excuses will not hold water. The international proletariat has known all the bitterness of tribulation caused by the split in the working class, and becomes more and more convinced that the united front, that the proletariat's unity of action on a national and international scale are both necessary and perfectly possible.

*—The Black Panther*, July 17, 1969

## SDS Resolution on the Black Panther Party

Editor's Note: Following is the full text of a resolution entitled "The Black Panther Party: toward the liberation of the colony," passed by the SDS (Students for a Democratic Society) national council meeting in Austin, Texas, on March 30, 1969. It was presented by Ed Jennings, Chicago Circle Campus SDS.

The sharpest struggles in the world today are those of the oppressed nations against imperialism and for national liberation. Within this country the sharpest struggle is that of the black colony for its liberation; it is a struggle which by its very nature is anti-imperialist and increasingly anticapitalist. The demand for self-de-

termination for the black colony—a demand which arises from the
most oppressed elements within the black community—is anti-imperialist and anticapitalist insofar as it challenges the power of the
ruling class. Furthermore the black liberation movement consciously
identifies with and expresses solidarity with the liberation struggles
of other oppressed peoples.

Within the black liberation movement the vanguard force is the
Black Panther party. Their development of an essentially correct
program for the black community and their ability to organize
blacks around this program have brought them to this leadership.
An especially important part of the Panther program is the Black
People's Army—a military force to be used not only in the defense
of the black community but also for its liberation. Given the military
occupation of the black community, it is especially true that "without a people's army the people have nothing." A second important
part of their program is their efforts to organize black workers. They
are increasingly moving into the factories and shops, e.g., DRUM,[20]
Panther caucuses, Black Labor Federations, etc. It is important for
us to understand that the black worker is not only a "subject" in an
oppressed colony fighting for its liberation but that he is also a
member of the working class. Thus the black worker, as a result
of this dual oppression, will play the vanguard role not only in the
black liberation movement but also in uniting and leading the whole
working class in its fight against oppression and exploitation.

The fundamental reason for the success of the Black Panther party
is that it has a correct analysis of American society. They see clearly
the colonial status of blacks and the dual oppression from which
they suffer: national oppression as a people and class exploitation
as a superexploited part of the working class. The demand for self-
determination becomes the most basic demand of the oppressed
colony. And nationalism becomes a necessary and effective means for
organizing the black community and forging unity against the
oppressor.

We must be very clear about the nature of nationalism. If the
principal contradiction in the world today is that of the oppressed
nations against imperialism, then support for these revolutionary
national movements becomes the most important criterion for
dividing revolutionaries from counterrevolutionaries (and revisionists). To say that "in the name of nationalism, the bourgeoisie
of all nations do their reactionary and dirty work" is to obscure
the reality that in the name of national liberation the workers and
peasants of all oppressed nations will struggle against and defeat
imperialism. To say that "all nationalism is reactionary" is objectively
to ally with imperialism in opposition to the struggles of the oppressed nations.

**Nationalism**

But nationalism is not always revolutionary. There is a fundamental difference between revolutionary nationalism which is "dependent upon a people's revolution" and reactionary nationalism in which the "end goal is the oppression of the people." What do the Panthers say about the reactionary, cultural or "porkchop" variety of nationalism?

"We must destroy all cultural nationalism, because it is reactionary and has become a tool of Richard Milhous Nixon, and all the U.S. power structure which divides the poor and oppressed, and is used by the greasy-slick black bourgeoisie to exploit black people in the ghetto."

*—George Mason Murray*
*Minister of Education*
*Black Panther Party*

The Black Panther party is under no illusion that liberation for the black colony can be achieved while capitalism still exists. Their call for "liberation in the colony, revolution in the mother country" clearly recognizes the dialectical relationship between liberation for the black colony and socialist revolution for the whole society.

"It's impossible for us to have control of the institutions in our community when a capitalistic system exists on the outside of it, when in fact the capitalistic system was the very system that enslaved us and is responsible for our continued oppression. So if we want to develop a socialistic system within the black community, we're saying it's also going to have to exist in the white community."

*—Bobby Seale*
*Chairman*
*Black Panther Party*

The correct and uncompromising leadership which the Black Panther party has brought to the black liberation movement has brought down the most vicious repression from the racist pig power structure. When the leading black revolutionary group is continually harassed, its leaders jailed, hounded out of the country and brutally assassinated, when Panther members daily face the provocations of the ruling class and its racist pigs, when their blood has been spilled and their list of revolutionary martyrs—Huey, Eldridge, Bobby Hutton, Bunchy Carter, John Huggins—increases daily, then the time has come for SDS to give total and complete support to their defense efforts. To do less would be a mockery of the word "revolutionary." We must continually expose and attack the role of the pigs and the courts in oppressing the black community. We must publicize the inhuman, brutal and unjust nature of "justice" in this society.

**Fight White Supremacy**
We see clearly the need to join with the Black Panther party and other revolutionary black groups in the fight against national chauvinism and white supremacy. The development of the Panthers as a disciplined and militant group fighting for black liberation has had a tremendous impact on the white radical movement. No longer can we refuse to deal with the chauvinism and white supremacy which exists both in the larger society and in our movement. Toleration of any vestige of white supremacy in the schools, shops and communities must be seen as nothing less than "scabbing" on the black liberation movement and on possibilities for unity of the working class.

SDS declares:—its support for the Black Panther party and their essentially correct program for the liberation of the black colony;—its commitment to defend the Black Panther party and the black colony against the vicious attacks of the racist pig power structure; —its commitment to join with the Black Panther party and other black revolutionary groups in the fight against white national chauvinism and white supremacy;—its total commitment to the fight for liberation in the colony and revolution in the mother country.

**Implementation**
—Form Newton-Cleaver Defense Committees. The Black Panther party has requested that SDS join in setting up these committees. Huey P. Newton is "the key political prisoner in this country at the present time." The committees should first raise money for the defense of Newton, Cleaver and all other Panthers facing charges, and second, educate the people about the real nature of "justice" in this racist society.

—The SDS national office should be mandated to print and distribute information about the history, development and programs of the Black Panther party and other black revolutionary groups. Information about the repression directed against the black community should be kept up to date and distributed. Literature about the history of the black colony and its 400 years of unending struggle against oppression should be produced.

—The national office should be mandated to print and distribute information about the organizing of black workers. This would include Panther organizing in the factories, DRUM and other revolutionary black unions.

—This resolution should stimulate SDS chapters and regions to develop and/or strengthen informal and formal relationships with the Panthers. We must keep in mind that the Black Panther party is not fighting black people's struggles only, but is in fact the vanguard in our common struggles against capitalism and imperialism.

—This resolution should be seen as a formal repudiation of the resolution, "Smash Racism: Build a Worker-Student Alliance," which was passed at the December national council. This previous resolution with its refusal to recognize the colonial oppression of blacks in this country, its statement that nationalism is "the main ideological weapon of the ruling class" within the black liberation movement, and its inability to distinguish between revolutionary and reactionary nationalism, is at best nonrevolutionary. SDS must not be on record as supporting any resolution which considers revolutionary nationalism—the main factor which ties all oppressed nations together in their fight against imperialism—as a "weapon of the ruling class." Anything less than complete repudiation of this previous resolution is a cop-out on the support and solidarity which we must give to the worldwide movement of oppressed peoples for national liberation.

—*The Guardian*, April 19, 1969

# The Young Lords Organization on the Move: Interview with Rafael Viera

by Roland Young
Community News Reporter

On Saturday, February 7, I rapped with Rafael Viera who is the Chief Medical Cadre of the Young Lords Organization, a predominantly Puerto Rican revolutionary organization that is trying to Seize the Time.

ROLAND: Would you run down what the Young Lords Organization is all about, how you got together, where you are going, etc.?

RAFAEL: The Y.L.O. (Young Lords Organization) started in Chicago in 1956 as a street gang, but they came under so much pressure and were tired of being beaten up by the White people in the area that they had to reorganize on another basis. Before that it was just the hustle and bustle of the gang days. They would go out and kill White brothers one day, then they'd go out and kill Black brothers the other day, then they'd go out and kill Asiatic

brothers the next day, and then when they didn't have anybody
else to kill, they'd kill each other—that's what they were about at
the time. Then in 1967 Cha Cha Jiminez, who was the president
of the Y.L.O. at that time, reorganized the whole organization. It
became political and changed its name from the Young Lords to
the Young Lords Organization. They took over a church which they
still have right now. They started community programs to help
people in the streets and they just related to serving the people—
which was their motto at the time.

ROLAND: Was it just the motivation of one cat that brought about
the change or was it a lot of different cats?

RAFAEL: A lot of various cats had a lot of different experiences
together and they finally woke up. They said, 'we're out here killing
each other and we ain't even dealing with the system that's really
messing us up.' So they got it together and organized around that
main base, that is, they stopped killing each other. That was around
the time when the Black Stone Rangers became political and others
started getting it together.

In January, 1969, the Y.L.O. started in N.Y. There was an organization in N.Y. named after Pedro Albizu Campos (he was a nation-
alist-socialist revolutionary who started the first armed revolutionary
struggle in Puerto Rico, twenty years ago). They were a group of
college students and a lot of them had been going back and forth
from Chicago digging what the Y.L.O. was doing and decided to
start a chapter in N.Y. At that time they went out into the streets
and started rapping with "street brothers," because that's where it's
at. They got the support of a lot of dope fiends, hustlers, pimps
and everything else, and these street brothers started a period of
transformation, of transition. That was when the Y.L.O. got organized in N.Y. We then had to think of something to let the people
know that the Y.L.O. was there, not only there, but there to serve
the people of East (Spanish) Harlem. And so the thing that we
thought of, and this is where our creativity came in, was the GAR-
BAGE OFFENSIVE. We were out in the streets for three Sundays
sweeping the streets. We would take the garbage and put it into
garbage cans, cover up the lids and wait for the garbage men to
come, but the garbage men never came. The people saw this and
they said, "what's happening." On the third Sunday the people got
out into the streets and we put the garbage in the avenues. We
piled it up and overturned cars that were abandoned on the streets
as well as baby cribs and everything else we could find, and we
blocked-off the traffic. You know how it is in 90 degree weather when
all those businessmen want to go home, they were mighty upset.
We did this two Sundays in a row and on the third Sunday they
were going to lay for us. There were repercussions all along, like

the pigs did vamp on people and people were throwing bottles and stuff. On the third week we took care of business on a Friday. The pigs came down with guns in their hands, ready to shoot anybody and so we would put the garbage in the streets, then we'd leave and when they came we had taken off our berets, and we'd be standing on the corner asking "what's happening." That was our first offensive.

ROLAND: What are the conditions in East Harlem and how do they compare to the conditions with the rest of Harlem?

RAFAEL: The conditions are the same. The rats are so big that they pay rent, the cockroaches are hump-backed because they don't have room to move around. The buildings are completely messed up. Our children are dying from all types of diseases. One of the biggest problems is lead poisoning. Inside the apartments of Harlem, they painted them with cheap lead paint until a year ago when it was outlawed. Our children tended to take the peelings off of the walls and eat them, this caused lead poisoning which would kill them or cause them permanent brain damage. We went out in the streets and started doing something about that. This was our second offensive.

We went from door to door checking the children's urine and we organized a great deal around that. I'm the Chief Medical Cadre for the Y.L.O. and we've got doctors, nurses and medical students who would go into the streets and from door to door serving the people.

The oppression is there, the people see it but they don't know what to do about it, so that's why the Y.L.O. is there. We have people in East Harlem who live fourteen to a room and who have been denied public housing. The buildings in Harlem are from the 19th century and they should have been torn down a long time ago, but they're still there.

ROLAND: Is your base primarily among the East Harlem lumpenproletariat?

RAFAEL: Yes! The people who live in East Harlem are from the lumpenproletariat. But we do have a small group of Puerto Rican people who have "made it" up the so-called "ladder" and who are supposedly assimilated into the system, but they really aren't. Our people must remember that they are Puerto Ricans no matter what and that they should be out in the streets doing their stuff for their Puerto Rican people.

ROLAND: Is the Y.L.O. primarily a Puerto Rican organization?

RAFAEL: Yes, it's predominantly Puerto Rican, but we also have Black brothers, Asiatic brothers and some Chicanos. We refuse White people admittance into the Y.L.O. for the purpose that we are out there to serve the community, the Puerto Rican community.

If White people want to serve their community then there is the Young Patriots in Yorkville or other respective organizations. Unlike us, our people are still hung up on this thing of believing that it's not the system but that it's the White man who is oppressing them. It takes time and effort to teach people it is not the White man but it's the system that oppresses them.

ROLAND: Is the Y.L.O. based primarily in N.Y.?

RAFAEL: No. Our National Headquarters is in Chicago. We have an office in N.Y., Puerto Rico, one opening up in Hayward, Calif., one opening in "Philly" and a new one that just opened up in Newark. So we're expanding.

ROLAND: What kind of solutions does the Y.L.O. offer to the problems that confront Puerto Rican people in this country?

RAFAEL: We're getting down to the needs of the people, no matter how little they may be and no matter how big. The main problems right now are food and clothing. We've got four breakfast programs going. When a mother comes up to us and says that her children are hungry and they need shoes on their feet, we can't pull out a Red Book and say Mao says this, this, and this, cause the lady is going to close the door in our face or maybe laugh at us. So we go out and we tell them, "you and I together, we can put food in your children's stomach and we can put shoes on your children's feet, if we join together. You alone can't do it and we alone can't do it, but both of us together can do it."

ROLAND: Is there a group similar to yours in Puerto Rico and have any of your members recently arrived from or gone to Puerto Rico?

RAFAEL: We've got some brothers who are in Puerto Rico right now. I just got back a few months ago and I'm going back there next week.

They've got a lot of small organizations going in Puerto Rico. There is a group called LIBERATION that is organizing a lot of the grass roots people—JIBAROS. These are the people that all of us stem from. Jibaro is the man who would be cutting sugar cane, picking coffee, his coffee and his sugar. Felipe Luciano, our N.Y. State Chairman, has a poem that reads:

> Coming home with the smell
> of sweet sugar on you
> You don't need no perfume and
> no cologne
>     to bathe yourself in
> And your woman loves you—
> Jibaro

The biggest thing in Puerto Rico is the ARMED COMMANDOS FOR LIBERATION, who, in the past year and a half, have torn up $35 million worth of ameriKKKan enterprise. This organization is not underground, it's just people who represent the military fraction of the Puerto Rican liberation movement. They have done some beautiful things, but they have jumped one step ahead of the people. They started engaging in armed struggle before the people were educated to the need for arms. That's where organizations like LIBERATION come in, they educate the people.

ROLAND: Are a lot of brothers and sisters from Puerto Rico still coming to Harlem in large numbers?

RAFAEL: I would say that more are going back now. The people who came up from Puerto Rico looking for milk and honey found that the milk was sour and that there was no honey.

ROLAND: Would you run down some of the specifics relating to your recent bust.

RAFAEL: I was arrested March 29, 1969, in Detroit for the alleged murder of a policeman in Detroit, 147 of us were arrested after the attack upon the church. We were later released by Judge Crockett of Detroit. A week later I was re-arrested stemming from information given by a "concerned citizen." This "concerned citizen" was David Brown, Jr., from Compton, Calif., who is a 19 year old "Mod Squad nigger." He said that he saw me shoot the policeman, but all the evidence is completely contradictory in itself. I spent five months in jail and I'm out now on $5,000 bail, pending second degree murder charges. My trial starts March 2 in Detroit.

ROLAND: Are any demonstrations planned in Detroit or elsewhere?

RAFAEL: What we're trying to do is organize a whole month of demonstrations for all political prisoners throughout the month of March. A lot of brothers and sisters are on trial now and their trials will be running all through March; the Panther 21, Rap Brown's trial will start in March, the Brooklyn 19 trial will start in March, Huey's appeal comes up this week which might run for a while, Los Siete de la Raza's trial starts February 16. We are going to try and organize around all these trials. The reason all these trials are in March is so they could split up the support into different factions. We want a month long demonstration to support all political prisoners.

ROLAND: Before we close would you run down some of the things the Y.L.O. plans to do in the future?

RAFAEL: We plan to try and get our church back, plus we are organizing hospital workers and hopefully soon we are going to take over a hospital. That's most likely our next offensive.

One of the main reasons Rafael came to the West Coast was to

raise funds to help defend their political prisoners, all contributions
may be sent to:
The Young Lords Organization
1678 Madison Ave.
New York, New York 10029

ALL POWER TO THE PEOPLE
SEIZE THE TIME

—*The Black Panther,* February 17, 1970

# Young Lords Block Street with Garbage

In a display of community strength and support of the YOUNG
LORDS ORGANIZATION, the people of East Harlem (El Barrio),
and the YLO closed the streets of Third Ave. from 110th, across
to 112th and down to Second Ave. on Sunday, July 27.

For two weeks previously, the YOUNG LORDS had been cleaning garbage from the streets and into garbage cans to show the
people that the department of garbage (Lindsay's department of
sanitation), or D.O.G., does not serve them. At first, communication with the people was slow. Then, as the barriers broke down
and everyone got their thing together, the people saw that even a
nothing department like D.O.G. looks upon Puerto Ricans and
Blacks as though they are something lower than garbage. These dogs
at D.O.G. have forgotten that they must SERVE THE PEOPLE.
And it all blew up Sunday.

By July 27, the original operation had grown to such a large
number of people, not just including LORDS, that the brooms and
shovels we were using were not enough. So four LORDS—the
Deputy Ministers of Finance, Information and Education and an
information photographer—went to the nearest D.O.G. hole at 108th
St. After some Bureaucratic Bullshitting they steered us to the
D.O.G. hole at 73rd St. Dig it! Two miles away, while a hole is
sitting three blocks away.

After playing the man's game of red tape, the LORDS brought
it all back home. We ran it down about what happened and a
course of action was developed. As fast as it takes a streetlight to
change, all the People—Lords, mothers Li'l Lords placed cans of
garbage across Third Ave. at 110th St. The pigs, who have been
eyeing the LORDS for the past few weeks in New York, came to the

scene in a matter of seconds. Sources on the blocks say the pigs had trucks waiting a few blocks away.

But the pigs found out that the spirit of the people is greater than all the man's pigs. At least 1,000 Puerto Ricans turned out to cheer the LORDS on as they woofed the pigs to their pens. Brothers and Sisters on 111th and 112th caught that old revolutionary spirit, last seen in '66, and blocked their streets, too.

When the garbage truck finally did show, the man vainly tried his game once more. For all those streets filled with garbage, D.O.G. sent one (1) Puerto Rican Brother. The people wouldn't fall for this cheap trick, and finally two white garbage men patted the junk into place while the brother hustled it into the truck. Afterwards a rally was held at 112th St. The cats in the street agreed to that.

The streets belong to the People!
The moon belongs to the People!
Power to the People!
  PALANTE!
  Yoruba
Dep. Minister of Information
New York State YLO

—Y.L.O., January, 1970

# Young Lords Party
# 13-Point Program and Platform

**The Young Lords Party Is a Revolutionary Political Party Fighting for the Liberation of All Oppressed People**

1. WE WANT SELF-DETERMINATION FOR PUERTO RI-CANS—LIBERATION ON THE ISLAND AND INSIDE THE UNITED STATES.

For 500 years, first spain and then united states have colonized our country. Billions of dollars in profits leave our country for the united states every year. In every way we are slaves of the gringo. We want liberation and the Power in the hands of the People, not Puerto Rican exploiters.
QUE VIVA PUERTO RICO LIBRE!
2. WE WANT SELF-DETERMINATION FOR ALL LATINOS.

Our Latin Brothers and Sisters, inside and outside the united

states, are oppressed by amerikkkan business. The Chicano people
built the Southwest, and we support their right to control their
lives and their land. The people of Santo Domingo continue to fight
against gringo domination and its puppet generals. The armed liberation struggles in Latin America are part of the war of Latinos against
imperialism.
QUE VIVA LA RAZA!
3. WE WANT LIBERATION OF ALL THIRD WORLD
PEOPLE.
    Just as Latins first slaved under spain and the yanquis, Black
people, Indians, and Asians slaved to build the wealth of this country.
For 400 years they have fought for freedom and dignity against racist
Babylon (decadent empire). Third World people have led the fight
for freedom. All the colored and oppressed peoples of the world
are one nation under oppression.
NO PUERTO RICAN IS FREE UNTIL ALL PEOPLE ARE
FREE!
4. WE ARE REVOLUTIONARY NATIONALISTS AND OP-
POSE RACISM.
    The Latin, Black, Indian and Asian people inside the u.s. are
colonies fighting for liberation. We know that washington, wall
street, and city hall will try to make our nationalism into racism;
but Puerto Ricans are of all colors and we resist racism. Millions of
poor white people are rising up to demand freedom and we support
them. These are the ones in the u.s. that are stepped on by the
rulers and the government. We each organize our people, but our
fights are the same against oppression and we will defeat it together.
POWER TO ALL OPPRESSED PEOPLE!
5. WE WANT COMMUNITY CONTROL OF OUR INSTITU-
TIONS AND LAND.
    We want control of our communities by our people and programs
to guarantee that all institutions serve the needs of our people.
People's control of police, health services, churches, schools, housing,
transportation and welfare are needed. We want an end to attacks
on our land by urban removal, highway destruction, universities and
corporations.
LAND BELONGS TO ALL THE PEOPLE!
6 . WE WANT A TRUE EDUCATION OF OUR CREOLE
CULTURE AND SPANISH LANGUAGE.
    We must learn our history of fighting against cultural, as well as
economic genocide by the yanqui. Revolutionary culture, culture of
our people, is the only true teaching.
7. WE OPPOSE CAPITALISTS AND ALLIANCES WITH
TRAITORS.
    Puerto Rican rulers, or puppets of the oppressor, do not help our

people. They are paid by the system to lead our people down blind alleys, just like the thousands of poverty pimps who keep our communities peaceful for business, or the street workers who keep gangs divided and blowing each other away. We want a society where the people socialistically control their labor.
VENCEREMOS!
8. WE OPPOSE THE AMERIKKKAN MILITARY.
We demand immediate withdrawal of u.s. military forces and bases from Puerto Rico, Vietnam, and all oppressed communities inside and outside the u.s. No Puerto Rican should serve in the u.s. army against his Brothers and Sisters, for the only true army of oppressed people is the people's army to fight all rulers.
U.S. OUT OF VIETNAM, FREE PUERTO RICO!
9. WE WANT FREEDOM FOR ALL POLITICAL PRIS-ONERS.
We want all Puerto Ricans freed because they have been tried by the racist courts of the colonizers, and not by their own people and peers. We want all freedom fighters released from jail.
FREE ALL POLITICAL PRISONERS!
10. WE WANT EQUALITY FOR WOMEN. MACHISMO MUST BE REVOLUTIONARY . . . NOT OPPRESSIVE.
Under capitalism, our women have been oppressed by both the society and our own men. The doctrine of machismo has been used by our men to take out their frustrations against their wives, sisters, mothers, and children. Our men must support their women in their fight for economic and social equality, and must recognize that our women are equals in every way within the revolutionary ranks.
FORWARD, SISTERS, IN THE STRUGGLE!
11. WE FIGHT ANTI-COMMUNISM WITH INTERNA-TIONAL UNITY.
Anyone who resists injustice is called a communist by "the man" and condemned. Our people are brainwashed by television, radio, newspapers, schools, and books to oppose people in other countries fighting for their freedom. No longer will our people believe attacks and slanders, because they have learned who the real enemy is and who their real friends are. We will defend our Brothers and Sisters around the world who fight for justice against the rich rulers of this country.
VIVA CHE!
12. WE BELIEVE ARMED SELF-DEFENSE AND ARMED STRUGGLE ARE THE ONLY MEANS TO LIBERATION.
We are opposed to violence—the violence of hungry children, illiterate adults, diseased old people, and the violence of poverty and profit. We have asked, petitioned, gone to courts, demonstrated peacefully, and voted for politicians full of empty promises. But we

still ain't free. The time has come to defend the lives of our people against repression and for revolutionary war against the businessman, politician, and police. When a government oppresses our people, we have the right to abolish it and create a new one.
BORICUA IS AWAKE! ALL PIGS BEWARE!
13. WE WANT A SOCIALIST SOCIETY.
We want liberation, clothing, free food, education, health care, transportation, utilities, and employment for all. We want a society where the needs of our people come first, and where we give solidarity and aid to the peoples of the world, not oppression and racism.
HASTA LA VICTORIA SIEMPRE! [22]

—*Palante*, Latin Revolutionary News Service


# Ten-Point Health Program of the Young Lords

1) We want total self-determination of all health services in East Harlem (El Barrio) through an incorporated Community-Staff Governing Board for Metropolitan Hospital. (Staff is anyone and everyone working at Metropolitan).
2) We want immediate replacement of all Lindsay administrators by community and staff appointed people whose practice has demonstrated their commitment to serve our poor community.
3) We demand immediate end to construction of the new emergency room until the Metropolitan Hospital Community-Staff Governing Board inspects and approves them or authorizes new plans.
4) We want employment for our people. All jobs filled in El Barrio must be filled by residents first, using on-the-job training and other educational opportunities as bases for service and promotion.
5) We want free publicly supported health care for treatment and prevention. WE WANT AN END TO ALL FEES.
6) We want total decentralization—block health officers responsible to the community-staff board should be instituted.
7) We want "door-to-door" preventive health services emphasizing environment and sanitation control, nutrition, drug addiction, maternal and child care and senior citizen's services.
8) We want education programs for all the people to expose health problems—sanitation, rats, poor housing, malnutrition, police brutality, pollution, and other forms of oppression.
9) We want total control by the Metropolitan hospital community-staff governing board of the budget allocations, medical policy along

the above points, hiring, firing, and salaries of employees, construction and health code enforcement.

10) Any community, union, or workers organization must support all the points of this program and work and fight for that or be shown as what they are—enemies of the poor people of East Harlem.

—Y.L.O., January, 1970

# The Patriot Party
# Speaks to the Movement

The Patriot Party is a revolutionary Party for poor and oppressed white people. We recognize that the struggle here in Babylon is a class struggle; the haves against the have nots; the oppressed against the oppressor and the exploited against the exploiter.

For some time now, the so called white "movement" in this country, has failed to recognize or support the Patriot Party—this includes: radical groups and radical papers. The Patriot Party is not playing; we're drawing that clear line of demarcation between our enemies and our friends, so the "movement" had better make up its mind which way it's going to go. The Patriot Party is moving too fast to be concerned about those holding the people back from their freedom.

The Patriot Party is dealing with the survival of our people—the poor and oppressed white people. We're sick and tired of certain people and groups telling us "there ain't no such thing as poor and oppressed white people," that's where the Patriot Party comes in—we're that "no such thing"—we're people from all over Babylon— north, south, Appalachia—where our children die at four because of starvation and indecent housing—the poor and oppressed white people. The so called "movement" better begin to realize, that— first of all—we're human beings, we're real; second—we've always been here, we didn't just materialize; and third—we're not going away, even if you choose not to admit we exist.

The "movement" seems to be more interested in Class-Clown, Abbie Hoffman, than kids getting food in their stomachs, or medical needs. They are more interested in Abbie Hoffman—the actor, making his film debut in "Prologue." Well, we've got something for Abbie Hoffman—he'd better turn that money over to the people. That's what we've got to say to Abbie. He talks about Revolution for the fun of it. Well, this is no game. We've got 30 class brothers

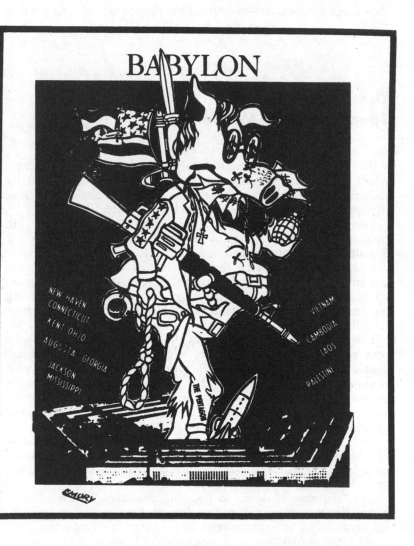

killed already. 32 to be exact. When we talk about Brothers being killed and murdered, we're talking about Panthers, Patriots and Lords—the oppressed people's warriors being killed. And if he thinks this is a revolution for the fun of it, he's either a fool or a pig.

Abbie Hoffman and the rest of the Conspiracy 7 now get paid to speak about their famous trial. Well, we have something to say to the rest of them too; those defendants who stood by and watched the Chairman of the Black Panther Party be handcuffed and gagged in that courtroom. If there were Patriots at that trial with the Chairman, they would have had to gag and chain 8 of us down. We're talking about Brothers and Sisters who stand in solidarity, who go down together—not make fool movies about it. Nobody calls us Brother unless they can take that step—that's solidarity! We know damn well if there were Patriots at that lynching (trial), they would have had to shoot us. We would have gagged that fascist Hoffman, and all his lackeys and, while we would have been gagging them, we would have been educating the people. The only educating that came out of that trial was by Chairman Bobby. The rest of the defendants didn't educate, they made a circus out of it. They showed that the only leader was Bobby Scale because as soon as Bobby left the trial, the only ringmaster was Fascist Hoffman. The seven defendants had never been so honored in their lives than to have Bobby Seale in the same courtroom with them, and they'll never be so honored again. That's what the Patriots have to say to them.

Most of the so-called "movement" states that they recognize our Brothers and Sisters of the Black Panther Party as the Vanguard Party—however, they do not follow their ideology or practice. The Patriot Party recognizes the Black Panther Party as the Vanguard by our practice. The people learn by observation and participation. The "movement" doesn't even recognize that we exist. They are racist toward oppressed white people. The Patriot Party comes from the people who have been down, and when you're down, the only place to go is up toward freedom, and anybody who stands in our way, and tries to stop us, is the enemy.

The Patriot Party grew out of the old Young Patriot Organization in Uptown Chicago. We split from the Young Patriot Organization because they were concerned with old friendships, individuals, rather than the masses of people in Uptown. They would rather be friends with a few people and indulge in drinking than listen to the community's cry for help. These old friends were holding the people's party back, and they became more important than the masses. The Young Patriot Organization was guilty of extreme liberalism—"For the sake of peace and friendship, when things have clearly gone wrong." A few programs were started by the Y.P.O. in Uptown Chicago. However, the People were not being educated to the struggle, so they had the effect of being reformist programs. People all over the country were calling for the Patriots; the People in Richmond, Va. were calling for us; the people in Carbondale, Ill. were calling for us, the people in Eugene, Oregon were calling for us; the people in Cleveland, Ohio were calling for us, and the people in New York, N.Y. were calling for us. Yet the Y.P.O. would rather relate to some old barroom friends than the masses of the people. So, a few of the Y.P.O. members said, "we've got to move with the people. We can't relate to old friends that are actually hurting our people." We knew that a revolutionary Party could not tail behind the people, but has to lead, and show the people by example. So we left the Y.P.O. and formed the Patriot Party. Let it be clear that we did not leave the people of Uptown Chicago, only the organization, that is misleading and confusing the people. Uptown Chicago is the home of our people, and we will serve our people's needs.

The Patriot Party has become a National Party with over five branches already functioning, and others in training. We don't relate to "Serve the people," "Power to the people," only in words, we are putting these terms into practice. Our programs range from Free Breakfast for Children to the Free Lumber Programs (in Eugene, Oregon—for the people's stoves in the mountain areas). The Patriot Party is working in oppressed communities.

In New Haven, Conn., the Patriot Party is now serving 30–40 children breakfast per day, and they're moving on a medical clinic already. It's heightening the contradictions and making the people aware of the system's faults. They're practicing Socialism. We recognize that this is the last thing the pigs want to see, and we know that we're educating the white community around the trial of our brother, Chairman Bobby Seale of the Black Panther Party. The pigs are uptight about that too, the white community coming out in support of Bobby Seale. Then they couldn't use racism to separate the people. When we say white people coming to support the trial, we don't mean the usual crowd of hippies with helmets, they're always there. We're talking about the community people— people nobody's ever seen before being moved and beginning to scream til they release Bobby Seale, because they understand by class oppression how Bobby's being framed, the same way they see Tom Dostou, our Field Marshal as their white brother being framed. They see Bobby Seale being framed as their black brother. So we know the pigs in New Haven are uptight, so we're going to make them more uptight.

As Fred Hampton said, "come down from that mountain top into the valley with the people." What we're saying is that "movement" people better stop fooling around, because we ain't fooling around.

If they're serious about revolution, if they're serious about change, well then come on down. You dig? The Chairman of the Patriot Party calls what they're doing petty bourgeois arrogance—all along, they've had all the education, they had all the schooling and put all that smoke in their brains. They made their pea brain grow into a watermelon you dig? And now that watermelon is confused because the people who never had the education, those who kept their pea brain, are now teaching them revolution. They can't dig that. They can't dig their own white niggers teaching them about Class Struggle.

So, Brothers and Sisters, we must get together. We have Chairman Bobby Seale facing a murder charge. Do people realize that? That he's on trial for his life in New Haven, Conn.? But, he ain't going to go, we'll tell you right now—you can quote the Patriot Party on that.

If Chairman Bobby is not set free—that's it! That's it as far as the Patriot Party is concerned. We say—ALL POWER TO THE PEOPLE OR ELSE. Bobby Seale is going to be set free, or else. And that goes for any of our leadership—Panther Party or Patriot Party. We're not taking it any more, they're not ripping off our leadership anymore. If any more of our leadership gets ripped off, there are going to be some political consequences, or physical alienation of the Problem.

ALL POWER TO THE PEOPLE—OR ELSE
PATRIOT PARTY
NATIONAL HEADQUARTERS
1742 Second Ave.
New York

—*The Black Panther*, February 17, 1970

# Latinos Walkout

by Doug Monica

Richmond California. The home of Standard Oil. Black, brown, and working whites. A racist school board, and no money for the schools.

September 16th was the date set for a nationwide walkout of Chicano youth at The National Chicano Youth Conference held in Denver last March. That date, in the Bay Area, coincided with a wide series of demonstrations at the International Industrialists Conference in San Francisco. The target of the Richmond demonstrations was Safeway stores, which was prominently represented at the Conference, which continues to sell California grapes and has been hit by many boycotts, and rips off everyone.

In Richmond, several hundred high school, junior high, and elementary school students walked out. At one junior high the administration tried to keep students in by locking all the gates. By that time, large numbers of students were already in the streets, and when they got to that junior high, students from inside would run out, and climb over the fence to join the ones outside.

### Jailbreak

At one school, one girl had gotten left behind and didn't know how to catch up, so she called her mother, who came and picked her up to drive her to the demonstration. There were many Chicanos among the marchers, but also many black and white allies. They marched with raised fists down to a local Safeway. Seeing few policemen on the streets they rushed into the Safeway, threw all the grapes on the floor and stomped all over them. The action went off smoothly and the march continued.

The march passed another high school, gaining strength, and then headed for another Safeway. When the march was a few blocks away from the store, pigs moved in and started busting Chicano students. Many students were busted on so-called truancy raps. Others managed to get away, and made it to the Safeway, where they found that the manager had locked the store. For a time pigs continued cruising, busting any brown youth they could, including one Chicano who was riding in a car with a city official observing the arrests.

Later, at the police station the pigs hassled Chicano parents who came to get their children. That only made the parents more angry. The parents organized and succeeded in having all the charges dropped, and in getting all students who were suspended from school back in.

In organizing the action in Richmond, reliance was placed on the masses of students. Students, not non-students, wrote the leaflets, determined the nature of the demonstration. Being familiar with other students and the schools, they had to take the leading role. Not all aspects of the demonstration were perfect, but there would have been no action except for the leading role of many students.

And the leading role played by women. Brown women, at several key points in the demonstration pushed ahead and acted as the vanguard. At one school, several hundred students were milling around in the schoolyard undecided about whether to walk out a gate flanked by deans and teachers taking names. It was the women who broke the indecision, who walked defiantly through, and the rest soon followed. When there was a brief argument and tussle at the door of the Safeway that was entered, it was the women who knocked the manager aside and led the rest of the students to the grapes.

The idea that this was part of a planned nationwide action helped bring the reality of a brown liberation movement home to many students. By tying in Safeway, the boycott, and the meeting of the imperialists, the enemy was well defined. By making Safeway, as a local arm of imperialism, the target, there was support from large numbers of black and white kids. This unity was a big step in schools that last spring were the scene of heavy racial fighting.

Students grasped the situation, and began learning how to move in a disciplined way against the enemy. And they're on the move.

—*The Movement*, November, 1969

## Getting Together

The young people in Chinatown are afraid and confused. We don't know what to do with our lives. There seems to be no hope in the future. Many of us join groups. We join groups for security and friendship. With the war eating up more men, with no good jobs and with boring and useless schools, no wonder more people are looking towards the groups.

There have been a lot of stabbings and shootings lately and everybody is confused and afraid because the pigs are picking up suspected troublemakers. Because pigs are racist they come down on everybody because "all Chinese look alike." (Just like at Songmy where the pigs killed all the Vietnamese because they couldn't tell them apart.) [23] Just last week four brothers were picked up and falsely charged with conspiracy and attempted murder. The pigs are using the courts and the legal system to jail the four brothers by setting excessively high bails and lengthy court procedures. Because of the high bail they have to rot in jail.

Why are the pigs coming down now? Because more and more young people are looking towards groups and because the groups of people are really together. The pigs are afraid of people getting together.

We have to get ourselves together and this means not only that all Chinese should unite but also that we unite with our Puerto Rican and Black brothers and sisters. The fighting amongst ourselves is used by the rich white people in the government and in the schools to keep the Chinese and Puerto Ricans in their places.

They figure if these non-white groups fight among themselves the problems of 1) crowded, run-down, roach infested apartments, 2) mothers working long hours in the sweat shops for 75 cents an hour, and 3) bullshit education given by racist teachers, will not have to be dealt with. But they are wrong because some of the young people in Chinatown are seeing through this bullshit and instead of fighting with Blacks and Puerto Ricans who share the same problems we do are now uniting in order to fight the real enemies—the establishment and schools for more decent lives. Young people in Chinatown realize that it is not the Blacks and Puerto Ricans who are oppressing them, that divisions among non-white people are used by the white man to further screw us and by fighting in the schools against Puerto Ricans is playing right into the hands of these pigs (big shots) who oppress the Chinese people and exploit the Chinatown community.

Recently, these fights have become greater in intensity and numbers. Many injuries, some serious ones, result from these fights. At this point we've got to ask ourselves: What are these gang fights doing for the Chinese people and our community? Are they helping us in *any* way?

People join gangs and fight because they are angry at something. They are right in being angry. Who wouldn't be angry with all this poverty, unemployment, racism, stupid war and hard life? So all of us Chinese, especially the young Chinese *should* be angry. And we *should* fight, and *fight hard*. But let's make sure we fight against the real enemy—the rich whites who run this country and who profit from the war against the Asian people. NOT against our own brothers in Chinatown, and NOT against our Black and Puerto Rican brothers!

ALL POWER TO THE PEOPLE!
ALL POWER TO THE BROTHERS & SISTERS WHO LOVE THE PEOPLE & FIGHT THE REAL ENEMY!!

—*Getting Together*, February, 1970

# Ten-Point Program and Platform of the Black Student Unions

We want an education for our people that exposes the true nature of this decadent American Society. We want an education that teaches us our true history and role in the present day society.

We believe in an educational system that will give our people a knowledge of self. If a man does not have knowledge of himself and his position in society and the world, then he has little chance to relate to anything else.

1. *We want freedom. We want power to determine the destiny of our school.*

We believe that we will not be free within the schools to get a decent education unless we are able to have a say and determine the type of education that will affect and determine the destiny of our people.

2. *We want full enrollment in the schools for our people.*

We believe that the city and federal government is responsible and obligated to give every man a decent education.

3. *We want an end to the robbery by the white man of our black community.*

We believe that this racist government has robbed us of an education. We believe that this racist capitalist government has robbed the Black Community of its money by forcing us to pay higher taxes for less quality.

4. *We want decent educational facilities, fit for the use of students.*

We believe that if these businessmen will not give decent facilities to our community schools, then the schools and their facilities should be taken out of the hands of these few individual racists and placed into the hands of the community, with government aid, so the community can develop a decent and suitable educational system.

5. *We want an education for our people that teaches us how to survive in the present day society.*

We believe that if the educational system does not teach us how to survive in society and the world it loses its meaning for existence.

6. *We want all racist teachers to be excluded and restricted from all public schools.*

We believe that if the teacher in a school is acting in racist fashion then that teacher is not interested in the welfare or development of the students but only in their destruction.

7. *We want an immediate end to police brutality and murder of black people. We want all police and special agents to be excluded and restricted from school premises.*

We believe that there should be an end to harassment by the police department of Black people. We believe that if all of the police were pulled out of the schools, the schools would become more functional.

8. *We want all students that have been exempt, expelled, or suspended from school to be reinstated.*

We believe all students should be reinstated because they haven't received fair and impartial judgment or have been put out because of incidents or situations that have occurred outside of the school's authority.

9. *We want all students when brought to trial to be tried in student court by a jury of their peer group or students of their school.*

We believe that the student courts should follow the United States Constitution so that students can receive a fair trial. The 14th Amendment of the U.S. Constitution gives a man a right to be tried by a jury of his peer group. A peer is a person from a similar economical, social, religious, geographical, environmental, historical and racial background. To do this the court would be forced to select a jury of students from the community from which the defendant came. We have been and are being tried by a white principal, vice-principal, and white students that have no understanding of the "average reasoning man" of the Black Community.

10. *We want power, enrollment, equipment, education, teachers, justice, and peace.*

As our major political objective, an assembly for the student body, in which only the students will be allowed to participate, for the purpose of determining the will of the students as to the school's destiny.

We hold these truths as being self-evident, that all men are created equal, that they are endowed by their creator with certain inalienable rights, that among these are life, liberty and the pursuit of happiness. To secure these rights within the schools, governments are instituted among the students, deriving their just powers from the consent of the governed, that whenever any form of student government becomes destructive to these ends, it is the right of the students to alter or abolish it and to institute new government, laying its foundation on such principles and organizing its power in such form as to them shall seem most likely to effect their safety and happiness.

Prudence, indeed, will dictate that governments long established should not be changed for light and transient causes, and accordingly all experiences have shown, that mankind are more liable to suffer, while evils are sufferable, than to right themselves by abolishing the forms to which they are accustomed. But when a long train of abuses and force, pursuing invariably the same object, reveals a design to reduce them to absolute destruction, it is their right, it is their duty, to throw off such a government and to provide new guards for their future security.

—*The Black Panther*, February 2, 1969

# The Black Panther Party and Revolutionary Trade Unionism

Speech of Ray "Masai" Hewitt, Minister of Education, Black Panther Party, to the Revolutionary Labor Conference

Power to the people, definitely all power to the workers. What we want to do, we definitely want to put forth the Black Panther Party's correct ideology and try to make the workers a class for itself instead of a class in itself. But we know that it's been tried before. Now that the workers made some attempts that failed, does not mean that the analysis of the class struggle no longer applies. There's many attempts now-a-days to apply any other kind of analysis, religious analysis, race analysis, all kinds of idealism and metaphysics are being applied to the struggle of the workers including sell-outs, bootlicking, ass kissing, back stabbing.

The Panther Party has already implemented in some areas, concrete revolutionary Marxist-Leninist principles, put them into practice to make the workers a class for itself, to make the workers a strong political organ for themselves. Without revolutionary theory, this is impossible. To think that correct revolutionary principles are going to drop out of the sky, or that they're born innate in the mind really borders on the ridiculous. As students say, into a television set.

The Black Panther Party is definitely willing to work in cooperation to help put into practice anything that will take the workers to the conscious level and organize economic and political struggle. We're not talking about rampant unionism, or separatism by occupation, by race, by salary. We're talking about making the workers a political tool, a real political force because the student movement gets a hell of a lot of publicity, what they like to call the militants and the radicals and the so-called black militant movement gets a hell of a lot of publicity. But it should be quite clear to anybody that has done a little research and has a reasonable amount of practice that only the workers can free the workers. And that to do this the workers will have to become a strong political force with a party based on correct revolutionary principles to guide them.

Now the vanguard position of any political struggle, is not something that's bestowed by the heavens, or snatched up by some lucky opportunists. The vanguard position is objectively earned through struggle and usually organizations or people who earned the vanguard position, only find out about it when they realize that they're wearing out the steps in the jails and the courts. The jailhouse doors are getting rusty from slamming and opening and slamming and opening. There won't be any alternative for the workers except to become a strong militant revolutionary political force. The students cannot free the workers, the workers cannot free the students. Black folks cannot free White folks, White folks cannot free Black folks. The Black Panther Party has a very clear understanding of these concepts. And we say that for all the workers the first point of demarcation which seems to have been forgotten in this country, is that there has to be a correct recognition that the primary struggle is the class struggle. Once this line of demarcation has been departed from the workers usually become turned on each other, or they become in many cases the champions of reform. With the type of unions that we've had in this country, it's been understandable why this weird phenomenon has come about. Another thing that we would like to make clear in the very beginning, is that we do recognize the need for a degree of self-determination, of self-rule for militant Black workers. This is not in any way to endorse racism. The Party has a very clear line on that point. But there is a need among Blacks, who are the most oppressed and exploited people within the confines of this Babylon they call America to have self-rule, this is not independent rule, independent of others, located geographically together, but self-rule. And there's also an equal need for these Blacks to work in very close working coalition and close communication with their class brothers, regardless of color, regardless of whether you're for or against intermarriage, whether you want to live in Beverly Hills or Watts or Oakland or Washington, D.C., it doesn't make any difference. The need is for a constant maintenance of a correct class line. And there's some unions that profess this in lip-service and then they take it as far as their local community, say Los Angeles, or the San Francisco area. Then these same unions that claim to be workers unions, forget one of the basic Marxist-Leninist principles, which Lenin put down, is that the interest of the local proletariat should be subordinate to the interest of the world proletariat. That's the advent of unionism there, they start selling out their working class brothers all around the world, even on the other side of the city. The Black Panther Party is against this kind of separatism, opportunism, individualism, this very subjective approach to a problem that is in reality a worldwide problem. The workers that catch a collective hell and try to deal with it in an individual manner, we see them as suicidal, nonsensical, and very backwards politically. So when we talk about self-rule this does not negate the need for a very close working coalition with class brothers, because the main problem in the United

States is not the race contradictions but the class contradictions. It's made that way by the royal fucking that the working class gets in this country. This is not the exclusive right of any ethnic group in this country. But racism does exist to such a high level in this country, that the people have to deal first on a level that goes from step by step, taking it from a lower to a higher level. There's no need of going into whether or not we think it has to always be like this. No we don't, we hope it doesn't. That the day when the workers will all belong to one working class association, when that day comes we'll all be much happier. But until then that's the way it has to be.

Another point of clarification is the role of the white radical workers. The white radical workers are the ones best suited to fight racism, ignorance and the political backwardness that exists in the whole community. We definitely cannot expect any working brothers from the Panther Caucuses or DRUM or other Black revolutionary groups to go among the white workers when racism is still so rampant. It would be like myself and these four brothers here going down to clean up the white folks in Mobile, Alabama. Not only would it probably be sheer suicide, it would be lunacy, it would be an apolitical move, but there is a role. We find that many times the white mother-country radicals among the workers would like to come into the Black community and do their thing or come in among the Black workers and do their thing. The sentiments are beautiful, but it's not very practical at all. For one thing to assume that the Black workers don't have enough brains to take care of themselves, is really a racist fallacy, the manifestation of a real racist attitude. For another the purpose of the working class as a whole can best be served by each going into his own community, because this mosaic that's passed off as a melting pot, this ethnic mosaic is a mixed-up mess. Racism is institutionalized to a degree that it has never been institutionalized in the history of mankind, I mean it's bounced off telestar and shot around the world. They pipe it under the ocean in cables, it's in the comic books, it's in Sunday papers, it's in television and radio. So it's rampant idealism to try to ignore this. But it's very foolhardy and politically backwards to ignore the fact that the primary struggle is the class struggle, this goes for Blacks and Whites alike. Now we can start with that basic degree of understanding and we can probably accomplish something.

Another thing that has to be understood is that if we get away from unionism, then the working class group, the group that professes to be for the worker is going to have to have a very concrete and practical platform and program. And I would say that the Black Panther Party's 10-point Platform and Program exemplifies the type of program that a revolutionary group needs. We're not going to confine ourselves just to the factory and divorce the factory from the community, that's a metaphysical approach, and that's not our theory. I think we'll have a question and answer period later on, so I won't try to take up too much of your time. Thank you.

—*The Black Panther*, May 4, 1969

# Black Caucus Program: An Interview

MOVEMENT: The Black Caucus has a 7 point program: What is it?

WILBERT: The first point is that the Black Caucus will attack all forms of discrimination and racism among workers. Immediately upon any of this shit being perpetrated by the International, the local leadership, or the boss, we'll be there to fight it and explain how racism goes against the interests of the workers.

The second point is that the Black Caucus is against the individual acceptance of special privileges and favoritism. We understand how Toms and lackeys are developed, by getting special privileges. By getting jobs that have less work to them. And people get these positions because of their loyalty to the policies of the union leadership. With the union leadership working only for its own and the bosses' advantage, they need some workers within the workers to perpetuate their position. We have workers in Local 250A who are Toms and lackeys. When the black caucus runs down a progressive line or expose something, these workers run some madness to confuse the membership. And they get paid for this. We're against special privileges. Period.

José: To add to that. The special privileges don't come down so much from the union leadership, but from the bosses. The bosses set up these so-called special duty jobs. It's a special privilege to be in the dispatchers' office, you do less work and make the same money as platform employees. These jobs are given to people who adhere to policies set down by the management and these policies are endorsed by the union by the mere fact that the union does not attack this practice. We say: if there's an opening for a dispatcher then there should be examinations given for dispatcher. We say open up the ranks. Not using a position to play on favoritism and cause dissension among the workers. The bosses play that game: divide and conquer.

WILBERT: The third point of the program is the Black Caucus will actively support all unions working in the best interest of the workers. We don't support a union that turns its back on its membership, just because the membership is politically ignorant. If the leadership of a union sees the membership is ignorant politically, and it is educating the membership, and struggling together with it, we support it.

MOVEMENT: Have you supported any unions in this area?

JOSÉ: Not any specific union. There have been workers from many local unions that we have stood in solidarity with.

The fourth point of the program is that the Caucus will support or select members seeking political office in the union after we've run a background survey of his history, union activities, sincerity, then we will support him if he will work in the interest of the workers.

MOVEMENT: Does the Caucus itself run candidates?

WILBERT: Should members and central committee people run for office? Members ask us why we haven't, when we've raised so many questions about how fucked up things are. We say that our main purpose is to raise the consciousness of the workers, and then they'll vote for men among themselves who are not opportunists, and who understand the necessity for strong unions. If the membership wanted us to represent them, and a particular situation arose where we felt this would serve their needs then we would. The whole union leadership is up for election in May and this is what the caucus is about right now, raising the political consciousness of the members so that when people come campaigning for different positions, they will be able to judge whether they'll serve them or not.

JOSÉ: One way we can do that is specify exactly what our black president now is doing that's not in the workers' interests. That way they'll understand clearly that when he says, "I'm doing this for you", he's not.

DUCHO: The fifth point of the program is that we reject all rumors or hearsay that are not given the official word of the Caucus. We had to make this point because of all the rumors being spread about us and what we stood for among the drivers. That's another reason why we came out with the paper.

JOSÉ: The sixth point is that the caucus does not recognize the union as being above constructive criticism. Criticism is to be administered in an educational manner, not to destroy, but to build and strengthen. Through criticism we expose the union leadership and educate.

The seventh point is that it is not the intention of the Black Caucus to disrupt the workings of the grievance procedures, which this union with honor has achieved in the past. Every grievance that comes forth from the membership to the extent that the union has dealt with it and the members were satisfied, we say right on to that. The objective of the Black Caucus is to unite the workers for the purpose of bringing about positive and concrete changes in the laws, rules, conditions, and their application. When laws, rules and policies do not serve the workers, we attack them.

MOVEMENT: Are there black caucuses in other transport unions? What about link ups with other black caucuses?

WILBERT: Right now we have a working coalition with the Black Panther Caucus of the U.A.W. in Fremont, California. Other than that we have no bonafide coalitions at this time. We are working with people in several different locals, and we are constantly making contact with people who are having problems within their local unions and are trying to come up with strategy and tactics to handle the problems.

In New York City there's a revolutionary element in the Transit workers union who are trying to start an independent union because of the shit that's coming down between the TWU and the Transit Authority. We keep in touch with them, although at this time we don't intend to split the union out here or start an independent union . . . but, we're revolutionaries and we'll do what's necessary.

MOVEMENT: What's the relationship to the Black Panther Party?

WILBERT: I myself am a member of the Black Panther Party, and these other brothers here on the Central Committee are very dedicated brothers and practice the Party ideology, the ten-point platform and program of the Party. That's what our relationship is with the Party, we feel we are one, and if that shakes anybody, well right on. Our objective is to show people by practice what our politics are, and they are the politics of the rank and file exercising their right to change the system, the politics of revolution in this country, and the politics of oppressed people all over the world gaining liberation from this imperialist pig that we here in Babylon are strategically close to.

—*The Movement*, November, 1969

# Petition to the United Nations [24]

We, the undersigned citizens of the United States, gravely concerned with the continued racist persecution, conscious and unconscious, and centuries-old denial of Constitutional rights and respect for human dignity to men, women and children of red, brown, yellow and particularly black Americans, assert that:

The savage police activities, based upon official policies of Federal,

State and City governments, has resulted in innumerable beatings, frameups, arrests and murders of black Americans, the classical example of which is the Black Panther Party. The murderous attacks on Black youth in Chicago Illinois, Orangeburg South Carolina, Augusta Georgia, Jackson, Mississippi, and the innumerable beatings, legal frameups of Brown, Red, Yellow and Black youths are not only in violation of their legal rights, but as well of this government's commitment under the Charter of the United Nations.

The Genocide Convention adopted by the General Assembly of the United Nations on December 9, 1948, defines as genocide "killing members of the group and any intent to destroy in whole or in part a national racial or ethnic or religious group". And further, according to the Convention, "Causing serious bodily or mental harm to members of the group" is Genocide.

We assert that the Genocide Convention has been flagrantly violated by the Government of the United States. We further assert that the United Nations has jurisdiction in this matter, to hold otherwise is to repudiate its position regarding apartheid in South Africa and as well its universal Declaration of Human Rights, and its Convention for the Prevention and Punishment of Genocide.

The racist planned and unplanned terror suffered by more than 40 millions of black, brown, red and yellow citizens of the United States cannot be regarded solely as a domestic issue. The continuance of these practices threatens the struggle of mankind throughout the world to achieve peace, security and dignity.

On the basis of simple justice, it is time for the Human Rights Commission of the United Nations to call for universal action, including political and economic sanctions against the United States. We further demand that the United States government make reparations to those who have suffered the damages of racist and genocidal practices.

NAME

Huey P. Newton

Bobby Seale

UNDER THE AUSPICES OF: *The Committee to Petition The United Nations,* of the Conference Committee, 33 Union Square W., New York, N.Y., 10003, Room 907

# APPENDIXES

# I. THE PERSECUTION OF THE BLACK PANTHER PARTY

## The Old Rules Do Not Apply

A Survey of the Persecution of the Black Panther Party by Charles R. Garry

In July, 1969, the Black Panther Party told the American people and, indeed, the entire world, that all who opposed fascism must unite against it and its encroachment first on the lives of the Black militants and the Black people as a whole and then on the lives of White radicals. Unfortunately, many people did not pay much attention to this appeal and warning. In fact, few Americans took it seriously, regarding it as mere rhetoric.

Since July, 1969, events have borne out the validity of the warnings of the Black Panther Party.

In December, 1969, the records of the Panthers who had been murdered and harassed since its early years were compiled. Unfortunately, the Party did not begin to keep records at its inception of the men and women who were harassed and killed, and the demand for such statistics was so great that they had to be compiled hastily. Nevertheless, even the incomplete records tell a story of systematic arrest and harassment of men and women in Los Angeles county alone for a period of almost two years. A man or woman or a group of men and women would be charged with murder, be held in jail for five or ten days, or twenty days, and all at once, the charges against them would be dropped. The familiar buzz-saw would be "attempted murder" or "resisting arrest."

The pattern in Los Angeles is the same pattern that has emerged throughout the United States wherever the Black Panther Party has set up chapters and commenced operation.

In a period of two years—December, 1967 to December, 1969—the Black Panther Party expended in bail-bond premiums alone—just the premiums, that is, money that would never be returned—a sum in excess of $200,000! How many breakfasts or lunches for hungry children, how much medical attention sorely needed in the ghetto communities would that $200,000 have furnished?

In the same two-year period, twenty-eight Panthers were killed. And we have documented all of these cases. Since then other Panthers have been murdered. How many more men and women will have to be murdered before the American people will wake up to their responsibility, and assert without equivocation that they are not going to permit fascism and a police state in this country?

Let me cite some additional statistics, though for the complete record, I would recommend you consult the special issue of *The Black Panther* (February 21, 1970) entitled, "Evidence and Intimidation of Fascist Crimes by U.S.A." Between May 2, 1967 and December 25, 1969 charges were dropped against at least 87 Panthers arrested for a wide variety of so-called violations of the law. Yet these men and women were kept in prison for days, weeks, and months even though there was absolutely no evidence against them, and they were finally released. At least a dozen cases involving Panthers have been dismissed in court. In these cases, the purpose has clearly been to intimidate, to frighten, to remove from operation and activities the Panthers, and to hope that the hysteria against the Black Panther Party would produce convictions and imprisonments.

A few Panthers have walked out of courtrooms as free men, having won acquittals in trials. One was Ralph Cobb who was acquitted on April 28, 1970 in a trial in Essex County, New Jersey. Cobb had been charged on the sole statement of one witness with three counts of kidnapping, assault and extortion. Furthermore, the prosecution openly implied that he had committed these crimes under orders from the Black Panther Party. At one point, the prosecution introduced the Party's 10-point program as evidence. As Milton H. Friedman, Cobb's lawyer, pointed out during the trial, had Cobb not been a Panther the evidence on which he was arrested would not have warranted his being brought to trial. In this case, the frame-up was too crude, and Judge Antell displayed a respect for the law, in sharp contrast to the conduct of judges most Panthers have had to face.

As I write this, one of the most beautiful, selfless human beings that I have ever known, one of the world's greatest revolutionary leaders is sitting in a penitentiary in San Luis Obispo, confined in prison for a crime he did not commit, and despite the fact that the Appeals Court of the State of California has ruled that he should have been acquitted. Huey Newton's conviction has been reversed. But already he has spent over three years in the penitentiary for a crime for which most people would have to spend six to nine months at the most. He now has to face another trial.

Eldridge Cleaver is widely acknowledged to be one of the most brilliant writers in contemporary American literature. Yet this man who Maxwell Geismar called "one of the best cultural critics now writing," and of whom Robert Coles in the *Atlantic Monthly* described as being "full of Christian care, Christian grief and disappointment, Christian resignation, Christian messianic toughness, and hope," will have to spend the rest of his days—unless a radical change occurs—in exile.

I did not personally know Mark Clark from Chicago who was murdered by the police. But I did know Fred Hampton, and he was a brilliant, aggressive, down-to-earth young man with tremendous understanding combined with great affability. As everyone knows, he was murdered when the Panther headquarters were raided in the wee hours of the morning. But who will pay for these deaths?

Twenty-one Panthers in New York have been kept in prison in New York under abominable conditions on all kinds of wild charges. The bail for the 21 is $2,100,000,000!

Because he exercised his rights under the First Amendment, David Hilliard, Chief of Staff of the Black Panther Party, now stands before the bourgeois world as Public Enemy No. 1. His bail premium was $30,000 and 190% collateral for the $30,000, before the bail bondsman would put up the bail. Even then it was impossible to get any Bay Area bondsman to write, and we had to import a man from Los Angeles to do it. He had to have 190% collateral so that he would put up $30,000—plus the $3,000 premium. And while all of this was being transacted, David Hilliard had to spend an additional four days in a cell block in the Oakland courthouse where the only ventilation comes through a small vent underneath the cage. This is the same cell in which Huey Newton was confined for seven months. Eldridge Cleaver, who spent four hours in this same cell, told the court in Alameda County that in all of the twelve years he had spent in prison, this was the worst hell-hole he had ever known.

In the over thirty years I have been practicing law, I have never experienced the type of persecution faced by the Black Panthers. The old rules do not apply to the Black Panther Party. There are new sets of rules, new requirements, new methods of harassment. I find that the judges are gutless, without any backbone. To be sure, there is a judge here and there who has guts and stands up against the onslaught of the police state. But most of them are frightened, and most of them are racists. The pathetic part of it is that they do not realize that they are racists.

Day after day in the courtroom in Chicago, Bobby Seale demanded the right to defend himself. After five weeks of begging and pleading for the right to exercise his right under the sixth amendment of the United States Constitution, he finally told that judge, "You are a blatant, fascist pig. You are trampling over my constitutional rights. You are not worthy to sit on that bench and decide the fate of men and women." For that he was gagged, chained like a wild animal. And when public opinion began to turn against that judge, what did he do? He declared a mistrial on Bobby Seale. He took advantage of his cloak and his oath of office and his responsibility to humanity. In vindictiveness, in anger, he sentenced Bobby Seale to four years in a federal penitentiary.

The judge could not do this legally. But this clever little judge worked out a little scheme. He knew that the United States Supreme Court had held that anyone who is imprisoned more than six months is entitled to a jury trial. This little man knew that. So he took 16 different charges, and sentenced Bobby to 3 months each which added up to 48 months. He was confident he would get away with that, and he will unless the people arise.

Whenever a Panther speaks in public, agents of the police department, the FBI, the CIA and other similar organizations are present taking notes on what is said, and then they proceed to take sentences out of context. Here is a concrete example. In December, 1969 I asked the court to permit David Hilliard to travel the length and breadth of the United States. All hell broke loose. The representative of the government objected strenuously. He said: "To permit Mr. Hilliard to be out of the district of North California would enable him to foment strife and continue to threaten the life of the President of the United States." The judge then asked why Mr. Hilliard had to be treated any differently than any other defendant. The two experts from the Attorney General's staff in Washington who were brought here to San Francisco finally had to admit that there would be no reason to treat Mr. Hilliard differently. I was asked to prepare an order, and one was prepared along the lines that the judge had indicated. We came to the court at one o'clock. Mr. Hilliard was not present, because all that was to be submitted was the order to be signed.

It was finally signed by the judge at 5:30 in the afternoon. But not before we had to face more harassment. In the afternoon in came two fat cats with an affidavit to be submitted to the judge. I said, "May I see the affidavit?" One of the cats said, "No." I said, "I'd like to see it." The judge said, "Give Mr. Garry a copy of the affidavit." The affidavit said that in a speech at the Glide Memorial Church on Sunday night, December 14, 1969, David Hilliard had said again, "We will kill the President." This was signed by an agent of the Federal Bureau of Investigation.

Those who had heard David Hilliard at the Glide Memorial Church know that the statement made by that FBI agent was a lie. All Hilliard did was to explain the language which he used in his speech on the 15th day of November, 1969, and the history of rhetoric in relationship to the dialectics of American history in connection with the oppression of the men and women in the Black ghetto.

When the judge would not consider the affidavit, the government demanded that the copy that had been shown me be taken from me. I had to give it back to them because I wanted the judge to sign the order for travel. But the record shows how statements of Panthers are continually being distorted as part of the deliberate campaign to exterminate the Party.

The telephone lines of the Black Panther Party and of anyone who regularly converses with that organization are constantly being tapped. The authorities know, before the members know, what the Black Panther Party is going to do next.

Let us look briefly at the case of Bobby Seale in Connecticut. There was a man named Rackley who was a Black Panther and who was murdered. We have every reason to believe, and intend to prove, when the time comes, that Rackley was murdered by police agents. Bobby Seale went to New Haven, Connecticut on the 19th day of May, 1969, at the request of Yale University, to speak. He received an honorarium for his expenses and speech. He left New Haven in the early morning, around five A.M., of the 20th. Rackley was murdered on the 21st day of May. No one mentioned Bobby Seale until the 21st day of August, 1969.

The papers submitted in Sacramento for the extradition of Bobby Seale to Connecticut carried the following statement by the intelligence officer: "Bobby Seale arrived in New Haven, spoke at Yale University, we picked him up there, and he went to the BPP headquarters at midnight." They also followed him to another place and until he left New Haven at five o'clock on the morning of May 20th. When, I ask, would he have had time to commit a murder, or to plan a murder, or to get involved in any way either directly or indirectly—especially with a man he did not even know and had not even heard of before? And yet today Bobby Seale is facing the death penalty.

The story of the Connecticut Panthers illustrates how constitutional rights fly out of the window when the Black Panther Party becomes involved. On the basis of information they claimed to have received from an informant whom they refused to identify, the police burst into the New Haven headquarters of the Black Panther Party, and arrested the people found inside. They were all taken to the police station, where they were denied the right to have their attorneys present. All eight people arrested were thus extensively questioned in violation of their constitutional rights.

The arrests were made without warrants. A heavily armed squad of police broke down doors at party headquarters, entered bedrooms where women and children were sleeping, ransacked the office, seizing personal items as well as money collected for the children's breakfast programs. On May 22 the arrests were widely and sensationally publicized, with much illegal discussion of evidence and items seized. Mug shots of eight defendants were spread beneath a banner heading announcing the arrests in a New Haven paper.

Connecticut law states that bail should be granted even in a capital case unless the evidence against the accused is very great. It has been held that an indictment is not prima facie proof of this "very great" evidence; the state must come forth with more. Despite that provision all defendants but one (Frances Carter) were denied bail. As of this writing, virtually all of the defendants will have been in jail for over a year. Three of the women—Frances Carter, Rose Smith, and Loretta Luckes—were pregnant at the time of arrest, and have had their children while in custody.*

It should be clear, then, that in the case of the Black Panthers the old rules simply do not apply. Any methods will be resorted to, in defiance of the constitutional rights of the Panthers, in the drive to destroy that Black Panther Party. But we will not sit by and allow these onslaughts on American democratic rights to continue. We have demanded that there be a special Congressional investigation of the actions of all the police departments, together with the Department of Justice and its auxiliary agents. And not by the House Committee on Un-American Activities or by the House Internal Security Committee, or whatever else such bodies call themselves, but by men and women in Congress who we feel have some integrity. There are not very many of them, unfortunately, but there are some in Congress who should do the investigating and the other work that is necessary to bring out the facts. We also intend to file a petition with the United Nations charging violation of human rights by the government of the United States.[24]

America is at the crossroads today. The people are not going to put up any longer with the existing state of affairs. They are not going to tolerate a society that is being run by 76 corporations and their stooges they pick to run the country. They are not going to be satisfied in having Tweedledee and Tweedledum for their next governor or their next president.

As for myself, if we are going to have fascism for everyone—as we already have fascism for the majority of the people in the Black ghetto and the Brown ghetto, and particularly for the Black Panther Party, and if it becomes impossible to stand before a courtroom and defend one's client, I will withdraw from the Bar. (That may make a lot of people happy.) But I do not ever intend to be a fixture in a courtroom, in order to give the semblance of due process of law, and say "Heil Hitler."

* These events are related in the "Memorandum for [Yale] Law Students on the History and Current Status of Panther Cases as of April 18."

# News Release Issued by the American Civil Liberties Union, December 29, 1969

"The record of police actions across the country against the Black Panther Party forms a prima facie case for the conclusion that law enforcement officials are waging a drive against the black militant organization resulting in serious civil liberties violations," the American Civil Liberties Union said today.

"First Amendment and due process guarantees have been breached in numerous instances," the ACLU reported in disclosing a spot check survey of ACLU affiliate offices in 9 major metropolitan centers.

The national survey, prompted by the recent Chicago and Los Angeles police raids on Black Panther officials, suggests that a pattern of harassment exists and describes the nature of the civil liberties violations involved. ACLU affiliates, in individual cases, have defended the rights of Black Panther groups when civil liberties issues have arisen.

"Quite aside from the killing of Panthers and police which we abhor, ACLU affiliates have reported that the style of law enforcement applied to Black Panthers has amounted to provocative and even punitive harassment, defying the constitutional rights of Panthers to make political speeches or distribute political literature.

"In San Francisco, Los Angeles, Chicago, Philadelphia and New York, police have made repeated arrests of Panthers for distributing papers without a permit, harassment, interfering with an officer, loitering and disorderly conduct—stemming from incidents where police have challenged Panthers as they attempted to distribute their newspaper or other political materials. Seldom have these charges held up in court, often they have been dropped by the prosecutor prior to trial, and in one New York case the arresting officer acknowledged that he had no evidence but had been instructed to 'get on the books' the arrest of a particular Panther who was already on the books of an adjoining county. We view this style of law enforcement as applied with prejudice to the Panthers, as inflammatory, and very susceptible to escalation into violent confrontations.

"ACLU affiliates in New York and Indiana report infiltration by government informants into black groups thought to be Panthers for the purpose of entrapment. The evidence indicates that government agents have attempted to induce black militants to burglarize, in one case offering automatic weapons, in another providing a map of the likely target, a getaway car and the offer of weapons. This is an abominable tactic for officers of the law to undertake. Police are supposed to prevent crimes, not encourage them.

"A common police procedure reported to us by ACLU affiliates in New York, Pennsylvania, Connecticut, Illinois, Indiana, California and Wisconsin is that of excessive traffic stops by police of Black Panther Party members. These challenges by police are so frequent in number and so forceful in manner as to be unconstitutional. They have rarely resulted in traffic violations, arrest of a known fugitive or charges of illegal possession of weapons. They more often produce the traditional catch-all charges of the police roust—disorderly conduct, interference with an officer, resisting arrest.

"Other police actions which bear out charges of harassment are reported from Chicago where police and FBI agents undertook a June 4th dawn raid on Panther headquarters with an arrest warrant for George Sams, but no search warrant. Upon smashing down the door of the office and failing to find George Sams, enforcement officials broke up furniture, confiscated literature, lists of donors and petitions and arrested eight Panthers on charges so flimsy they were later dismissed. The following day a similar raid was made in Detroit, the door broken down, documents photographed, three Panthers arrested on specious charges and later released.

"Our reports do not prove a directed national campaign to get the Panthers. However, even if not a concerted program of harassment, high national officials, by their statements and actions, have helped to create the climate of oppression and have encouraged local police to initiate the crackdowns. For example, the Vice President has called the Panthers a 'completely irresponsible, anarchistic group of criminals;' the Assistant Attorney General, Jerris Leonard has said, 'The Black Panthers are nothing but hoodlums and we've got to get them;' FBI Director J. Edgar Hoover has called the Panthers 'the greatest threat to the internal security of the country [among] violence-prone black-extremist groups;' and Attorney General John N. Mitchell has ruled that the Panthers are a threat to national security, thus subject to FBI surveillance by wiretapping.

"This official federal posture makes it easy for the president of the Cleveland Fraternal Order of Police to suggest, 'the country doesn't need the Black Panther Party, to my way of thinking, they need to be wiped out.'

"We believe the climate of anger and the specific cases of police harassment against the Black Panther Party warrant intensive investigation. We are therefore consolidating the case materials, letters and notes from ACLU affiliates for submission to the Commission of Inquiry into the Black Panthers and Law Enforcement Officials convened by 28 eminent Americans and national organizations and headed by former U.S. Supreme Court Justice Arthur Goldberg. The ACLU is a participating organization in the Inquiry."

The ACLU statement was released by John de J. Pemberton, Jr., Executive Director. Mr. Pemberton commented:

"Law enforcement officials symbolize the rule of law and have an extra responsibility to abide by lawful procedures. Peaceful resolution of conflict, through the fair application of law, must be preserved as the mainstay of the democratic process. No matter how inflammatory a political program is perceived to be, policemen and their superiors cannot decide to exceed their legal authority, even in treating specific violations of the law. For police excesses lead to tyranny of law and sow the seeds of a police state.

"It is therefore essential that reports supplied by ACLU affiliates be fully probed so public and legislative officials may know the special qualities of police behavior in their confrontations with the Black Panther Party."

# Resolution Adopted by the New York Group of the Society for Philosophy and Public Affairs, May 23, 1970

At its May 23 meeting, the New York group of the Society for Philosophy and Public Affairs adopted the following resolution concerning the Trial of the New York Panther 21:

The treatment of the New York Panther 21 by courts of the State of New York represents what we regard as a judicial outrage. The evidence brought against the defendants seems far from conclusive; yet the defendants have been placed under excessive bond that they have no chance of meeting, and that is far greater than the bond imposed on other defendants in New York charged with similar crimes and confronted with greater evidence against them. Eleven of the defendants have spent the past year in jail. In jail they have been the victims of gross brutality. In courtrooms they and their lawyers have been constantly harassed and have been denied elementary rights necessary for the conduct of a fair trial.

We believe the defendants in this case must immediately be granted bail that they can afford to pay. Also we believe that Justice Murtagh, who is conducting the pre-trial hearings in the case, has shown himself to be prejudiced against the defendants and should be disqualified from presiding at further proceedings. If, as we sadly believe is very possible, the defendants cannot be given a fair trial in any court of this state, then the charges against them must be dismissed. Also we believe that official investigations must be conducted into all aspects of the handling of this case by police, the courts, penal institutions, and the district attorney's office. Unfortunately, it would appear necessary in the course of any thorough investigation to consider the possibility that this case is part of a nationwide "police conspiracy" to destroy the Black Panther Party.

The crimes committed against these defendants by our judicial system not only endanger the lives of the defendants and the Black Panther Party, but also endanger the very legitimacy of the courts of our state. In the face of this crisis of legitimacy the New York chapter of the Society for Philosophy and Public Affairs believes that militant nonviolent actions, including acts of civil disobedience and symbolic contempt of court, can be permissible means to help secure for these defendants their rights to a fair trial and to be free on reasonable bail until proven guilty, and the chapter calls upon its members to establish or join committees on their respective campuses to raise money for and give other appropriate aid to the Panther 21.

Kai Nielsen
President, New York Chapter
Society for Philosophy and Public Affairs
and Chairman, Department of Philosophy
Washington Square College
New York University

*—New York Review of Books,* July 2, 1970

# II. CALL FOR REVOLUTIONARY PEOPLE'S CONSTITUTIONAL CONVENTION, SEPTEMBER 7, 1970, PHILADELPHIA, PA.

## Message to America

Delivered on the 107th Anniversary of
the Emancipation Proclamation at Washington, D.C.
Capitol of Babylon, World Racism, and Imperialism
June 19, 1970 by The Black Panther Party

As oppressed people held captive within the confines of the Fascist-Imperialist United States of America, we Black Americans take a dim view of the position that we, as a people, find ourselves in at the beginning of the 7th decade of the Twentieth Century.

We find ourselves in a very dangerous world-situation. White America has always adhered to a very racist attitude in its policy towards people who have color. This has been true in the past and it is true today. We see very clearly that whereas White America has escalated its policy of repression and containment of Black people inside the United States itself, on a world scale, the United States is playing the leading role in organizing the White race against the people of the world who have a color. Resolving contradictions between White Protestants and White Catholics, between White Christians and White Jews, between White Capitalists and White Communists, between White Eastern Europeans and White Western Europeans, between White Archeo-Colonialists and White Neo-Colonialists, wherever we look, the picture is one and the same. White racist America, which domestically has adopted the policy of open fascism in order to put down the uprisings of oppressed people of color and those few Whites who take a stand against the grizzly reality of the Babylonian scene, this same White racist America has projected its domestic racist perspective onto the international scene and has organized world imperialism along racist lines. Within the domestic confines of the United States of America, we see clearly that a well-planned, calculated Fascist Genocidal Conspiracy is being implemented against our people.

Black people within the domestic confines of the U.S.A. have reached another cross road. This is a time for the most serious decisions that we, as a people, have ever been called upon to make. The decisions that we make in our time, the actions that we take or fail to take, will determine whether we, as a people, will survive or fall victims to genocidal extermination at the hands of the FAS-CIST MAJORITY which the Nixon clique are rapidly mobilizing into a beastly vigilante weapon to be unleashed against us.

### The U.S.A. Monster

The United States of America is a barbaric organization controlled and operated by avaricious, sadistic, bloodthirsty thieves. The United States of America is the Number One exploiter and oppressor of the peoples of the whole world. The inhuman capitalistic system which defines the core of reality of the U.S.A., is the root of the evil that has polluted the very fabric of existence within the U.S.A. Exploitation of man by man; the rule of man over man instead of the rule of the laws of Human Rights and Justice; savage wars of aggression, mass murder, genocide, and shameless slaughter of the people of the world; impudent, arrogant White Racism; and a naked, brazen attempt to perpetuate White Supremacy on a world scale—these are a few of the unsavory characteristics of the U.S.A. Monster with which we have to deal.

We did not ask for this situation. We did not create it. And we do not prefer it but we must deal with it.

### The Emancipation Proclamation

Today, June 19th, is the anniversary of the issuance by President Abraham Lincoln of THE EMANCIPATION PROCLAMATION during the Civil War, officially dated January 1, 1863. The end result of the EMANCIPATION PROCLAMATION was supposed to be the freedom and liberation of Black people from the cruel shackles of chattel slavery. And yet, 100 and 7 years later, today, Black people still are not free. Where is that freedom supposedly granted to our people by THE EMANCIPATION PROCLAMATION and guaranteed to us by the Constitution of the United States?

Is it in the many "Civil Rights Bills" that have been passed to try to hide the irrelevance of the Constitution for Black People?

Is it in the blood-shed and lives lost by Black People when America brings "Law and Order" to the ghetto in the same fashion and by those same forces that export "Freedom and Democracy" to Korea, to Vietnam, to Africa, Asia, and Latin America?

Is it the right to "political activity" when the U.S.A. attempts to legally murder Bobby Seale, Chairman of the Black Panther Party, for his political beliefs?

Where was that right when brother Malcolm was murdered, when Martin Luther King was gunned down?

Where is Freedom when a people's right to "Freedom of Speech" is denied to the point of murder? When attempts at "Freedom of the Press" brings bombings and lynchings? Where is Freedom when the right to "peacefully assemble" brings on massacres? Where is our right to "keep and bear arms" when Black People are attacked by the Racist Gestapo of America? Where is "religious freedom" when places of worship become the scene of shoot-ins and bomb-ins? Where is the right to vote "regardless of race or color" when murder takes place at the voting polls? Are we free when we are not even secure from being savagely murdered in our sleep by policemen who stand blatantly before the world but yet go unpunished? Is that ". . . equal protection of the laws"? The empty promise of the Constitution to "establish Justice" lies exposed to the world by the reality of Black Peoples' existence. For over 400 years now, Black people have suffered an unbroken chain of abuse at the hands of White America. For 400 years we have been treated as America's footstool. This fact is so clear that it requires no argumentation.

**The Constitution**

The Constitution of the U.S.A. does not and never has protected our people or guaranteed to us those lofty ideals enshrined within it. When the Constitution was first adopted we were held as slaves. We were held in slavery under the Constitution. We have suffered every form of indignity and imposition under the Constitution, from economic exploitation, political subjugation, to physical extermination.

We need no further evidence that there is something wrong with the Constitution of the United States of America. We have had our Human Rights denied and violated perpetually under this Constitution—for hundreds of years. As a people, we have received neither the Equal Protection of the Laws nor Due Process of Law. Where Human Rights are being daily violated there is denial of Due Process of Law and there is no Equal Protection of the Law. The Constitution of the United States does not guarantee and protect our Economic Rights, or our Political Rights, nor our Social Rights. It does not even guarantee and protect our most basic Human Right, the right to LIVE!

**Implementing Point No. 10 of the Black Panther Party Platform and Program**

Point No. 10 of the Black Panther Party's Platform and Program addresses itself to the question of the National Destiny of Black people. We feel that, in practical terms, it is time for Black people as a whole to address their attention to the question of our National Destiny.

Black people can no longer either respect the U.S. Constitution, look to it with hope, or live under it. The Constitution is the social contract that binds the American people together into a sovereign nation and defines authority and the distribution of power, rights, and privileges. By shoving the Constitution aside, rendering it null and void, in order to carry out fascist oppression and repression of Black people, the fascists have, by that very fact, destroyed even the false foundations of authority in this society. We live in a lawless society where racist pigs have usurped the Legislative, Judicial, and Executive branches of government and perverted them towards the prosperity of their private interests. We repudiate, most emphatically, all documents, Laws, Conventions, and Practices that allow this sorry state of affairs to exist—including the Constitution of the United States.

For us, the case is absolutely clear: Black people have no future within the present structure of power and authority in the United States under the present Constitution. For us, also, the alternatives are absolutely clear: the present structure of power and authority in the United States must be radically changed or we, as a people, must extricate ourselves from entanglement with the United States.

If we are to remain a part of the United States, then we must have a new Constitution that will strictly guarantee our Human Rights to Life, Liberty, and the Pursuit of Happiness, which is promised but not delivered by the present Constitution. We shall not accept one iota less than this, our full, unblemished Human Rights. If this is not to be, if we cannot make a new arrangement within the United States, then we have no alternative but to declare ourselves free and independent of the United States. If it is our national destiny to follow the latter course, then we must declare ourselves into self-governing machinery, and seek the recognition of the freedom-loving nations of the world.

The Black Panther Party fully realizes that the two roads open to us as set forth above involve monumental undertakings. But we are trapped in a monstrous situation that requires a monumental solution. And no task, however great, is too much to deal with when the very welfare, survival, and national destiny of our people are at stake. Having already struggled up from the dismal depths of chattel slavery, no obstacles can be too high for us to surmount in order to liberate our people and take back the freedom and security that was taken away from us and denied us for so long.

### Call for a Revolutionary People's Constitutional Convention

The hour is late and the situation is desperate. As a nation, America is now in the middle of the greatest crisis in its history. The Black Panther Party believes that the American people are capable of rising to the task which history has laid before the nation. We believe that the American people are capable of rejecting the fascist solution to the national crisis which the fascist Nixon clique, the George Wallaces', Lester Maddoxes', Ronald Reagans', Spiro Agnews', etc. hold out to the people.

WE THEREFORE, CALL FOR A REVOLUTIONARY PEOPLE'S CONSTITUTIONAL CONVENTION, TO BE CONVENED BY THE AMERICAN PEOPLE, TO WRITE A NEW CONSTITUTION THAT WILL GUARANTEE AND DELIVER TO EVERY AMERICAN CITIZEN THE INVIO-LABLE HUMAN RIGHT TO LIFE, LIBERTY, AND THE PURSUIT OF HAPPINESS!

We call upon the American people to rise up, repudiate, and restrain the forces of fascism that are now rampant in the land and which are the only real obstacles standing between us and a rational resolution of the national crisis.

We believe that Black people are not the only group within America that stands in need of a new Constitution. Other oppressed ethnic groups, the youth of America, Women, young men who are slaughtered as cannon fodder in mad, avaricious wars of aggression, our neglected elderly people all have an interest in a new Constitution that will guarantee us a society in which Human Rights are supreme and Justice is assured to every man, woman, and child within its jurisdiction. For it is only through this means that America, as a nation, can live together in peace with our brothers and sisters the world over. Only through this means can the present character of America, the purveyor of exploitation, misery, death, and wanton destruction all over the planet earth, be changed.

**Warning to America**

We are from 25 to 30 million strong, and we are armed. And we are conscious of our situation. And we are determined to change it. And we are unafraid. Because we have our guarantee. If the American people, as a whole, do not rise up, reverse the present course of this nation, which, if unchecked, holds out only fascist repression and genocide for Black people, then we, Black people, will be forced to respond with a form of War of Salvation that in the chaos of carrying it out and the attempt to repress it, will gut this country and utterly destroy it. Before we accept Genocide, we will inflict Total Destruction upon Babylon.

It had best be understood, now, that the power we rely upon ultimately, as our only guarantee against Genocide at the hands of the Fascist Majority, is our strategic ability to lay this country in ruins, from the bottom to the top. If forced to resort to this guarantee, we will not hesitate to do so.

FOR THE SALVATION, LIBERATION, AND FREEDOM OF OUR PEOPLE, WE WILL NOT HESITATE TO EITHER KILL OR DIE!

ALL POWER TO THE PEOPLE

—*Quicksilver Times*, June 23–July 3, 1970

# Notes

1. The reference is to the Pact of Zanjon which ended the Ten Years War (1868–1878) of the Cuban people to gain independence from Spain. Maceo refused to sign the Pact mainly because it did not include the abolition of slavery and issued his famous Protest of Baragua in which he announced his determination to continue the war. However, he was soon forced to leave Cuba because of limited resources. He never surrendered to the Spaniards.

2. The quotation is from Regis Debray's book, *Revolution Within a Revolution*.

3. The reference is to the sending of marines to the Dominican Republic by President Johnson ostensibly to protect American lives but in reality to prevent the coming to power of Juan Bosch and the liberal-radical forces he headed.

4. Robert Williams, president of the Republic of New Africa, had just returned to the United States from exile. The Republic of New Africa's blueprint for black liberation called for the setting up of a black Republic in the United States which would declare its independence from the "mother country." This Republic was to have its own economy, army and navy in five Southern states.

For an exposition of Williams's views, see the interview with him in *The Black Scholar*, May, 1970.

5. For Bobby Seale's report of his tour, see *The Black Panther*, March 31, 1970. For his speech in Scandinavia, see *ibid.*, Oct. 25, 1969.

6. During the summer of 1969, Stokeley Carmichael announced from Africa that he had resigned from the Black Panthers because of their work with white radicals. Carmichael asserted that the only path to liberation lay in effecting a united front of black people in Africa and in the United States.

Ron Karenga and his organization, US, also feel that Afro-Americans must fashion their own plans and conduct their own programs apart from any involvement with white radicals. Karenga and his organization have been bitter enemies of the Black Panthers, and the Panthers view them as agents of the white power structure.

7. The reference is to the president of San Francisco State College, who won wide approval in the reactionary press because of his actions in calling in police to smash the student-faculty strike at the College.

8. The reference is to the American Federation of Teachers.

9. The reference is to the Mayor of San Francisco.

10. The Black Legion was an anti-labor, anti-black pro-fascist terrorist organization founded during the depression years of the early 1930's.

11. For a full discussion of this incident, see Bobby Seale, *Seize the Time: The Story of the Black Panther Party and Huey P. Newton*, New York, 1970, pp. 99–105.

12. PL refers to Progressive Labor, a group of radicals who split off from the Communist Party.

13. For Eldridge Cleaver's remark referred to, see page 113.

14. This is a variation of the famous remark of José Martí, the Cuban revolutionary leader who spent fifteen years in the United States from 1880 to 1895 and wrote in 1892: "I have lived inside the belly of the Monster and know him from within."

15. Gabriel Prosser was the leader of the slave conspiracy of 1800 in Virginia. Denmark Vescy, a slave who succeeded in purchasing his freedom, led the slave conspiracy in Charleston, South Carolina, in 1821–22. Nat Turner led the great slave uprising in Virginia in 1831. Toussaint L'Ouverture was the slave leader in the uprising against the French in Saint Domingue in the 1790's which led to the establishment of Haiti, the first black Republic in history and the second Republic in the New World.

16. William Kunstler, a famous civil rights lawyer, was one of the two attorneys for the other seven defendants in the Chicago conspiracy trial. He had been appointed by Judge Hoffman to represent Bobby Seale after the Judge refused to postpone the trial until Charles R. Garry could defend him. Schultz and Foran were the prosecuting attorneys for the government in the trial.

17. Seale is referring to Title 42 US Code Section 1981, which was a statute passed during Reconstruction granting black men equal protection under the law. The reference to 1892 is incorrect.

18. While Seale is correct in making the statement that Benjamin Franklin owned (and dealt in) slaves, Franklin was a founder and president of the Pennsylvania Society for Promoting the Abolition of Slavery, the Relief of Free Negroes Unlawfully Held in Bondage, and for Improving the Condition of the African Race. His last public act was to sign a memorial to Congress for the abolition of slavery.

19. The Fugitive Slave Act of 1850 was passed by Congress, not by the Supreme Court. It was part of the Compromise of 1850.

20. DRUM refers to the Dodge Revolutionary Union Movement, a Black Caucus formed by black members of the Dodge local of the United Auto Workers who accuse the union leadership of neglecting the interests of its black membership.

21. On July 18–20, 1969, the Black Panther Party sponsored the United Front Against Fascism Conference in Oakland, California.

Four thousand people, representing a wide variety of organizations, attended the conference in response to the appeal that Americans regardless of race, creed or color make a stand against "the rising tide of fascism in America."

22. *"Hasta la victoria siempre"* ["Ever onward to victory"], the phrase Che Guevara used in his farewell letter to Fidel Castro.

23. On March 16, 1968, at My Lai between 450 and 500 Vietnamese—most of them women, children, and old men—were brutally massacred by American soldiers of the Charlie Company.

24. The idea of an appeal by black Americans to the United Nations began soon after the international organization was formed. The NAACP presented the document "An Appeal to the World" to the UN in 1947. Written under the editorial supervision of W. E. B. Du Bois, the document was subtitled "A Statement on the Denial of Human Rights to Minorities in the Case of Citizens of Negro Descent in the United States of America and an Appeal to the United Nations for redress." In 1951 the petition "We Charge Genocide" was presented to the UN by William L. Patterson, national executive secretary of the Civil Rights Congress. The petition was a catalog of lynchings and other acts of violence against Negroes and asked for UN action under Article II, the Genocide Convention. In 1964 Malcolm X attended the conference of the Organization of African Unity to urge African nations to bring the question of Negro rights to the United Nations. On July 19, 1964, Jesse Gray, leader of the Harlem Rent strike, told the press that he planned to lead a demonstration at United Nations Plaza "to ask the UN to intervene in the 'police terror in the United States.'" On June 15, 1964, at a forum sponsored by the Association of Artists for Freedom at Town Hall, John O. Killens, the black novelist, declared that black Americans had to "place our case before the United Nations . . . since it is a case of denial of human rights. I believe there is a Human Rights Commission."